DON'T MURDER YOUR MYSTERY

24 Fiction-Writing Techniques
To Save Your Manuscript
From Turning Up ...

D.O.A.

Chris
Roerden

REVIEWERS ARE SAYING...

Enthusiastically recommended.
— *Midwest Book Review*

Noteworthy small press book....Get a copy. — *Southern Review of Books*

One of this volume's greatest strengths is that it grows out of a large body of experience.... [It] is smarter, more comprehensive, more effectively targeted, and more accessible than most books on writing. — *Kate Flora, ForeWord Magazine "In the Spotlight"*

This book is good.... I highly recommend this title to anyone wanting to publish any type of novel.
— *Jane Cohen, reviewed for DorothyL*

A wealth of good advice, supported by excellent examples from published writers.
— *Jon L. Breen, Mystery Scene*

Don't let the title fool you. This book is not just for mystery writers. ALL fiction writers can benefit.... 5 stars. Don't miss this one! — *Catherine Chant, Futures Mystery Anthology Magazine*

I highly recommend *Don't Murder Your Mystery* as a useful and enjoyable guide to moving from someone who writes to someone others want to read.
— *Kim Malo, MyShelf*

PUBLISHED AUTHORS ARE SAYING...

Experienced writers may also find its tips helpful and inspiring if they have hit a roadblock.... I went back and re-wrote an entire first page after reading [this book].
— *PJ Parrish, 7 Lewis Kincaid mysteries, N.Y. Times best-selling author*

A must-have for all aspiring mystery writers. — *Anne Underwood Grant, 4 mystery novels*

Highly recommended.
— *Vicki Lane, 4 mystery novels [made DMYM required reading for her writing students]*

I have shelves filled with how-to-books about writing, but *Don't Murder Your Mystery* instantly surpassed them all and became my #1 guide. — *Sandra Parshall, The Heat of the Moon; Disturbing the Dead*

Basic enough for beginners, thorough and deep enough for seasoned writers, and humorous enough to read just for fun—the best how-to I've read.
— *Betty Beamguard, recipient of over 30 writing honors and awards*

Of all my books on writing, this is the one I would not part with.
— *Phil Hardwick, 7 mystery novels*

A superb book. Lots of good information, even for experienced writers, presented with wit.
— *Cynthia Riggs, 7 Martha's Vineyard mysteries*

An indispensable tool.... I've learned more from it than any of the numerous other instructional manuals I've read.
— *Scott Nicholson, 9 fantasy novels*

A terrific job; the book will be a great service to experienced writers as well as newbies.   —*Jeanne Dams, 14 novels, Agatha Award-winner*

One of the best writing tools I've ever read.—*Craig Faris, Carrie McCray Literary Award, Best Short Fiction*

It all looks wonderful!
— *Libby Fischer Hellmann, 4 novels; past president Sisters in Crime*

A solid entry that belongs on a mystery writer's reference shelf.
—*Steve Brown, 15 novels in 3 genres*

Outstanding guide to improving one's critical reading and writing skills.   —*Alix Dobkin, feminist singer-songwriter, author of forthcoming My Red Blood*

Great book. I will be recommending it to new writers.—*Michael Allen Dymmoch, award winner, 7 novels*

A valuable reference work.
—*Sara Paretsky*

Not only do you tell the secrets of writing outstanding mysteries, you also show how successful writers have done it. Great book!
—*Ann Prospero, Almost Night*

You explain a number of writing errors that I haven't seen mentioned in other books. — *Alex Matthews, 8 Cassidy McCabe mysteries*

Your whole approach is so original ...I'll certainly keep recommending it, beginning with a fiction workshop I'm teaching.
—*Nancy Means Wright, 6 novels*

I bought two copies and gave one to (my co-author). I told her I thought it was the best book on its subject out there. She agrees.
—*Michael Mallory, co-author with Marilyn Victor, Death Roll*

EMERGING WRITERS ARE SAYING...

I believe libraries ought to add this book to their collections for patrons who are writers or who teach writing. A terrific resource.
— *Linda Lemery, Mary B. Blount Library, Averett Univ., Danville VA*

I used most every technique in your book recently. I was stunned by how much better even my first draft was when I did what you suggested.
—*Heather Hutchins, Chicago, IL*

ALSO BY THIS AUTHOR

Collections from Cape Elizabeth, Maine (1965)
On to the Second Decade (1977)
Oops'n'Options (1981), a game
Open Gate: Teaching in a Foreign Country (1990)
What Two Can Do: Sam & Mandy Stellman's Crusade for Social Justice (2002)
and four ghostwritten nonfiction books

DON'T MURDER YOUR MYSTERY

24 Fiction-Writing Techniques
To Save Your Manuscript
From Turning Up D.O.A.

Chris Roerden

Published by Bella Rosa Books
P. O. Box 4251 CRS, Rock Hill, SC 29732
www.bellarosabooks.com
A Mystery Writers of America approved publisher

Publisher's Cataloging-in-Publication

Roerden, Chris.
    Don't murder your mystery : 24 fiction-writing techniques to save your manuscript from turning up D.O.A. / Chris Roerden.
    p. cm.
    Includes bibliographical references and index.
    ISBN 1-933523-13-1

    1. Editing. 2. Detective and mystery stories—Technique. 3. Fiction—Technique. I. Title.

PN162.R62 2005   808.3'872
                                  QBI05-600178
LCCN 2005938873

12 11 10 09 08 07   3 4 5 6 7 8 9 10

DEDICATION

To the writers, already published
and still submitting, who have
trusted their best efforts to me and
asked for assistance:

You taught me what you need.

This book is one way I can show my
gratitude for your trust and pay it
forward.

TABLE OF CONTENTS

PRECAUTIONS: *For long-lasting relief* 1
NOT ABOUT RULES 2

PART I: DEAD ON ARRIVAL
THE JUDGES 3
   Screener-outers—what they look for
THE PLAINTIFFS 9
   Writers—what you hope for
THE DEFENDANTS 11
   Agents and publishers—why they want what they want
CORRECTIONS FACILITIES 15
   Self-editors—show to do what you need to

PART II: EVIDENCE COLLECTION
TERMS OF THE WILL 21
   A legacy of technique-speak
WITH PURPOSE AFORETHOUGHT 25
   With density and richness for all

PART III: FIRST OFFENDERS
CLUE #1: HOBBLED HOOKS 27
   Replace with high-tensile lines that stretch your holding power
CLUE #2: PERILOUS PROLOGUES 41
   Beware: May lead to low-tension, post-prologue, backstory ache
CLUE #3: BLOODY BACKSTORY 53
   Hide the evidence by slicing, dicing, splicing

PART IV: KILLING TIME
CLUE #4: FATAL FLASHBACKS 63
   Caution: braking and shifting in reverse risks collision
CLUE #5: TOXIC TRANSCRIPTS 71
   Watch those verbatim stories-within-the-story
CLUE #6: DECEPTIVE DREAMS 79
   Make the character wake up before the reader does
CLUE #7: CRAZY TIME 85
   Prevent whiplash from wacky sequencing

PART V: THE LINEUP
CLUE #8: DASTARDLY DESCRIPTION 93
   Revoke the driver's license and come out of the clothes closet
CLUE #9: POISONOUS PREDICTABILITY 103
   Get therapy for cases of arrested development
CLUE #10: DISAPPEARING BODIES 113
   Why introduce what isn't worth mentioning again?

PART VI: CHANGE OF VENUE

    CLUE #11: SHIFTY EYES 121
        Danger ahead: slipping and sliding point of view
    CLUE #12: UNSETTLING SETTINGS 133
        Oh, no, not just another pretty place
    CLUE #13: INSUFFICIENT GROUNDS 143
        Satisfy the hankering for anchoring

PART VII: THE USUAL SUSPECTS

    CLUE #14: SLOW DEATH 151
        End adverbosity, adjectivitis, and other fatal infections
    CLUE #15: BURIED AGENDAS 163
        Expose a tension deficit disorder
    CLUE #16: DYING DIALOGUE 175
        Quit pretending it's dialogue just because you put it in quotes
    CLUE #17: TREACHEROUS TAGS 187
        Snip—like embarrassing price tags worn in public

PART VIII: ROGUES GALLERY

    CLUE #18: MULTIPLE IDENTITIES 199
        Fight confusion profusion
    CLUE #19: STRANGLED SPEECH 211
        Do you hear what I hear?
    CLUE #20: KILLED BY CLICHÉ 223
        Avoid like the plague
    CLUE #21: GESTURED TO DEATH 231
        Stamp out body language illiteracy

PART IX: LOOSE ENDS

    CLUE #22: SNITCH VS. SPY 243
        Telling vs. showing: long time no see
    CLUE #23: MYSTERY DYSTROPHY 251
        Strengthen weak style
    CLUE #24: WORDS & MISDEMEANORS 263
        Insidious abuses and mis-uses

PART X: POST-MORTEM

    Supporting Testimony ... *Endnotes* 273
        Exhibit A .... *Standard Manuscript Format* 276
        Exhibit B .... *Recommended Nonfiction* 278
        Exhibit C .... *Popular Internet Sites* 280
        Exhibit D .... *Bibliography of Fiction Cited* 282
    Cross-examination .... *Index* 287
    The Witness Box .... *Acknowledgments* 292
    The Perpetrator .... *About the author* 293

"The number of authors who are irritated
by copy editors, brush off their queries, and
can't be bothered to work with them only
serves to demonstrate to publishers that
many authors are in fact amateurs.
[The copy editor's] only aim is to make
the writer look as good as possible."

Clarkson Potter
Who Does What and Why in Publishing

PRECAUTIONS

For long-lasting relief, apply this remedy
to drafts that have finished digesting.

Attempting to revise while still
writing can lead to double vision
accompanied by intermittent paralysis of
the hands. The writer's nervous system
may develop the classic two-steps-
forward one-step-backward syndrome,
which has been known to produce dry-
well disorder.

Complications include a mild ache in
the shoulder, as if an editor were looking over it. Severe cases are marked by
schizophrenia, in which the voice of an
editor is heard, temporarily blocking the
writer's voice.

Use caution when applying any
writing remedy.

NOT ABOUT RULES

Despite my parody of a prescription warning, I don't call myself a book doctor. To me, the term implies that a writer's work is sick. Neither do I talk about good and bad or right and wrong. Those terms presume the existence of rules. This book is not about rules. It's about effectiveness.

What counts in any work of fiction is its effect on readers. How writers bring that about is a matter of technique. Some techniques are more effective than others.

Helping writers with technique is the role of the manuscript editor and writing coach. That's me. Editing has been my full-time day job for more than forty years. I love my work, though I'm saddened by witnessing the same techniques murdering one manuscript after another year after year.

My goals in this book are to help all writers of fiction:

1. find and fix the clues to those deadly techniques, and
2. survive the first cut of the submission process so plot and characters get a fair reading.

Why send your manuscript off to commit suicide?

PART I: DEAD ON ARRIVAL

"Idealistic young scribes who insist their work is for them alone will disagree, but a writer without readers is like shouting in an empty room."
Leonard Pitts Jr., syndicated columnist [1]

THE JUDGES

How long do you listen to a telemarketer's pitch before saying "no thanks" and hanging up? When dinner is interrupted night after night by strangers who mangle your name and inquire about your health, you develop the ability to tell, in an instant, that you are not interested in whatever is being offered.

Despite the telemarketer's having scarcely begun to pitch the product, you recognize the clues right away. There's no point in listening further.

The same destiny faces the majority of submissions that flood literary agencies and publishing houses day after day. In the same way that you've developed your own shortcuts for rapidly screening telemarketers—or spam in your e-mail—the publishing industry has developed its own shortcuts for rapidly screening submissions.

One form of flood control is the literary agency, the industry's first responders. Whether your manuscript lands in a pile at an agency or a pile at a publishing house, the screening process is essentially the same. An optimistic book lover known as the first reader has the job of lowering the leaning tower of printouts as efficiently as possible—all the while hoping to rescue the rare beauty that may be imprisoned within.

First readers work rapidly, spotting the clues that separate the manuscripts with no chance of publication from those that might be worth a second look. These gatekeepers know what to screen for. In reality, they know what to screen *out*. Think of them as screener-outers.

The piles of manuscripts are large; made larger still by multiple copies of the same submissions making the rounds of agents and royalty publishers all across the country. Think what's involved in simply *handling* those thousands of manuscripts, much less attempting to read them. Most of us can barely handle an evening's worth of telemarketers.

SPEEDY EXECUTION

When busy screeners pick up your 12-point Courier, double-spaced, laser-printed, return-receipted-priority-posted manuscript, they do what you do when you pick up a ringing telephone. They go on instant alert for the earliest clue that will give them a reason to quickly disconnect.

At this make-or-break moment in which the first impression is the only impression, appearance is everything. Submissions that merely *look* unprofessional get shoved back in the bubble wrap, unread.

Because appearance involves mechanics, not *writing,* you'll find information about formatting at the end of this book (Exhibit A of the POST-MORTEM).

> "Despite the statistics that we are a country suffering from functional illiteracy, we seem to be producing an extraordinary number of imaginative, interesting writers. The problem is that they can't get anyone to read what they write."
>
> Rayanna Simons, about her
> four years as first reader
> for Macmillan[2]

Another rapid disqualifier is wrong category or genre. A sci-fi/fantasy house won't buy a cozy mystery, no matter how well written. A literary press won't redirect its editorial and marketing strategies to publish a private-eye novel, no matter how cleverly crafted. For your book to reach the audience most likely to buy it, your submission must aim for the publishing pros who court that market.

Just as you know which over-the-phone products don't interest you, agents and publishers know which genres don't interest them.

To learn who's interested in what requires homework. Check the submission guidelines that agents and publishers post on their Web sites and happily send you for the courtesy of a self-addressed stamped envelope (SASE). Then:

1. Follow each set of guidelines, even if the variations from one to another seem minor.
2. Send your work to only those agencies or publishing houses that state an interest in your genre.
3. Identify the genre in your cover letter, and your subgenre if you know it.

A surprisingly large number of writers submit their work to anyone in publishing whose address they happen to come across. My spy thriller is so good, thinks the aspiring writer, surely *every* publisher will want it.

Nonsense.

Disregarding the stated preferences of agents and royalty publishers ensures that a submission will be dead on arrival, added proof that the writer is not a professional. Because matching a manuscript to the interests of its recipient takes common sense, not writing skill, you'll find information about genre among the sources listed at the back of this book (Exhibit B of the POST-MORTEM and endnote #3).

A GOOD FIT

If your submission passes the qualifying trials of appearance and category, it becomes eligible for the opening round of the main event. That's where your manuscript begins to be read. That's where your writing skills begin to be judged. The entire process is publishing's version of the survivor-based reality show.

For an agent to represent you, your submission must be a good fit for the agency. For an acquisitions editor to offer you a contract, your submission must be a good fit for the publishing house.

You may scoff at the words "good fit," hearing them as weasel words.

"Whatever those people want to call it," you say, "I know rejection when I get it."

Without discounting any writer's feelings of rejection, I wish to reframe the situation.

TIP: THE FITTING ROOM

Let's say you need a new pair of slacks. Whatever store you start with, you are eliminating all the merchandise offered by all the other stores—at least for the time being. Isn't that rejection? Maybe it's only prioritizing, like shifting some manuscripts to the bottom of the reading pile to look at later.

On entering your favorite emporium, you ignore half the clothing solely because it's intended for the opposite sex. You also walk past jewelry, shoes, toys, and hardware *without even looking* at what they offer. Isn't that rejection?

When you arrive at sportswear, you brush past racks of slacks with budget-busting prices and sizes from a past life. Nothing is wrong with those thousands of trousers; they simply don't fit your needs—like the thousands of manuscripts that don't fit the needs of every agent and publisher.

Fast-forward to the fitting room. You're about to try on six promising selections—not unlike the agent who asks to see a full manuscript based on a promising synopsis and first chapter.

If none of the try-ons fits well enough to buy, you're prepared to start over at another store. But one pair of slacks happens to fit just right, so you leave the other five candidates hanging in the dressing room, pay for your purchase, and head home.

There, crammed into your mail slot, sits one of your own self-addressed stamped envelopes. Your manuscript has come home—again. You can feel rejected, or you can feel that much nearer to the next step.

You slip into your new slacks, check your e-mail, and browse the latest postings on your favorite writers' list serve. One e-subscriber is asking, "Why did they ask for my whole manuscript if they were only going to reject it?"

At that very moment, an army of underpaid department-store clerks is cleaning out fitting rooms from coast to coast, grumbling, "Why do they take so many clothes to try on if they're going to buy only one?"[4]

SUDDEN DEATH

The manuscript that's always a poor fit is one that seems unlikely to sell enough copies to push revenues well above the break-even point. What sells books (besides a celebrity name) is enthusiasm: booksellers telling customers, "Here's a mystery you'll enjoy," and customers telling friends, "I loved this book!" That's word-of-mouth. That's *buzz*.

A promising indicator of buzz is the enthusiasm that a submission generates in wary literary agents, cautious acquisitions editors, and skeptical marketing and accounting decision-makers. Mild interest won't do it.

I know, I know; the industry is famously poor at predicting the success of the titles it releases. High-advance celebrity books lose millions, while best-selling authors admit to a history of so many rejections they had grown dizzy with despair.

In spite of cloudy crystal balls, publishing pros do foresee with some accuracy one type of failure: *average writing.* It's usually called *amateur.*

As unkind as the word "amateur" seems, it's entrenched throughout the industry. It is used to distinguish the typical writer of average skills from the professional: the one in a hundred whose work shows that the writer has studied the craft, practiced it, and appears able to make money at it.

Sadly, the overwhelming majority of submissions deserve the amateur label. That's why the industry's first readers must be efficient screener-outers. The sooner they can spot a clue to average writing, the sooner they can stop reading and go on to the next piece of writing. Before you can say "give my piece a chance," it goes from the slush pile to the "no" pile.

"No" is a rapid decision, despite your manuscript's having scarcely begun to make its pitch. You may have spent a year or more in labor to bring your own 350-page bundle of joy to life, but your effort miscarries. And you don't know why. So you keep looking for the one agent or publisher who will listen to what your writing has to say.

But all are alert to the same clues.

It doesn't matter that you have a suspenseful plot and intricate subplots spinning themselves from beginning to end. Most manuscripts aren't read far enough for the plot to reveal its intricacies. It doesn't matter how skillfully you develop the relationship between protagonist and antagonist. Screener-outers don't hang around long enough to see how you develop your characters.

A manuscript screener is the quicker picker-upper: a professional reader who picks up the earliest clues that separate the amateurs from the pros.

What are those clues?

That's what the next twenty-four chapters are all about.

A REPRIEVE

No doubt you have seen works of fiction that made you wonder how they ever made it into print. The reaction "I can do better than that" probably spawns more new writers than all the writers conferences put together.

As your own reading proves, not every piece of writing deserving of obscurity is rewarded with it. There's an exception to everything.

Luck may play a part, though few writers care to pin their hopes on being picked from fortune's fickle barrel. Most want to do everything they can to improve their work to survive its first, sometimes *only* screen test, with a screener-outer who is the publishing police, judge, and executioner rolled into one.

Cruel? Even the kindest, most optimistic agents and acquisitions editors, after years of seeing the identical weaknesses and poor writing habits, cannot help but feel cruelly treated by those who expect to enter a skilled profession without learning its craft.

With more self-improvement resources available today than ever before, publishing pros wonder how writers can remain oblivious to the many ways they sabotage their own submissions.

"We write all these books and how-to articles in writers' magazines," they groan. "We travel all over the country giving workshops and telling writers what to do and what not to do. Are these efforts making a difference?

"No," they moan. "Our offices are still being flooded with the same kind of amateur work."

To deal with the deluge, agencies and publishers respond to submissions with brief form letters or postcards saying thanks-but-no-thanks, here's wishing you success . . . elsewhere.

If you receive one of those "elsewhere" advisories, you might feel like spending the rest of the day lying on your couch in a blue funk. "How could they reject my story," you cry. "What do those people *want?*"

D.O.A.

THE PLAINTIFFS

Before we look at what publishers want, take a few moments—since you're stretched out on the couch anyway—to contemplate a want of your own. An end to those unsaintly "elsewhere" notes? That, too. What I have in mind, though, is the secret desire that lurks deep in the unconscious of the unhappily unpublished.

Like many who yearn for publication, you may be nurturing a dream in which your manuscript lands on the desk of a kindly benefactor able to look past any rough edges and recognize raw, undeveloped talent. This visionary is so taken by your *potential* that he or she shows you how to fix whatever little flaws might be getting in the way of your success.

Wouldn't it be wonderful to encounter a nurturing mentor willing to mold you into the accomplished writer you know you can become?

Like any fantasy, this secret desire is based on an unreal premise—the result, perhaps, of growing up with all those inspiring biographies in the school library that told of misunderstood geniuses who struggled and eventually made good. Biographies are by definition inspiring; few of us hear of the poor soul who didn't succeed at *something*.

In publishing, mentors and fairy godparents exist, but they are rare. Teaching writers their craft is not the job of an agent or a publisher's in-house editor.

> "[P]eople tend to think, I can take this horrible mess of a manuscript to a benevolent genius who is going to turn it into a masterpiece and teach me how to write. The function of the [in-house] editor is not to run a writing school; it is to edit and publish books."
>
> Justin Kaplan, editor of
> *Bartlett's Familiar Quotations* [5]

CALCULATED GAMBLE

Royalty publishers are professional gamblers. They bet on an acquisition's netting a large enough profit to make their risk worthwhile—larger by far than their outlay for production, marketing, distribution, and the author's modest advance and equally modest royalty.

Agents are risk-takers, too. They gamble on the acquisition's generating a large enough advance plus royalties to produce a worthwhile commission. Other than client reimbursements for postage and photocopying, agents receive no income for the time they invest in seeking homes for the manuscripts they agree to represent.

As a result, a reasonably well-written story that generates mild *but not wild* enthusiasm is unlikely to attract either an agent or a publisher if the ROI (return on investment) seems only fair to middling, *even when the manuscript has nothing wrong with it.*

Moreover, if this nicely written manuscript does get published and nets only a small profit, that profit can be considered a loss. To grasp the concept of a small profit being a loss, we have to consider what's known in all business ventures as the *opportunity cost*—more accurately, the venturer's *lost* opportunity cost. That is, a decision to publish Book A means not publishing Book B, which *might* have done much better.

So you can see why agents and publishers who risk their time and energies on an untested writer must feel passionate about that individual's chances for success. How often do you feel passionate enough to gamble thousands of dollars on an unknown investment touted by a total stranger?

For agents and royalty publishers, gambling is a given. Not so for those whose job is to help writers learn their craft, such as the professional writing instructor, coach, book consultant, and independent manuscript editor. Those fee-for-service providers are paid at the time they render their professional services. Now that publishers no longer subsidize the editorial costs they once did, the burden of who pays for editing has shifted. The writer is expected to do whatever it takes to come up with a profitably publishable manuscript.

Writers serious about their work are well advised to put aside their fantasies, get up from the couch, and learn as much as possible about the craft of writing *before* subjecting themselves to possible disappointment.

THE DEFENDANTS

We can now look at what publishers want. Writers are always being told, write what *you* want, not what you think publishers want, unless you're a writer for hire. "The first person you should think of pleasing, in writing a book, is yourself," advised best-selling author Patricia Highsmith. She felt strongly enough about this issue to put it on page 1 of her classic *Plotting and Writing Suspense Fiction.*

However, Highsmith and others are not saying write whatever you want. They are saying don't try to second-guess the next trend. "Are they still buying cozies?" asks the *trendinista.* "Has the serial killer been overdone?" "Chick-Lit seems hot right now. Maybe I'll try it."

Pleasing yourself applies to selecting genres and topics. It does not apply to *writing well,* which never goes out of style.[6]

Sometimes the letters that accompany returned manuscripts say what a specific publisher is looking for.[7]

> "What's sought is a fresh voice, a magical individuality that is both unique and indefinable. . . ."

Magical? Indefinable? Maybe the next rejection letter is more helpful:

> "We are always looking for the writer with that extra pizzazz."

Is this clearer? Stay tuned—we place our order for pizzazz later.

BACK TO BASICS

To review, publishing is a profit-driven business based on a gamble in which the odds favor no one. Most new titles have short, unprofitable shelf lives of twelve to thirteen weeks. Many lose money, their losses offset by the earnings of books that do well.

How many other industries turn out between 50,000 and 85,000 *different* product lines every year? Only a small number of these titles earn extra dollars by being reissued in film, paperback, and foreign reprints. Note that book revenue comes from *new* units sold; not a penny from the huge market in used books goes to authors, agents, or publishers. (Raise your hand if you buy only brand new books.)

> Because the goal is to get through the pile, literary agent Noah Lukeman says that agents and editors read "solely with an eye to dismiss a manuscript."[8]

In contrast, Hollywood produces a little over 300 films a year for theatrical release,[9] which earn residuals whenever they are licensed to TV, video, and DVD *whether or not the original did well at the box office.* Furthermore, film has no competition from sales of used movie tickets.

These realities force the publishing industry's risk-takers to select manuscripts likely to spill less red ink than previous gambles. That's why the odds-pickers attempt to maximize the sales potential of their already-established high earners, and to:

a. minimize risks by taking on a small number of new writers who look like winners;
b. cut further losses by dropping existing authors whose sales are not stellar; and
c. ignore the rest: those whose work reveals evidence of *average* writing, aka *amateur.*

Everything else that can be said about publishing comes down to these abc's. The industry cannot afford to gamble on writers who are still developing their potential, who show little evidence of having studied the craft of the profession they aspire to, or who fail to reflect the preferences that publishers and agents state in their submission guidelines.

TIPSHEETS

Submission guidelines, also known as tipsheets, do more than specify genres of interest; they spell out house rules for submitting, including required formatting and other dos and don'ts.

Often they state the need for fresh characters, plausible plots, and lively dialogue.

They do not tell you how to correct implausible plots, avoid stale characters, and eliminate other signs of amateur writing. That's not the job of a tipsheet—it's yours. So is the indefinable magic and pizzazz.

Your most valuable resource for learning the craft of writing is the work of other authors. Steep yourself in books of all kinds. Read and reread the authors you feel an affinity for and study their techniques. Analyze the way they set their scenes, construct dialogue, develop characters, build suspense.

Reading a novel or a short story for the second or third time keeps you from getting caught up in the what-happens-next. Instead, you can concentrate on the how-to of creating the effects you admire.

Effective techniques, when added to your own natural ability to spin a great story, prepare you to give publishers what they are really looking for: *good writing.*

Jason Epstein, publisher of Anchor Books and a founder of the *New York Review of Books,* writes that when he got his start in publishing at Doubleday, for several weeks he was given "no further assignment than to read unsolicited manuscripts, which I soon learned could be disposed of on the evidence of a paragraph or two."[10]

BEYOND TIPSHEETS

1. Join organizations of writers, attend their meetings and conferences, and participate in their online discussions. (See Exhibit C of the POST-MORTEM.)

2. Take courses on technique at local colleges and online. Learn which courses are worthwhile by asking your online discussion buddies.

3. Join a local writers' support or critique group or start one. Some writers find such groups extremely helpful; others find them addictive, absorbing time and energy that could better be used for writing. (There's a reason that Milwaukee's Redbird Studios has a waiting list for its "Shut Up and Write" program.)

4. If possible, work with a professional writing coach or personal editor to build your writing strengths, identify your weaknesses, and produce a manuscript with promise.

5. Read books about the craft of writing, and not merely one or two, because no book has all the answers. Advice ranges from how to write and market your book to how to edit it, and from "My way is the only way" to "See all the options you have."

6. Read novels in your genre and others and soak up the sound of good writing.

7. Use the quick FIND & FIX checklists throughout this book.

CORRECTIONS FACILITIES

Now that we've considered some of the fundamentals that drive the publishing business, we can look at the factors you have some control over.

Whether you love revising or hate it, revision is where the real writing takes place. Step 1 is to put your completed first draft aside for a week or more to gain a fresh perspective of it. The longer its forced exile, the fresher your vision.

For Step 2, some writers prefer revising each scene or chapter before writing the next one, to rethink where they've been and where they're heading. They recommend not revising from the beginning until the first draft is finished.

Other writers tackle revisions by reading only for plot on their first pass through, taking notes but making no corrections. On their next pass, they focus only on characters. They recommend reading for specific elements on each subsequent pass. Why work over the phrasing of a sentence when the whole scene might be dumped?

Both approaches have merit, as do other methods. What I recommend depends on how much experience you have with writing a full-length novel. First-timers can benefit from trying several methods, because I believe in revising, revising some more, and revising again.

Between revisions put your manuscript out of sight and read a good novel. Let the voices of skilled writers expand your sensibilities. The moment you feel inspired, stop reading and get back to your manuscript. Without these mind-cleansing interludes, a too-frequent self-edit of your draft can counteract the fresh approach gained by its temporary exile.

Should you reach revision overload, try an about-face. Work your way from the last scene to the first. A change in sequence breaks the continuity of the plot and keeps you from missing the same weaknesses again.

An altered perspective reveals action, dialogue, and characters who contribute nothing and scenes that go nowhere.

Whatever works for you, go for it.

NO "RIGHT WAY"

When the subject of revision comes up at writing conferences, occasionally a successful author puts forth his way as "The Way." Hearing this makes me uncomfortable. The audience is filled with writers eager to believe that any advice from an author who glitters is gospel. When aspiring writers, already insecure, realize they aren't doing things the way they think a *real* author is supposed to, they have one more reason to feel inadequate.

The truth is, no one way is the right way. Revising, like writing, is a creative process, too complex to reduce to a formula.

As convinced of this truth as I am, I was nonetheless gratified to come across support for it from the award-winning author Jan Burke. Her essay "Revision" appears in the Mystery Writers of America handbook edited by Sue Grafton.

> "Revision is one more process through which each writer must
> find his or her own way, and while it may take some time and
> experimentation to learn what method works best for you,
> mastering this part of the craft of writing will be well worth it."
>
> Jan Burke, in *Writing Mysteries*   [p. 182]

Revise as much as you can before handing your manuscript off to an agent or publisher. Do the same even when the only one looking at your draft is your personal editor or writing coach.

Wait a minute—can't you expect the editor you hire to take care of all those little details? Yes, and many editors do, but most are able to see the forest *and* the trees more clearly if you get rid of the dead stumps and underbrush.

It's a fact: certain issues become evident only as smaller obstructions are removed.

The more problems you keep from murdering your manuscript, the more attention a writing coach or manuscript editor can pay to:

- reinforcing your writing strengths, and
- helping you overcome the weaknesses that are invisible to a critique group and to you as a self-editor.

The professional editor takes no pleasure in fixing what you can be taught to find and fix yourself. By mastering the two dozen techniques in this book, you not only protect your manuscript from instant rejection but also free your editor to focus on the subtler challenges that help you grow as a writer. Professional editors get a kick out of witnessing the development of new talent. I know I do.

THE BIG STUFF

Chances are you've been concentrating most of your efforts on perfecting your characters, weaving your plot and subplots, and refining other large-scale, whole-book concepts. These big-picture elements comprise your manuscript's content—what your novel is *about.* Slight one and you have no story.

This book does not focus on those large-scale concepts. One reason is that many other books do. Another reason is that problems with character and plot are not easy to find and fix by yourself.

Besides, you know that outstanding characters and a great plot determine what gets published. You expect those major concepts to speak for themselves when read. But for the majority of submissions, the screener-outers never read far enough to evaluate character or plot—which is my main reason for not examining those whole-book concepts.

"Most cuts are made in the first three pages. The 'yes' pile is cut two more times."

Barbara Gislason, literary agent [11]

As you now realize, the most efficient way for agencies and publishing houses to process mountains of submissions is to stop reading at the earliest clues to average writing.

THE SMALL STUFF

At the opposite end of the spectrum from the big picture is the small stuff: *mechanics*. This includes formatting, which affects appearance, and what I call PUGS: punctuation, usage, grammar, and spelling.

I don't analyze mechanics in this book, either, though I must emphasize their importance. The bumper-sticker philosophy of don't sweat the small stuff does *not* apply to submissions. A few errors in PUGS, or a failure to mirror formatting guidelines, gives the busy screener the first and often the only reason to say, "Whew, another four-pounder I don't have to read."

Why give screener-outers such an easy pass? (Let 'em work for it, right?) Most editors-for-hire can do a decent job of cleaning up PUGS for you. Scores of books and magazines advise you on the protocols of submission. So do the free tipsheets from publishers and agents.

All tipsheets are similar but not identical, so follow the standards specified by your intended recipient. Customize each submission accordingly. Evidence of a writer's flouting a requirement might not disqualify a submission immediately, but it does peg the writer as a possible prima donna. No one wants to begin a working relationship with a pain in the neck.

IN THE MIDDLE

Between the large-scale concepts of plot and character development and the small-scale PUGS and mechanics, a vast middle ground exists. That's my focus in this book.

Picture a pyramid. Its base represents the major whole-book concepts that call for macro-editing. This is the province of acquisitions and developmental editors. The top of the pyramid represents the small stuff that demands the narrow, finicky approach of micro-editing. This is the province of copy editors and proofreaders.

In between lies the wide-ranging province of the line editor. It encompasses large amounts of both developmental editing and copy editing, but it is especially attuned to helping writers shape their techniques and sharpen their writing.

WHY THESE CLUES

You and I know that turning out a publishable manuscript goes well beyond the ability to master two dozen writing techniques. Some are more important to a story than others. However, as early indicators of average writing skill, all twenty-four are dead giveaways.

1. Their misuse is pervasive. They contribute to a style that reads as if the same person wrote ninety-five percent of all submissions.

2. Clues to their presence frequently remain invisible to the writer until pointed out.

3. The same clues are equally invisible to one's writing buddies, who usually address the big stuff, and to the English major in everyone's life, who tends to tinker with the small stuff. (Take no offense, please; I'm a past English major and a life member of Tinkerers Anonymous.)

4. Screeners quickly spot these clues.

And now for the good news.

5. The problem techniques these twenty-four clues reveal are the easiest to learn to find and fix yourself.

ABOUT THE EXAMPLES

By way of demonstrating how others successfully deal with the same techniques that challenge all writers, I review excerpts from 150 published novels, mostly mysteries. Where possible, these excerpts are also from first novels, because I believe that an emerging writer might identify more readily with authors at the beginning of *their* publishing careers.

Every passage bearing an author's name is offered as a positive example. The few nameless ones I wrote, using the identical phrasing and construction that I encounter repeatedly in unpublished manuscripts. Only the identifying details are changed, because I have no wish to embarrass anyone. Writing is difficult enough, and the professional skills a writer must demonstrate to be taken seriously in a highly competitive marketplace involve a long and difficult process of development—much longer and more difficult than new writers imagine.

The extracts I present make up my show and tell. The rest is opinion, mostly mine, based on a lifetime of editing and teaching. I do not expect every reader to agree with my opinions or admire every example I review.

Each selection focuses on a specific technique and how it is used to create its effect. Some caveats:

- I don't claim to know what effect its author intended—only the effect on me and what my years in publishing have shown me is the effect on others.

- By offering specific examples that I find especially effective, I am not necessarily endorsing the books from which they come or all the techniques within their pages.

- Each selection I review is meant to stimulate your imagination and inspire your experimentation—not imitation.

- In no way am I laying down *rules*. In fiction, there are no absolutes. There are, however, guidelines.

"Never start a sentence with a comma." That's the only rule in publishing, said Bill Brohaugh, former editorial director for Writer's Digest Books, speaking at a Mid-America Publishers Association conference. "Everything after that is up for discussion."[12]

What's more, in all things editorial:

- No solution is right for every situation. Evaluate my suggestions in relation to what is most effective for your own work.

- There's an exception to everything—a caveat that bears repeating.

- The choices are always yours, no matter what I or any editor recommends at any stage of your manuscript's development.

PART II: EVIDENCE COLLECTION

However good the content, it's technique that makes the difference. What keeps today's classical music lover from being totally transported by the voice of Enrico Caruso is the scratchy needle.

TERMS OF THE WILL

Writers in every genre inherit a legacy of terminology from past generations of writing professionals. They add to it, modify it, and pass it along to the next. Ordinarily, a glossary of terms is stuck at the back of a book, where readers discover it long after they make assumptions about the author's meaning.

So here is a brief overview of some of the terminology I use in this book. If you are already familiar with this legacy of writers' technique-speak, please skip ahead.

Of the narrative forms available for presenting a story, the easiest to recognize, but the most difficult to write well, is **dialogue**.

The least understood narrative form is **action**, because action is not whatever moves. It is behavior that reveals character, advances the plot, and provokes reactions, tension, and conflict. At the opposite end of the action continuum are gestures and body language—behaviors that show a character's feelings and attitudes.

Description is another narrative form. So is **thought**, also known as **self-talk, monologue,** and **interior dialogue**.

Everything else is **exposition**, sometimes called by the general term **narrative**. Exposition is highly efficient for condensing, explaining, and summarizing content. Action and dialogue are less efficient but more compelling, showing behavior that lets readers interpret meaning for themselves.

The main or lead character is the **protagonist**. He or she is often the **viewpoint character**, whether the story is narrated from a first- or third-person **point of view** (abbreviated **POV**).

Today's audiences favor a **developing character**—one who experiences an internal change in the course of overcoming external opposition.

In a crime novel, the **antagonist** is always a person, although the protagonist might be challenged by additional forces; for example, by nature, or—in fiction with elements of **woo-woo** or **fantasy**—by paranormal phenomena.

Motivation is not limited to the antagonist's reason for committing a crime; motivation accounts for whatever each character wants.

Conflicts between those wants produce the story **situation**, also known as the problem or **predicament**. Motivation propels characters to change that situation or adapt to it, resulting in a new predicament to be resolved.

Plot is carried out through **scenes**, fiction's basic building blocks.

Every scene includes one or more characters, action, and a **setting** in time and place. Each scene is propelled by a **goal** and an **obstacle** to that goal, which causes **conflict**. The plot is advanced by a scene's outcome or **resolution**.

The preferred scene-ending for moving the story ahead is a **setback** or **redirection**, often the result of a **red herring**: a false lead that takes the protagonist further from the goal.

> "It's interesting that the word 'plot' can mean a place for the dead, an evil intrigue, or a story line."
>
> Sandra T. Wales, author of the Warrior Queen series[13]

The plot's forward movement toward its conclusion is known as **progression**. The rate of progression is controlled by **pacing**.

A story's pace, action, and tension reach their height in the **climax**. This penultimate scene is followed by a very brief **dénouement** to explain and tie up any loose ends.

A **beat** is a statement that takes the place of a *he said/she said* **tag**. It usually accompanies dialogue and shows a gesture that identifies and **grounds** or **anchors** the speaker in the setting.

Fiction is typically written in the past tense, which indicates current reality for its characters. **Story time** is real time for them.

Background is information that was or continues to be true.

Backstory tells of events that occurred before story time.

The opening lines that grab attention and get readers involved in the story situation are called, appropriately, the **hook**.

The desirable literary quality known as **density** comes from story elements that serve more than one purpose.

Author of *The Sterile Cuckoo,*
John Nichols, talks of writing his
first draft very quickly, then
rewriting and rewriting—loving
the process. For him, "really
writing" is that final stage in which
he dwells on lines and words.[14]

WITH PURPOSE AFORETHOUGHT

Every element of the novel—that is, every character, scene, setting, action, image, description, detail, and word—serves a purpose. Elements that serve more than one purpose or function at a time enrich your writing by multiplying its *density*.

Evaluate the density of your writing by seeing how many of the following purposes are served by each of your novel's elements.

advancing the plot
dramatizing action
evoking mood
introducing tension
escalating conflict
sketching a description
revealing a buried agenda
thwarting someone's goal
raising the stakes
supplying information
establishing a sense of place
embedding a first reference
making a second reference
increasing a character's insight
identifying a speaker
furnishing visual interest
appealing to the other senses:
   sound, smell, taste, touch
offering another perspective
grounding or anchoring characters
grounding again or re-anchoring
setting up a surprise
introducing irony
adding humor

portraying character
hooking interest
indicating motivation
building emotion
intensifying suspense
establishing attitude
causing a reaction
triggering a counter-reaction
differentiating characters
changing tempo or pace
transitioning in time, place
suggesting elapsed time
misdirecting
expressing a relationship
planting a clue
providing texture
comparing or contrasting
   with similes or metaphors
extending a metaphor
symbolizing meaning
creating counterpoint
constructing parallel actions
developing theme
enriching the writing style

At a conference of writers, Elizabeth Daniels Squire,
author of the Peaches Dann mystery series, shared
what a publisher told her a manuscript had to do to get
his attention. He suggested watching readers in a
bookstore deciding which book to buy.

They look first at the jacket, which is largely out of the
author's control, and the first page. Writers, he said,
have the first page at most to sell the reader.
"So you have even less space than that to sell me." [15]

D.O.A.

PART III: FIRST OFFENDERS

"In the book publishing business, an observer can reasonably conclude that there are an infinite number of manuscripts chasing a finite number of opportunities to publish with established publishers."
John B. McHugh, publishing consultant [16]

CLUE #1: HOBBLED HOOKS

Every submission needs a hook—something sharp to catch the attention of a busy screener. A celebrity byline is a strong hook, but if you don't yet own that particular bait, you have to lure the reader into your story with an interesting, intriguing opening line.

As in fishing, an effective hook not only arouses curiosity but also holds on to it, not letting it get away, not even letting it . . . uh, flounder.

The typical submission begins effectively enough with a line or two of dialogue or action about a predicament. But it soon drifts into backstory and description, telling us of the character's past instead of continuing to *show the character in action in the present.*

By the time the writer gets around to picking up the opening action where it left off, the screener-outer is picking up the next submission.

When you edit your opening, determine whether it fulfills its primary function of making readers want to read the next line, and the next, and each line after that. Sustaining interest is important when the busy screener is looking for the earliest excuse to stop reading.

To heighten the effect of your action opening, omit description and background or limit it to the fewest words. Work those few words in with the main action, never upstaging dialogue and action, the two narrative forms that involve readers directly with the main character. Include a mere suggestion of the setting.

> "He was murdered upstairs, in that front bedroom where you sleep, Ashley dear," Binkie said.

This line opens *Murder on the Candlelight Tour,* Ellen Elizabeth Hunter's first mystery novel. Dialogue introduces the main character (Ashley), briefly sets the scene (in the house where she sleeps), and makes the powerful statement that someone was murdered in her bedroom.

Opening with the word "he" indicates that Binkie and Ashley are in the midst of discussing the murdered man, a technique for creating a sense of dropping into a scene *in medias res*—in the middle of things. This kind of opening immerses readers in the story situation right away.

FAST START OR SLOW

To increase the feeling of a fast start, use short sentences and paragraphs and open with action or with quick, punchy dialogue. Begin more slowly if you are establishing a mood that foreshadows danger and intrigue, as the next example does.

> The row of Victorian houses loomed dark in the early June fog. I put my hand on the cold iron railing and started up the stairway from the street. As I pushed through the overgrown front yard, blackberry vines reached out to tear at my clothing.
> Marcia Muller, *The Cheshire Cat's Eye*

Fast start or slow, verify that your main character appears as soon as possible and is faced with an immediate situation that raises the questions who, what, where, when, how, and why.

The night Vincent was shot he saw it coming.
Elmore Leonard, *Glitz*

The world never ends the way you believe it will, Ronnie Day thought.
Scott Nicholson, *The Red Church,* first mystery novel

In *The Basic Formulas of Fiction,* Foster-Harris defines the hook as "the first brief, potent statement of what is the matter with the central character, what his problem is, what difficulty he is facing."[17]

"I can't do it." Kate's hand tightened on her father's with desperation. "I don't want to even talk about it. Do you understand? Don't ask me, dammit."
Iris Johansen, *Long After Midnight*

My eyes weren't fixed on the direction I was driving, but on the words "Nigger Landlord" slashed in bright neon paint across the ribs of the oak tree that stood in front of my new home.
Gammy L. Singer, *A Landlord's Tale,* first mystery novel

For your first step in revising, examine your hook to see that it gets readers caught up in your protagonist's problems from the get-go.

DOING IT ALL

If these recommendations seem too numerous for any hook to support, here's an opening line that covers them all in a single sentence. It's from *Dead Over Heels,* Charlaine Harris's fifth Aurora Teagarden mystery.

My bodyguard was mowing the yard wearing her pink bikini when the man fell from the sky.

Despite some playful details, we know a murder has been committed, since no self-respecting mystery fan would believe that a body falls from the sky by accident. Harris's multi-pronged opening line raises all the important questions: whose body is falling, whodunit, how, and why.

A minimum of description raises enough additional questions to pique our curiosity and prompt us to read further. Why is a bodyguard performing yard duty? Why is she doing so in a bikini—a pink one, no less—and how come she's a she? Who *is* this narrator that she needs a bodyguard?

Now that you've seen how many questions can emanate from a tightly worded opening line, compare Harris's sentence with one I'm making up to show the kind of writing I see all the time:

> I was lazily watching my tall, well-built bodyguard mowing the lush green lawn in her bright pink bikini when I heard a loudly buzzing small, private airplane flying overhead. When I looked up I saw the scary sight of a man's body falling from the cloudless sky.

What's wrong with this picture? Everything. It's awkward and wordy. A monotonous rhythm pulsates from the pile-up of adjectives that precede each noun: "tall, well-built"; "lush green"; "bright pink"; "small, private"; "scary"; "cloudless." The adverbs "lazily" and "loudly" add nothing. The narrator's actions are buried in redundancies: "I was watching," and "When I looked up I saw. . . ."

Wordiness counteracts the impact of a hook. How many readers will be motivated to endure such unimaginative prose for the length of a novel? Besides Mom. Cramming multiple actions into a single sentence can make even a well-written hook sink of its own weight. One exception: where the weight of repetition creates a deliberate effect.

> Claire Jenson was out back in her favorite part of the garden, the section where she'd tossed seeds here and there this past spring, nothing structured, nothing formal, just scattered here and there the way her grandmother had taught her, when the call came from Chicago telling her that her youngest daughter had been murdered.

This line begins *Murder Online,* the first mystery novel by Beth Anderson, a Frankfurt Award nominee. With a leisurely pace and a homey setting, Anderson makes us feel at ease, laid back, off guard. We're picturing a favorite place and a familiar routine performed with a casualness learned from grandma, a figure associated with love and old-fashioned stability. The mood is one of security, calm, and normalcy, when . . . WHAM! Readers are slammed into the worst scenario any parent could imagine, made more powerful by Anderson's use of contrast.

CONTRADICTION

Anderson's opening sentence illustrates a concept that underlies all mysteries: *nothing is as it seems.* A contradiction or paradox adds intrigue. Look for the contradiction in this opening to *Deadly Deception,* the first mystery novel from Susan P. Mucha.

> The perfect windless day kept the tear gas hovering near the ground.

How can a day be perfect if tear gas is hovering? Find the incongruities lurking in the following openings.

> On an otherwise ordinary Tuesday in the year 2012, First Sergeant Matthew Storey bled to death from a gunshot wound after an ill-considered charge on the Confederates. It was his worst death in several months.
>
> Leah Carson, *The Sons of Lazarus*

> Of course Molly would live; anything else was unthinkable. But Anna was thinking it.
>
> Nevada Barr, *Liberty Falling*

> We approved of the first murder.
> We applauded the second.
> By the third murder, I think we would have given the killer a ticker-tape parade.
> But the fourth death, that was different.
>
> Elaine Viets, *The Pink Flamingo Murders*

> I was home, and the mouth of the corpse was open wide.
>
> Phillip DePoy, *The Devil's Hearth*

> Few murder streets are lovely. This one was.
>
> Jonathan Kellerman, *The Clinic*

> He was the man every woman dreams about—in her worst nightmares.
>
> Edna Buchanan, *Miami, It's Murder*

TONE

When you edit your hook, decide what tone you want to communicate—amused, cynical, angry, worried, or something else. Tone sets the mood for the type of story to come. Whereas a humorous opening signals a lighthearted story ahead, for a dark drama it would mix the message. Tone reflects the attitude of the protagonist toward his situation and puts readers in a frame of mind to accept his response to that situation.

The tone of Charlaine Harris's fell-from-the-sky opening is whimsical; that of Beth Anderson's in-the-garden hook is soothing—at first. What's similar about the next two openings—and what's different?

> Things got off to a rotten start when I found Cousin Otto dead in the ladies' room.
>
> Mignon F. Ballard, *Shadow of an Angel*

> She had often dreamed of her little sister floating dead beneath the surface of the ice, but tonight for the first time, she envisioned Hannah clawing to get out.
>
> Jodi Picoult, *Plain Truth*

These first lines are similar in content, and both make use of understatement. Yet they are very different in tone. Sometimes, an opening gets its edge from only one word or phrase.

> Jack Drucker didn't recognize his death when he saw it coming in the rearview mirror of his car.
>
> Michael Kronenwetter, *First Kill,* best first novel in the Private Eye Writers of America/St. Martin's Contest

> Lying always came easier to me than telling the truth.
>
> D. W. Buffa, *The Prosecution*

> The Cross house was twenty paces away and the proximity and sight of it made Gary Soneji's skin prickle.
>
> James Patterson, *Cat & Mouse*

Ignoring content for a minute, which of the hooks you've read so far comes closest to the tone you want for your own story? Which evokes feelings similar to those you want your opening to evoke? Granted, I chose examples that I find most interesting. Many other kinds of hooks are equally effective. If the mood or tone of each example I present feels wrong for your story, see if you can explain *why* without resorting to liking or disliking it. Then analyze *how* each author achieves her or his effect.

SUSTAINABILITY

There's a reason "angling" is synonymous with fishing. Angling is defined as attempting to get something by *artful means.* In the creative arts, technique is the means. It includes selecting and manipulating content and mood until the desired effect is achieved.

To continue the angler's analogy, a mystery's first line should be a high-tensile line. *Tensile:* capable of being stretched or drawn out. An effective hook stretches our interest beyond the first sentence. It raises a question that teases us into seeking the answer in the next sentence. There, we learn just enough to want to learn more. The high-tensile line is sustainable. It keeps stretching, stringing us along, drawing us from one sentence to the next—preferably nonstop.

Many a manuscript comes close to hooking readers with an interesting line or two, but it doesn't sustain our curiosity. Faltering interest is reason enough for a busy screener to move on to the next manuscript, and from that one to the next—preferably nonstop.

To discover how far a high-tensile line can take you, look at the opening to Mary Saums' first mystery novel, *Midnight Hour.*

> The phone hit the far corner of my bedroom like a blast out
> of a shotgun.

This sentence is all action, no background. It raises the questions that we want answered—a want that keeps us hooked: what, who, when, how, and why. The "where" is already indicated: "my bedroom." The only description is "far corner." Is this violence really occurring in a bedroom? And to a *telephone?* To find out, we're obliged to read on.

> Its plastic parts slid down the wall and fell in a heap.

Yep, it *is* a phone, and there's the wall it hit. So much for the *what,* which makes us want to find out *why.* Let's read another sentence before deciding how far to let this hook take us.

> After a few seconds of quiet it sputtered a final electronic
> cough, then flat-lined like a dead man's monitor.

First there's a shotgun simile, now a dead man, images that resonate
with mystery fans. Who could quit now? Okay, one more sentence.

> "You deserved a slower death, you demon tool of iniquity!"
> I yelled. I tugged the straps of my push-up bra, part of a
> fancy set I'd bought specifically for the evening—a truly
> joyous occasion. It was my fortieth birthday.

Oops! We meant to read one sentence, and three whizzed by. How'd
that happen? What has Saums done to keep our eyes pasted to the page?

- ◆ Her structure continually provokes new questions because the hook
  keeps stretching, adding more interest, not letting go. To see where
  it leads, we have to read more, don't we?

- ◆ Her character is quirky—a desirable trait in any protagonist. Saums
  has her do to her phone what most of us only dream of doing to ours.
  We like this character already. Saums also has her character reveal
  intimate details about herself, strong personal feelings, and a hair-
  trigger mood—which anyone over twenty who turns a divisible-by-
  ten birthday can identify with.

Whaddya know, our emotions are engaged. We're starting to care about
this Ma Bellicose mangler and want to know what happens next.

> The dial tone was driving me crazy. I stomped across the
> room and slammed the receiver onto what was left of its cradle.
> Sitting down at my dressing table, I rubbed my face and tried
> to calm down. *To hell with that jerk,* I thought. I shook my new
> bottle of age-denying makeup and slathered it on.

What jerk? Something else to find out? Oh, all right, one more line.

> Much to my surprise the debris-that-once-was-my-phone rang.

Maybe that's the jerk calling. If so, we have yet another reason to stay
tuned—we want to hear him reamed out by this spitfire. Her name, Willi
Taft, we learn *after* she picks up the phone. That detail, plus other bits of

background and description, are worked in with the action.

You might ask, how much of all this activity is the hook itself? We keep being strung along into the next scene, and the next. It doesn't stop.

Precisely!

The function of an effective hook is *not* to stop but to draw us into the situation to a point of no return. The goal is to keep readers from putting the book down—especially its first reader, the busy screener. The plan is to build staying power. Tensile strength.

TURN OF THE SCREW

Many authors open more sedately than Saums and sharpen their hooks gradually, letting a slightly later sentence be the one to turn the screw.

> My name is Ingrid Anastasia Beaumont. My ex used to say
> that my initials stood for "I'm a bitch." True.
> > Denise Dietz, *Footprints in the Butter*

> Nathan Rubin died because he got brave. Not the sustained
> kind of thing that wins you a medal in a war, but the split-second
> kind of blurting outrage that gets you killed on the street.
> > Lee Child, *Die Trying*

> My name was Salmon, like the fish; first name, Susie. I was
> fourteen when I was murdered on December 6, 1973.
> > Alice Sebold, *The Lovely Bones*

Which openings make you want to keep reading? How does each author attempt to capture your curiosity? Which suggest incongruities? Ask the same questions of your own hook.

WEATHERING OPINION

Opinion is split on opening with the weather. One objection is the tendency to produce clichés—not as rusty, perhaps, as "It was a dark and stormy night,"[19] but close. Another objection is that weather reports often seem tacked on, like scenery, without evoking a mood related to the story.

Leann Sweeney reminds us that readers are interested in people. She says that for the weather to work as a "grabber," the character has to experience that weather.

The opening to the first of Sweeney's Yellow Rose mysteries, *Pick Your Poison,* shows how Abby Rose experiences the climate of Houston.

> The sun could have melted diamonds that day, and I spent the afternoon poolside, wasting away in Liptonville for the thirtieth time in a month.

Weather continues to play an important part in Sweeney's plot, as it does in *Act of Betrayal,* a thriller by Shirley Kennett, writing as Morgan Avery. The novel begins:

> It was hot in the apartment, but Cut was used to the heat. His lean body sweated freely and the undershirt he wore was soaked under the arms and down his back. The last week of July in St. Louis was bad enough when a person could lie in the deep shade of a tree and let the breeze take away the sweat. . . . Compared to an afternoon under a shade tree, the apartment was a little slice of hell.
> It would have been nice to open the window.

But he cannot open it, because the plot is intricately connected with the weather, and because he "always associated the summer heat with the day that his boy died."

Nature and the environment are especially effective for creating an atmosphere of foreboding, as in the following first lines.

> It was a land—hostile and unforgiving.
> Faye Kellerman, *Moon Music*

> Legend says that overcast skies are nature's way of hiding evil, protecting the gods from seeing sinister deeds.
> S. D. Tooley, *When the Dead Speak,* a first mystery

> The late morning blazed with blue skies and the colors of fall, but none of it was for me.
> Patricia Cornwell, *Black Notice*

> I had forgotten the smell.
> Sara Paretsky, *Blood Shot*

These lines paint no leisurely panorama of the sky, water, or landscape for their own sake. Rather, the environment is called upon to create an effect that's quick and sharp: nature with a twist.

If you open with the environment, check your follow-through. Is the opening connected with your plot? With your main character? Or is it mere background? Do readers sense what the character is feeling, both physically through selected sensory data, and emotionally through mood, tone, and anticipation of what lies ahead?

> "Weather is a literary speciality, and no untrained hand can turn out a good article on it."
>
> Mark Twain[18]

If not, take a hint from the developers of real estate and don't let your grand opening depend on the weather.

CLICHÉD OPENINGS

One of the most clichéd openings in crime fiction begins with the sleuth's being jolted awake by a ringing telephone, always too early, often too hung over to function. That hook was sharp in the early days of the hardboiled detective story. Today, hooks that start the morning demand originality—which the following examples provide.

> I had become so used to hysterical dawn phone calls that I only muttered one halfhearted oath before answering.
> "Peacocks," a voice said.
>> Donna Andrews, *Murder with Peacocks,* Agatha winner for best first novel

> I sat on my living room sofa at five o'clock in the morning with a copy of the mock-up of the front page of the day's *New York Post* in my hand, looking at my own obituary.
>> Linda Fairstein, *Final Jeopardy*

> Some days are better than others for walking in graveyards.
>> Nancy Pickard, *No Body*

> Mouse is dead. Those words had gone through my mind every morning for three months. Mouse is dead because of me.
>> Walter Mosley, *Bad Boy Brawly Brown*

Rapidly becoming a cliché is the hokey hook, one that's contrived for quick shock value but has no lasting power. After delivering its initial jolt it drifts into other topics, and continues to meander for a chapter or more before coming around to the opening incident. For example:

> The morning the severed finger arrived in the mail, I was still thinking about Hawaii. The blinding sun, the fragrance of yellow hibiscus, and Lola's sleek body riding the waves.
> We'd arrived on a balmy Tuesday evening after a long, sleepless flight listening to some moron in the seat behind us trying to impress the blonde traveling alone. A pretty woman, she wore. . . .

Eventually the writer gets around to picking up the story line that's hinted at in the opening sentence. The busy screener, recognizing the technique for its hokey pokiness, might skip ahead a few pages looking for the story line's reappearance.

Or not.

So don't hobble your hook with backstory, description dumps, meanderings, clichés, pile-ups of adjectives and adverbs, or the hokiness of a gratuitous shocker. Choose an opening action you are prepared to build from and sustain.

A hook does its job by continuing to engage our attention until we are firmly caught and cannot get away. Nothing should divert our attention or cause reader interest to . . . um, you know . . . flounder.

Caring about the main character is the ultimate hook.

> "Fiction does not exist on paper. It exists within the mind of the reader. Use just enough words to get the mind working. Don't let ego tell you otherwise."
>
> J. A. Konrath, author of the "Jack" Daniels mystery series

FIND & FIX CLUE #1: HOBBLED HOOKS

- See how many of the following characteristics are true for your hook:
    - arouses curiosity about who, what, where, when, how, and why;
    - introduces the main character as soon as possible and leaves no doubt about who is the lead;
    - begins with the problem, predicament, conflict, threat, or change;
    - plunges into the middle of the situation;
    - uses tone to create a mood without piling on adjectives and adverbs;
    - stirs emotions that keep readers identifying with the central character's feelings;
    - sets a tone consistent with the main character's attitude;
    - avoids being clichéd, boring, or hokey—not contrived solely for shock value;
    - sustains curiosity well past the first chapter;
    - keeps action going without submerging it in backstory or description;
    - suggests a contradiction of some kind.

"Give them no reason to reject your work."

Harry Arnston,
quoted by Peter Abresch

CLUE #2:   PERILOUS PROLOGUES

New writers may be surprised to learn that a mystery is not obliged to open with a prologue. Its absence is a good thing, because readers often skip what they see as a barrier to the story—along with all the other body parts known collectively as front matter: legal notice, acknowledgments, author's note, and so on. Nonfiction additionally conditions readers to skip the preface, introduction, and much-despised "How to Use This Book." Such behavior gives a whole new meaning to the term "page-turner."

Whenever I see the word "Prologue" I picture the public speaker who walks to the microphone, looks at the audience, and announces, "Before I begin. . . ." News flash: You just began.

Although walking out on a speaker's drawn-out warm-up would seem rude in an auditorium, prologue-skipping is common in a bookstore. Why should readers browse front matter when thousands of crisp new spines stand at attention waiting to be selected for active duty?

Meanwhile, back at the prologue, the author's carefully wrought hook lies undiscovered among all the other body parts.

REASONS OR EXCUSES?

Why do some mysteries open before Chapter 1? Here are the reasons I'm given when I ask.

- *My first chapter is not that exciting.*
  My reply: Let's work on your first chapter.
- *My editor made me do it.*
  Probably for the above reason. See above reply.
- *Writing the prologue was the easiest way to get started.*
  True, but even jumper cables are temporary.

Here's good advice on getting started from Denise Dietz, creator of the Ellie Bernstein mysteries and the Ingrid Beaumont mysteries:

> "Most of the time I write a prologue, then delete it
> later. For me, it's a way to get my act together (since I
> don't outline). For *Footprints in the Butter,* my
> prologue became my second chapter."

More reasons (or excuses) are:

➤ *I introduce my protagonist after the prologue because I have the whole book to develop interest in her.*
   Not exactly. The book develops the character; interest begins on page 1.

➤ *I thought a prologue was required.*

If your reason is equally lame but you are set on using this questionable device anyway, my next question is, are you willing to buck the bias?

BIAS?

What bias?

Agents and editors know all about the page-skipping that goes on in the aisles of the book nook and the privacy of the bedroom. Even mystery *writers* admit to not reading prologues.[20] At least one acquisitions editor makes no secret of shifting front-loaded manuscripts to the bottom of his pile. *And those are agent-referred!*

As someone who reads front matter even when I'm not being paid to, I agree that the majority of prologues are unjustified, unconnected, and unnecessary. So the rest of this CLUE presents four basic types of prologues, together with their pros and cons. Mostly cons.

Literary agent Jessica Faust finds that material put in a prologue seldom belongs there because it often gives away crucial plot elements too early and ties in to the main story too late.

"If you must use the device," she advises, "tie its content in with the main story almost immediately. For example, if the prologue introduces a time when the characters are children, at least one of them has to be introduced right away in Chapter 1."[21]

Let's see how your prologue, if you use one, measures up.

TYPE 1: BACKSTORY CONNECTION

The most immediate connection between a prologue and its main story, and therefore the most justifiable form of the device, occurs with the chronological or backstory prologue. The gap in time can be a few hours, as in Dan Brown's *The DaVinci Code,* or twenty-three years, as in Meg Chittenden's *More Than You Know.*

The latter opens with thirteen-year-old Nick Ciacia attending his father's funeral. He's given a tip that his father's killer might be a white-haired man known only as "the Snowman." Nick tells this to the police captain, who ridicules the tip. The boy vows to find the mystery man himself.

The prologue's tie-in to Chapter 1 is immediate. Nick, now an FBI agent, learns the Snowman's real name and begins tracking him. Same objective, same narrative POV, same central character. The only change is time.

Not all writers who open with a backstory prologue dramatize it. *Some present history in the form of news clippings or correspondence, often in italics. If you must italicize, keep the text as brief as possible, preferably under four lines. One hardcover I saw from a major publisher opened with fourteen pages set entirely in italics, despite the type style being notoriously unappealing to read at length. See?*

One alternative to opening with backstory is to select only essential bits of it and weave those bits into the main story a little at a time (discussed in CLUE #3). Or rename the prologue Scene 1 of Chapter 1.

A top candidate for renaming is *The DaVinci Code* because its prologue is structured no differently from many of its chapters.

- The time interval from the opening event to the main story is only a few hours, an interval that occurs between other chapters.
- The post-prologue switch to a different viewpoint character and a different setting also occurs at other times.
- The narrative uses a third-person POV throughout.

Renaming Brown's prologue Scene 1 of Chapter 1 would involve only the renumbering of chapters. Content would not be affected. If your prologue could as easily become part of Chapter 1, why not make it so? Although *The Da Vinci Code*'s prologue hasn't hurt the sales of this best-seller one little bit, if your novel is not even a first-seller, are you willing to put it at risk by opening with a device widely considered controversial?

TYPE 2: FUTURE CONNECTION

Alas, the most frequently used type of prologue is the least chronologically connected, and is therefore the hardest to justify. It's the flash-forward or peek-ahead prologue in which a high-anxiety event from later in the story is mounted on the front end, like a hood ornament.

Its purported purpose is to let readers in on certain facts from a temporary POV—either the villain's, the victim's, or the objective third person's—while keeping the protagonist in the dark until later in the investigation.

One problem is that by the time the plot catches up to the prologue's events, readers have forgotten the particulars. Should we plow on, hoping those details are unimportant?

In a mystery, details are always important.

Maybe we should stop, return to the beginning, and read the opening again. Seems a good reason for not reading the prologue the first time.

Advocates of the peek-ahead form defend it as the only method for keeping the sleuth's first-person voice consistent once the main story begins. Here lies the second problem: the case has yet to be made for using first-person at all. Frequently, the sleuth's POV can be made equally effective in third-person, with fewer restrictions. (More on POV in CLUE #11.)

> "I find that prologues are vastly overused in mysteries and almost always a mistake. They get in the way of a good story, rather than enhance it."
>
> Jim Huang, editor,
> *The Drood Review*[22]

First-person's benefits include intimacy, immediacy, and—theoretically, at least—a fair chance for readers to solve the mystery along with the sleuth. We enjoy the illusion of sharing a close, personal relationship with the sleuth-as-narrator, privy to his thoughts, feelings, and clues.

We expect to stay *in* step with the sleuth while he and the reader stay one step *behind* the killer—until the climax, that is. At this breakthrough moment we accept (sort of) being shut out of the sleuth's thinking as he puts the last piece of the puzzle in place, traps the villain, and wows us with his superior detecting abilities.

Which brings us to problem number three for this type of prologue. From the outset, peek-ahead information puts readers in a superior position to the protagonist, the one who is supposed to be the story's most clever and resourceful character. However, when readers know something the central character doesn't, the benefits of intimacy and fair play diminish. The story becomes a hybrid of two genres: mystery and thriller. Blending them is difficult for the writer who does not yet realize that the expectations for each genre are different.[23]

A more consistent way of keeping information from the crime-fighter—if that's necessary—is to merge the prologue with Chapter 1 and use third-person throughout.

There are no simple answers to questions about point of view. Writers demonstrate their skill by the choices they make—presumably *after* they experiment with alternatives.

Successful writers have boxes filled with such experiments. These are known in the business as first drafts.

CHEAP THRILL

Let's be honest. The reason for a mystery's peek-ahead prologue is to heat up a lukewarm opening.

Does it matter if this quick fix for a slow start gives away too much too soon, or is unrelated to the chapters that follow? Yes, it does. Imagine this: We are reading a mystery that plunges us into action on page 1, without our noticing the small type in the upper corner that says "Prologue." Heading, shmedding—form shouldn't call attention to itself anyway.

Just as we become interested in the high-anxiety threat to the character we believe is the protagonist, she suffers a gruesome, gory, graphic end. This evil deed barely pushes our emotional buttons, though, because so far we've had little opportunity to care about the victim. We may feel sympathy for her but not empathy. Not good.

We turn the page and the 48-point heading "Chapter 1" shouts the start of the main story. Now we cannot help but become aware of form. Worse, we seem to be reading a different novel: actions are unrelated to those of the prologue, time and place are ambiguous, and every character is a stranger. Our connection to the story just disconnected. *Click.*

What happened to our need to identify early with the main character? Our first relationship ended when she turned into the victim and got bumped off on page 2, 4, 6, or 8. *Now* who do we appreciate? Someone new is emerging as the possible protagonist, but we're slow to invest our emotions in this newcomer because the prologue's cheap thrill trifled with our emotions. What if this relationship turns into another brief fling? Will the real protagonist please stand up?

A bigger problem with the peek-ahead prologue is that after it raises the goose bumps, what follows has nowhere to go but down. Invariably, the opening action morphs into backstory and downshifts to description. Although a change of pace is usually welcome after a high-tension scene, we just got here. We are not completely hooked. We're not even sure who the main character is. This is too early for a meltdown.

Yet here we are, mired in the same slow-moving chapter that the thriller prologue was mounted in front of to keep the story from opening with originally. We've been had by a blatant appeal to sensationalism. The nightly news exploits the same principle: if it bleeds, it leads.

> "The well-told story, with characters who interest us, does quite well, no matter when the murder takes place."
>
> Pat Browning, author of *Full Circle*

I like an exciting opening as well as anyone. What is not desirable is the tension drop that takes place when a prologue disconnects from the main story. *Click click.*

Evaluators of prologues—agents, editors, and other astute readers—see the disconnect as ruining the novel's structural unity. The prologue-skipper finds Chapter 1 as dull as ever—one more unsold book. And the writer who uses this device keeps believing, mistakenly, that it's okay to follow a strong opening with a first chapter that suffers from chronic post-prologue, low-tension, backstory ache.

TYPE 3: BODY ON PAGE 1

A variant of the cheap thrill is the "body on page 1"—shorthand for the murder that takes place or is discovered in the opening scene. Writers who dramatize this event in a prologue believe that having a body on page 1 is a rule. It is not a rule. It's a precipitating event that kicks off an investigation—a sequence that's a natural for the mystery subgenre known as police procedural. Think *Law and Order.*

When the crime-fighter is a professional, the prologue might as well become Scene 1 of Chapter 1, because there is no disconnect between it and the main story. The investigation is supposed to proceed from the discovery of the corpse. This unfortunate fellow is not, however, under contract to pop up at the opening of *every* mystery.

When the crime-fighter is an amateur or "accidental" sleuth, her part in the investigation seldom begins immediately. The writer has to first justify why an ordinary citizen would become involved in tracking a dangerous killer. A delayed start allows the writer to meet three needs.

1. The sleuth's crime-solving ability or predilection has to be established, her background sketched, and her eccentricities demonstrated under normal circumstances.

2. Her motivation needs to be developed. (More on that in CLUE #15.)

3. To provide further credibility, she will at first resist being drawn into the investigation.

Typically, while all this is being developed, the high-tension action of the prologue skids to a halt at the threshold to Chapter 1, where it causes a noticeable disconnect. *Click click click.*

If this scenario resembles your own opening, begin at a more modest anxiety level so the drop in tension is less severe. Build up from there. Whatever you do, avoid divorcing your audience's emotional investment in your central character this early.

Murder does not have to open the story, but you might want to commit the wicked deed before page 100. Again, this is not a rule. (If it were, several fine mysteries would be disqualified.) It's an expectation. A mystery is in trouble if *something* doesn't cause tension from page 1. It's in bigger trouble if its *only* tension comes from a body on page 1.

THE HE-HE-HE VILLAIN

Crimes that take place in prologues usually conceal the killer's identity until the climax—a technique that lets the villain play a dual role throughout the story: a mysterious evildoer in private and an ordinary chap in public.

But some writers try so hard to conceal the identity of this Mr. Hyde that they go on, at length, about "the man," "him," "the dark figure," "he," "he," and "he." Before long, the profusion of indefinite pronouns becomes tedious and grammatically ungainly.

Jan Burke has the right idea in *Flight,* her eighth mystery featuring Irene Kelly and Detective Frank Harriman. Burke gives her unidentified murderer a specific nickname: the "Looking Glass Man." With a consistent third-person POV throughout, she periodically cuts to scenes that focus on this villain—starting with Chapter 2. In Chapter 1, before we meet him, Burke dramatizes his brutal attack on a father and two teenagers. A less-skilled writer would have framed that opening attack as a prologue.

Sol Stein, author and editor, points out that ideally, the protagonist should play an important role in the first scene so there's no mistaking another character for that primary role. He says that one mark of amateur writing is a "lack of early clarity as to whose story we, as readers, should be following."[24]

Wisely, Burke uses no such device. By opening with a fully developed chapter, she gives us the opportunity to care about the teenagers before they are assaulted.

CONTINUITY

Tell No One, Harlan Coben's tenth novel, begins with a variation of the body on page 1. The story opens with a sudden assault on the wife of the protagonist, David Beck. With her screams still ringing in his ears, he, too, is assaulted.

No heading identifies that opening scene as a prologue and no dateline appears. This sly evasion of truth-in-labeling lets us approach the story with no expectation of a disconnect—except for David's warning us on page 1: "There was my life before the tragedy. There is my life now. The two have painfully little in common."

Given the shocking attack that ends the opening scene, we might not recall David's observation about *before* and *now.* I didn't. So I was unprepared for the "Chapter 1" heading on page 9 and its "Eight Years Later" dateline. Not for long, though, because Coben quickly establishes continuity between the two scenes. Here's how.

1. Change is limited to one factor: time. Although the eight-year gap comes as a surprise (I can't be the only one), the dateline keeps readers from having to puzzle over the "when"—unlike many other writers make us do with their post-prologue settings.
2. The same POV continues, as with a true backstory-type prologue. (Three chapters later, David's first-person viewpoint shifts to third-person, but that's a different issue, dealt with in CLUE #11.)

3. The first words of the main story are: "Another girl was about to break my heart." These opening words acknowledge the events of the prologue and effectively connect the two scenes.

4. A few pages into Chapter 1, David begins making direct references to his efforts over the years to find some trace of his missing wife. This tightens the connection and unifies the story's structure.

Suppose you were to develop similar unifying features for your opening scenes. Would I then say, "Aw shucks, go ahead and use a prologue"? Not on your life. What I *would* say is, "Think. If your prologue is so well-connected to the main story that it could *be* Chapter 1, have you any reason for not making it so?"

TYPE 4: SUMMARY PROLOGUE

Another perilous prologue to become aware of is the summary, in which the narrator looks back on the experience about to be told. The summarized lessons learned express the story's theme.

A summary is not a scene, however, and philosophizing is not action. Moreover, summary prologues are usually so generalized that if page one fell to the floor of the book bindery it would never be missed.

Reflecting on lessons learned is a type of foretelling. While *foreboding* is a mood-setting technique, and *foreshadowing* legitimizes future events by planting early clues, *foretelling* is too similar to the aptly named had-I-but-known gimmick.

> Had I but known I'd be dangling from a ledge a hundred meters above the Pacific Ocean, I'd never have opened the lilac-scented envelope.

How suspenseful can a cliffhanger-dangler be if it reminds us that the narrator survived to tell of it? This once-fashionable foretelling device is today's object of ridicule.

In truth, slight foretelling is tolerated but not encouraged. Did you notice it in the quotation from *Tell No One* a couple of pages ago? Harlan Coben's opening combines elements of three kinds of prologues: the chronologically connected, the dramatized "body on page 1," and the summary.

Here is that opening in full. Notice how it begins with foreboding to establish a mood, slides into foreshadowing, summarizes the theme about violence altering everything, and concludes with foretelling.

> There should have been a dark whisper in the wind. Or maybe a deep chill in the bone. Something. An ethereal song only Elizabeth or I could hear. A tightness in the air. Some textbook premonition. There are misfortunes we almost expect in life— what happened to my parents, for example—and then there are other dark moments, moments of sudden violence, that alter everything. There was my life before the tragedy. There is my life now. The two have painfully little in common.

BREVITY COUNTS

Once in a while I come across a prologue that enhances the story it precedes but isn't a scene and might not work as part of Chapter 1. Instead, it's a looking-back summary—with two differences: it is short, and it uses specific images, not generalizations.

Here's the prologue to *A Woman's Place,* Linda Grant's fourth Catherine Sayler mystery. Its brevity and resulting white space on the page greatly increase the likelihood of this prologue's being read.

Grant uses only fifty-one words to evoke a mood, arouse our curiosity, and express the protagonist's fears—without giving away their source.

> I don't dwell on the past. No point in that.
> But I still can't stay in the same room with a man wearing Paco cologne. And there are times when a ringing phone makes my heart race. I read the newspapers, but I skip certain stories.
> The nightmares come less often.

This is the entire prologue.

I like to think that the line about not dwelling on the past is a playful slap at mysteries overloaded with backstory.

That's the next CLUE.

FIND & FIX CLUE #2: PERILOUS PROLOGUES

- If you use a prologue, be sure it serves a useful, well-integrated purpose essential to the story.
- Double-check that any prologue:
  - does not delay bonding with the protagonist;
  - ties into the main story right away;
  - exists for a reason other than a cheap thrill;
  - avoids giving away important developments from the middle of the book;
  - is not a disguise for a first chapter that sags with backstory and description.
- See if your prologue could more properly become Scene 1 of Chapter 1.
- Confirm that the character directly affected by your opening situation is someone readers will care about. Don't answer until you work through the issues raised in CLUES #1 and #3.

"My motto is, when all else fails—edit."

J. T. Ellison, author of the forthcoming thriller,
All the Pretty Girls

CLUE #3: BLOODY BACKSTORY

When you are introduced to strangers at a party, do you want to hear about their past if you haven't gotten interested in what they're like in the present? Yet writers are always interrupting their story's current action to relate a character's background. The past is history. In fiction it's called backstory.

Readers do need to know something about past events that affect the present story. Why, then, is backstory so maligned, so bloody unpopular? (That's *bloody* as in blasted, cursed, and damned.) Because the techniques used to present it are wretched. Instead of showing one event that would make us care about the protagonist *now,* writers tend to summarize a lifetime of facts, telling too much too soon. They stop the action before the reader has a chance to get wrapped up in the character or her predicament.

One thriller I edited killed off five victims, stopping after each killing to tell the story of that victim from childhood to adulthood. Those five life stories went on for at least four pages *each,* quickly chilling any thrill.

SATISFYING CURIOSITY

Fiction, especially mystery, is in trouble if it focuses attention on what's already happened instead of on what's about to happen. Backstory may advance the reader's store of data, but data does not necessarily advance the story. Most of what I see in manuscripts is not essential or even relevant. Rarely is it needed right after a scene opens or a character appears.

Once readers become invested in the main character's problem, you can insinuate backstory via one or two *sentences.* You don't want to satisfy reader curiosity—you want to increase it. Several *chapters* later, after your readers are committed to finding out what happens next, you can offer a paragraph or two of backstory. Be selective.

If events from the past are important to your plot, please remember that plot is unlikely to make its impression before the busy screener finds some other reason to stop reading. Too much backstory too soon is a great reason. So before you kill a screener's interest in your story:

- ❖ Edit your first two chapters to sustain the tensile quality of your hook.
- ❖ Force yourself to stop telling what already happened and show what is happening *now.*

By freeing yourself from explaining your characters, you can concentrate on the real work of character portrayal.

WHERE TO BEGIN

Where your story opens determines whether backstory is an issue. Begin too early and you bury your mystery in history. Begin too late and you have all that backstory you want to cram in. Where *is* the beginning, anyway?

It's where the first sign of trouble appears. It's where a change threatens to upset the status quo. Mystery author and literary agent Jack Bickham says, "Nothing is more threatening than change. . . . Identify the moment of change, and you know when your story must open."[25]

Memory Can Be Murder, the third Peaches Dann mystery by Elizabeth Daniels Squire, opens with these three sentences:

"I'm scared." The voice on the telephone wavered. "Maybe I'm losing my mind."

The story does not open with the telephone ringing and the too-conventional "Hello, who is this?" Neither does the action stop to unload backstory. Readers learn what led up to the caller's situation in the same way the sleuth does, from the action and dialogue that unfolds when Peaches goes to meet the phone caller. The narrative moves forward, not backward.

> "Only that part of *then* that is important to, that has a bearing on, *now* is worth being told."
>
> Robie Macauley and George Lanning,
> *Technique in Fiction* [26]

This forward movement is known as *progression*—a subtle but important element in a mystery. Progression builds a sense of inevitability—the conviction that once events have been set in motion, whatever follows moves inescapably, relentlessly toward the solution. Stopping the action for a backward glance interrupts the story's momentum and shatters the sense of inevitability.

BACKGROUND

Whereas backstory tells what occurred before the story opens, *background* supplies information that was or still is true. When you self-edit for backstory, start with your first three chapters and highlight all references to past events. Examine the evidence. Do you work the past in with dialogue and action? Or do you unload it in a *backstory dump*—a paragraph of exposition occurring shortly after each new character appears?

If you're a dumper, clean up the wreckage with some clever slicing, dicing, and splicing.

1. Evaluate how much of your backstory—which you just highlighted— is not vital to the story. Get rid of it (slice).
2. Take the remaining backstory and cut it into separate bits and pieces (dice).
3. Determine where in the story readers need which bits of information to understand what's happening *at the time*. Weave those relevant bits in with the action and dialogue (splice).

Don't let background dominate foreground or sidetrack the action. Adopt a less-and-later approach: give readers only what they need to know when they need to know it, not before.

SPLICING BACKGROUND

Sara Hoskinson Frommer splices a dozen background facts into the first two sentences that open *The Vanishing Violinist,* fourth in her Joan Spencer mystery series.

> Joan Spencer hadn't expected to marry again after Ken died. During the rough years when she was bringing up two children alone, she had occasionally let herself fantasize about a stranger with their father's slender build, dark curls, and pixie grin. Nothing could have been further from the man of her dreams than the one on her sofa, nibbling her ear after she'd fed him

lunch. Yet she felt absolutely right about planning to share the
rest of her life with the bulky blond policeman with crinkly eyes.

By the third sentence, we are watching the two characters in current
story time. Their interaction remains dominant while the next bit of background, Joan's job, is slipped in with another action.

> "Only don't rush me, Fred," she said.
> "Rush you!" Detective Lieutenant Fred Lundquist pulled
> away and patted her hand the way she occasionally patted the
> hands of the old ladies at the Oliver Senior Citizens' Center she
> directed. "I wouldn't dream of it. Now that you mention it, we'd
> probably better wait a few more years. You'll need grandchil-
> dren first, to throw rose petals."
> "You!" She punched him lightly on the shoulder. At the
> moment, she was feeling anything but grandmotherly.   [p. 7]

Smooth, isn't it, how the fact that Joan directs the senior center is sub-
ordinated to Fred's hand-patting? A novice might try to slide that fact into
the conversation: "As you know, Fred, I'm the director of. . . ." Dialogue
that informs the characters of what they are likely to already know is *phony
dialogue*, a corny device invented by the unimaginative for the convenience of the desperate.

A novice might also write a straight statement of background:

Joan Spencer directed the Oliver Senior Citizens' Center.

A line as brief as this would not seriously interrupt the flow of the story,
but as a direct statement of fact it's prominent. And flat. The information
simply lies there, like road kill.

Frommer reduces Joan's job to a comparison: *the way she occasionally
patted the hands [at the] Center she directed.* This roundabout mention
keeps background subordinate to Joan's feelings and to the interaction between the two characters. Even Fred's description is indirect, presented as
part of what Joan is feeling.

Add two character portrayals, and this opening is more multi-faceted
than it appears at first. It has density. Does yours?

BACKGROUND EXPLANATION

Assuming that your story begins at the perfect moment, can it go back to fill in the blanks? You do have to explain what warped your villain's psyche, don't you?

The short answer is no. The long answer agrees that all characters have a past and their life experiences form an integral part of who they are. You have to know all of it; readers don't. Although events occurring before the story opens may cause the problems that affect your characters now, readers can get the picture from a single sentence, like this one:

> "The neighbor told me of hearing the old man beating on the kid almost every night."

A brief reference like this is often sufficient to account for the way the kid turned out, with little need for his life's story. If possible, dramatize the character's actions in current story time so readers can observe his behavior and interpret it for themselves.

Another technique that substitutes for a backstory dump is the character's dropping hints about himself, never quite telling all.

Sometimes a writer sends me an e-mail that says, in effect, "I took out as much backstory as I could, like you said to, but I had to keep a lot because if I cut more, I'd have no story."

Unfortunately, that's true. Some writers begin writing with the unexamined assumption that backstory *is* the story.

If you feel that a considerable amount of information from the past has to be included for your story to make sense, take a hard look at what story you want to be writing, history or mystery. Maybe you are working in the wrong genre.

Long ago, when I first got hooked on books, long passages of explanatory background were common. Today's aspiring writers need to meet today's market expectations. Remember your genre: mystery, not history, not biography. Even the historical mystery, a subgenre of its own, is first a mystery.

The character profiles or bios you create are for your own guidance. Not every fact and personality trait in a profile can or should show up in your manuscript, any more than every job you've ever held should show up on your résumé.

BE SELECTIVE

The most important skill for any writer, I'm convinced, is the ability to be selective. The best time for a vigorous application of this skill is during self-editing. The key to being selective is the delete key. Use it to make your writing not merely shorter but *sharper.*

Begin the revision process by presuming that all backstory is unnecessary. Not all of it is, of course, but if you're not used to cutting your own writing, the process becomes easier when you approach your writing with that presumption.

MULTIPLE PURPOSES

The writer who develops a series knows that some readers forget background from earlier titles, some read titles out of sequence, and some read only one title in a series. Each book has to stand alone as well as preserve continuity from one title to the next. How much background should be repeated?

As little as possible. Refer to an occurrence from the past when it affects the current story. Also, briefly reestablish the protagonist's credentials as a crime solver. Minimize flat statements of fact. Avoid the phoniness of characters telling each other what they already know. Show relationships through action and dialogue.

In *Snipe Hunt* by Sarah Shaber, the second title in her Professor Simon Shaw mystery series, Simon's reputation as an investigator is relevant to the story. Shaber makes that fact known by having Simon's friend, Morgan, discuss it with a shopkeeper.

In an interesting twist, Simon is present while his reputation is being aired. The shopkeeper asks:

> ". . . Aren't you the history professor who figured out who killed that woman in Raleigh? The one that disappeared so many years ago?"
>
> Damn, Simon thought.
>
> "Yeah, that's him," Morgan said. "You probably saw the big article the *News and Observer* did. They called him a 'forensic historian.' A couple of national papers picked the story up off the wires and ran it, too."

"It was a slow news day," Simon said.

Morgan selected a twelve-pack of Miller draft and a jumbo bag of potato chips and took them to the cash register, chuckling.

"Next thing you know, *Newsweek*'s got a whole page on him and *People* wanted to do a profile—"

"That's enough," Simon said. He handed Morgan the Coke and a box of Goody's headache powders. "If you're going to embarrass me, you can pay." [pp. 21–22]

This brief exchange delivers background—and more. It establishes how and when the mom-and-pop shopkeepers learn that the visitor to their town is a forensic historian. It shows the relationship between two friends, whose give and take of protest and persistence adds a little lighthearted conflict to what might otherwise seem too mundane to dramatize: a trip to the store for a headache remedy.

Shaber remains in control of her material throughout, keeping the history brief and the facts few. Her focus stays on the interactions between her characters while she slips in bits of background. The result is a deceptively simple scene that works overtime to function on multiple levels. That's density.

ALL'S WELL THAT ENDS

My final example of double duty backstory comes from the fourth book in the V. I. Warshawski series by Sara Paretsky, *Bitter Medicine*. It's the last scene. The case is solved, loose ends tied up. But V. I. feels moody and lethargic, unable to put her feelings into words. Her protective neighbor believes he knows the reason.

Mr. Contreras was looking at me anxiously. "Life goes on, doll. When Clara died, I thought, boy, this is it. And we'd been married fifty-one years. Yep. We were high-school sweethearts. Course, I dropped out, but she wanted to finish and we waited to have the wedding until she did. And we had some fights, cookie, fights like you never saw the like of. But we always had the good times, too.

"That's what you need, doll. You need someone tough enough to fight with you, but good enough to give you the good times. Not like that ex of yours. . . ." [p. 258]

Mr. Contreras's brief summary of his background becomes relevant to the action by virtue of its provoking a reaction from V. I. That reaction leads Warshawski to think about her life—but not as her neighbor intends.

> I stiffened. If he thought not having a husband was troubling me. . . . Maybe I was just burned out. Too much city, too much time spent in the sewer. . . . Maybe I should get out of the detective business—sell my co-op, retire to Pentwater. I tried picturing myself in this tiny town, with twelve hundred people who all knew each other's business. A quart of Black Label a day might make it tolerable. The idea made me give a little snort of laughter.
>
> "That's, right, doll. You gotta be able to laugh at yourself. I mean, if I laid down and cried for every mistake I ever made, I'd a drowned to death by now. And look at the good side. We got a dog. At least, you got a dog, but who's going to walk her and feed her when you're out to all hours, huh?" [pp. 258–59]

Mr. Contreras misinterprets V. I.'s laughter as well as her lethargy. But the idea that occasioned her laughter lifts her mood. The book ends on a positive note, reflected in the word images associated with the playful golden retriever and an equally golden sunset.

> . . . "She'll be company—long as she don't pee on my tomatoes, huh, girl?"
>
> When Peppy realized he was talking to her, she dropped the stick she'd been gnawing to lick his hand. Then she bounded back to the stick, picked it up, and dropped it next to me, her tail making a great golden circle in the sun. She nudged me hard with her wet nose, slapping me with her tail to make sure I got the point. I pushed myself up to standing. While the dog danced herself into a crescendo of ecstasy, I picked up the stick and hurled it into the setting sun.   [p. 259]

Something else I'd like to say about this ending is the way that it reinforces two traditions in the genre—one thematic and one structural—each well-suited to a mystery's final scene.

Thematically, V. I.'s lifestyle reflects the literary tradition known as the "lone wolf," which originated with the single, male, professional private eye who has his fun and stays unencumbered. The reaction that Mr. C.'s advice triggers echoes the theme that V. I. is happier as a lone investigator, just like a guy P. I.

Structurally, the sequence of actions and reactions of the two series characters reverses V. I.'s discontent and gets her to stand up and join the game, which fulfills another tradition, one often cited to explain the popularity of mystery fiction. Mysteries let readers derive a sense of satisfaction from experiencing, vicariously, a world in which justice prevails, order is restored, and everything ends as it should.

FIND & FIX CLUE #3: BLOODY BACKSTORY

- Approach self-editing with the presumption that backstory is unnecessary.
- Highlight all passages of backstory and background in your first three chapters; then be selective and slice what's non-essential.
- Dice what's left into small, manageable bits.
- Splice those bits in with the dialogue, action, exposition, and description only where needed for readers to understand what is happening at the time.
- Determine the moment of change and begin your story there.
- Use background to serve more than one purpose.
- Replace the too-much-too-soon approach with a less-and-later restraint.
- Break the habit of inserting a background dump immediately after each new character is introduced.
- Verify that the story keeps moving forward with the least amount of stopping, side-stepping, or reversing.

"Anyone who is satisfied with first-draft writing
is either extraordinarily talented
or has low standards."

Arnold Melnick, D. O. [27]

PART IV: KILLING TIME

For the screener-outer, the first clue raises suspicion.
The second reinforces it. By the third clue, the
culprit's identity is sufficiently confirmed: the
perpetrator is an average writer, and the victim
is a rejectable manuscript.

CLUE #4: FATAL FLASHBACKS

A flashback is backstory dramatized. The power of this technique is tempting to harness, but publishing professionals strongly recommend that new writers not try to mount this particular charger. Even experienced writers have problems with it. Here's why:

1. Shifts in time challenge every writer; they're an invitation to crazy time.
2. Flashbacks don't merely apply the brakes to a story's forward drive, as any backstory does; they shift it into reverse. When the gears don't mesh, the collision can be fatal.
3. Material is often included that's not important to the story.
4. Readers need less history than some writers believe, and that small amount can almost always be presented less intrusively.
5. The longer the flashback, the greater the risk of destroying the story's momentum.
6. Any scene that occurs within another scene is difficult to get into and out of gracefully.

7. The hint that a flashback is beginning can prompt readers to skip ahead.

8. The device is often an indulgence used for the writer's convenience, not for its primary purpose—which, as editor and author Sol Stein says, is to *illuminate the present story in a significant way.*[28]

SMOOTH SEGUE

An excellent example of significant illumination is found in *Delayed Diagnosis* by Gwen Hunter, first in her series of medical thrillers featuring Rhea Lynch, M.D.

The scene is a hospital emergency room. Rhea silences a drunken bully and misogynist so she can tend to the injuries of his son, obviously abused. Action changes to thought as the doctor realizes that she'd rather be looking into the medical records of her lifelong friend, Risa, who lies badly beaten and comatose in another part of the hospital.

> Instead of paperwork, I pulled together layers of muscle
> and flesh and stitched up the laceration. And thought about the
> moaning child under my hands. He was so innocent and so at
> risk of being warped. Just as I had been at one time.   [p. 81]

With the theme of childhood vulnerability, the author draws a parallel between the little boy of the present and the little girl of the past. Hunter begins the process of moving us from the present into that past with a single paragraph.

> Risa and I were seven the year we met, and to this day it was
> the best year of my life. Better even than my senior year of med
> school, when John noticed me for the first time and began
> pursuing me as if I fit into his parents' upper-class lifestyle.
> Better even than the year I graduated medical school and was
> accepted into my first choice of residency programs. Better even
> than that perfect summer when John and I became engaged.
> Better because there were no butterflies, no uncertainties, no
> hormonal confusion, no stress, no self-doubt. No grown-up
> angst. Just childhood perfection.
>   We had met. . . .   [pp. 81–82]

Before we pursue the words "We had met" into the flashback itself, I want to acknowledge the richness of Hunter's technique. The repetition of "Better even than" creates a framework for backstory. With each major event in Rhea's life reduced to a small but specific chunk, the passage becomes a model of compression, and the compare-contrast method further doubles its density. The words "We had met" set the scene for that long-ago time and place where Rhea's mother had rented a house.

> Though fairly stable at the time of the move, Mama had been drunk since, and the groceries had run out. Her next trust-fund check wasn't due to arrive for a week. And it wasn't as though I could ask my daddy for money, as he had died before I was born. Even when Mama was sober, I was alone. . . .   [p. 82]

An alcoholic parent provides yet another parallel between the little girl of the past and the little boy of the present.

> Hungry, angry at the world, I had carried every rock, branch and construction remnant I could find to the creek and hurled them in. I had built a fine dam. Water had begun to swell and rise over the low banks, flooding the low-lying empty lot near the rental house where Mama snored in a pool of vomit on the bathroom floor. . . .
> And so I built a really fine dam with junk and angry frustration. Just as I dumped in an armful of wallboard scraps, I heard a voice.   [pp. 82–83]

Notice the switch from the past perfect tense ("I *had built*" and water *"had begun* to swell") to the simple past tense ("Mama *snored*"; "I *dumped*"; and "I *heard* a voice"). Backstory glides effortlessly into flashback, and we find ourselves *in* the past, where we see the world through seven-year-old eyes and feel the powerful emotions of a neglected child. We glimpse a personality taking shape in Rhea's proactive response to frustration and unmet expectation—ideal characteristics for a protagonist who solves crimes.

Hunter's flashback portrays the beginning of a lifelong friendship, and for the next two pages we see how unlike Rhea and Risa are in upbringing and lifestyle, yet how alike in their defiance of authority.

Because Risa's coma prevents our witnessing the interaction between these friends as grownups, the mechanism of a flashback offers the only way we get to see their relationship for ourselves. Through the flashback we experience the importance of that friendship to Rhea, which establishes a believable motive for her to investigate Risa's mysterious injuries.

RETURN TO PRESENT

The first three words of the author's next paragraph, "To this day," prepare us for the return to current story time. The actual return occurs four sentences later, effective in its swiftness.

> . . . To this day I can remember the crunch of that apple and the taste of the peanut butter and jelly. It was peach jam. I had never eaten peach jam, and it was wonderful.
>
> After lunch, Risa took off her sandals and waded in with me. Together we tore down my dam. I never built another.
>
> Carefully, I tied off the last stitch.   [p. 84]

In one smooth motion Hunter brings us back to the emergency room, where the doctor is continuing the same action as before the flashback.

Let's summarize a few of the author's techniques.

- Thematically, images of the boy's physical injuries parallel Rhea's psychic injuries.
- Structurally, the departure in time is fused smoothly with the main story, engaging our interest before we realize that a flashback is upon us.
- Transitions are seamless, with the same action at the point of departure picking up at the return.
- There's no overt setup for the shift in time, no clichéd "It stirred a memory of" or "My mind went back to that special day. . . ."
- The flashback is all characterization, presented mostly through dialogue and action with a minimum of description.
- Most importantly, it serves the function widely recognized as the only justification for a flashback: to illuminate the main story in a significant way.

Flashbacks work as effectively in third-person narration as in first-person, except where writers make excessively wordy shifts in time, such as "his memory took him" or "her mind floated back." Often, a nearly unnoticeable change in tense is all that's needed to complete the transition.

ALTERNATIVE PASTS

Instead of transporting your readers into the past, in many cases you can maintain your story's forward momentum by treating the content of the potential flashback as you would other backstory: by slicing, dicing, and splicing selected essentials into the main action in current story time. (Described in CLUE #3.)

Another option is the *recollection* or *flash memory,* a mini-flashback that evokes the feeling of a blast from the past. Mini-flashes are introduced at those moments when an incident in current story time would naturally trigger the character's recall of a past event. The device may offer readers new information or repeat old information in a new context—either of which creates new meaning.

A memory flash needs no transition or fanfare, no *he thought* or *she remembered.* Because each recollection is brief, it can be set off by italics to distinguish it from what's taking place in current story time.

Sandra Brown uses the technique in *The Alibi* to furnish the lines of dialogue she omits from key scenes dramatized earlier in the book. When we first experience those early scenes, we believe we are seeing and hearing all we need to. We are wrong.

Later circumstances cause Hammond Cross, Brown's protagonist, to recall the dialogue spoken earlier, and he comes to realize that his initial encounter with an attractive woman was not what he thought it was.

See how Brown integrates flash memories into a scene:

> . . . They had been together at the fair for at least an hour before he even thought to ask her name. They'd laughed because it had taken them that long to get around to what was usually the first order of business when two people meet and must make their own introductions.
>
> *"Names aren't really that important, are they? Not when the meeting is this amiable."*

> *He agreed. "Yeah, what's in a name?" He proceeded to quote*
> *what he could remember of the passage from Romeo and Juliet.*
> *"That's good! Have you ever thought of writing it down?"*
> *"In fact I have, but it would never sell."*
> From there it had become a running joke—his asking her name,
> her declining to tell him.   [pp. 166–67]

If this dialogue, recollected later, had been included in the earlier dramatization, our suspicions would have run ahead of Hammond's. That would have put readers in a superior position to him. The author's technique dupes both the reader and the protagonist, who—unlike the reader—possesses knowledge that he *failed to realize the significance of at the time*. By integrating the flashed memory seamlessly into the action, Sandra Brown raises our awareness simultaneously with Hammond's, which adds to our surprise.

If mini-flashes work for your mystery, you may find the technique easier to carry out than a fully developed flashback, and you avoid losing the momentum of your story in a time warp.

TENSING UP

Writers tell me they aren't sure what verb tense to use when introducing material from the past into the present, given that current story time is already being expressed in the past tense. Here's the easy part:

> Paul *announced* (past tense) that he *had* found (past perfect tense)
> the murder weapon.

This sequence of past tense followed by past perfect is appropriate for the first step back in time. However, if the past perfect were to continue, as I've seen done in numerous manuscripts, the result—though grammatically correct—would be cumbersome:

> Paul announced that he *had found* the murder weapon. This
> morning he *had gone* for coffee as usual and *had noticed. . . .*

Steer clear of cumbersome. Here's the same example, equally correct, which uses "had" only one time, and only to introduce the episode. From then on, the simple past tense prevails.

Paul announced that he *had found* the murder weapon. This morning he *went* for coffee as usual and *noticed.* . . .

The one-time use of the past perfect tense is usually sufficient to signal a transition to the past, especially when another transition clue is furnished, such as *this morning.* From that point forward, the simple past makes the long-ago action more immediate and less wordy.

To end the sequence and signal a return to story time, reintroduce "had" one last time, if necessary. Also add a reminder of the time or setting that exists before the flashback, as John Sandford does in the following scene from his first thriller, *Rules of Prey.*

Sandford's series character, police lieutenant Lucas Davenport, is flying from Minnesota's Twin Cities to Cedar Rapids, Iowa. When the woman in the next seat notices his death grip on the armrests, she volunteers a series of unwelcome platitudes, then adds:

> "Well, don't worry, we'll be there in an hour."
> Lucas cranked his head toward her. He felt as though his spine had rusted. "An hour? We've been up pretty long now."
> "Only ten minutes," she said cheerfully.
> "Oh, God."
> The police psychologist had told him that he feared the loss of control.
> "You can't deal with the idea that your life is in somebody else's hands, no matter how competent they are. What you have to remember is, your life is always in somebody else's hands. You could step into the street and get mowed down by a drunk in a Cadillac. Much more chance of that than a plane wreck."
>   [p. 200]

The author signals the flashback with the line, "The police psychologist had told him," a one-time use of the past perfect. From that point on the flashback stays in past tense.

> "I know that," Lucas said. "I want to know what to do about it."
> The shrink shook his head. "Well, there's hypnotism. And there are some books that are supposed to help. But if I were

you, I'd just have a couple of drinks. And try not to fly."

"How about chemicals?"

"You could try some downers, but they'll mess up your head. I wouldn't do it if you have to be sharp when you get where you're going."

The flight to Cedar Rapids didn't offer alcohol. He didn't have pills. . . .   [p. 201]

Without changing verb tense, Sandford brings us back to story time by reminding us of the current setting: "The flight to Cedar Rapids." He further links the past to the present by repeating, briefly, the psychologist's reference to alcohol and pills. Smoothly done.

If you use such time shifts in your fiction, stay in current story time with the simple past tense as much as possible. Minimize your use of the past perfect and always avoid cumbersome constructions.

FIND & FIX CLUE #4: FATAL FLASHBACKS

- If you must use a flashback, determine how *little* of the material from the past is essential, not how *much* can be stretched to fill a scene.
- Confirm that your flashback illuminates the main story in a significant way and stirs emotions that could not be evoked through other, less time-stopping techniques.
- Keep the same action going before and after any mid-scene flashback, and edit all transitions so they are clear, unobtrusive, and seamless.
- Experiment with the protagonist's quick flashes of memory.
- Avoid transporting readers into the past if you can incorporate certain highlights from the past into current action.

CLUE #5: TOXIC TRANSCRIPTS

You are sitting in a comfortable chair reading about a sleuth who sneaks away from a party and goes upstairs to look for evidence. She comes upon a roll-top desk in the study and quietly raises the top. The old wood creaks and she freezes. So do you. When her nerves calm down she resumes her rummaging and discovers a small diary tucked into a cubbyhole. She opens it, sits down in the desk chair, and begins reading. And reading.

So do you, because the text of this diary is reproduced verbatim within the pages of the novel you are holding in your hands. Maybe the author is intentionally slowing the pace of this scene to keep readers on edge for a surprise—such as someone discovering the nosy sleuth. But the pace is not slowing—it stopped, and it remains stopped until the sleuth finishes reading.

No plot development can justify bringing a scene to a standstill while a character does nothing for an extended period but sit and read. Better that our imaginations keep us skulking around the house in the shadow of the sleuth. But instead of maintaining our involvement with the protagonist's actions and emotional reactions to her surroundings, the author drags in a story-within-a-story device to give us a backstory dump. Bor-ing.

The busy screener looks ahead a page or two, and seeing no change in the sleuth's's reading habits puts the manuscript aside. It looks suspiciously like . . . uh-oh! The toxic transcript rides again.

SUSPENSION OF TIME

I'm not railing against a few lines of a letter interwoven with a story's action or dialogue. I *am* sounding the alarm for those multi-page transcripts dropped whole into a scene, from letters the sleuth finds in a hope chest to typed pages retrieved from a wastebasket; from old newspaper clippings that fall out of a book to e-mail downloaded from a computer.

Sometimes the quoted material is presented as a written police report, a lecture the protagonist listens to on tape, a luncheon speech she endures, or a folk legend narrated around a campfire.

At best, the effect of a story-within-a-story is similar to that created by a flashback—but with less to visualize. At worst, the effect is unreal, as when a purported letter or diary includes a full-blown dramatization, complete with action and dialogue.

> "Time present cannot stand motionless for too long or it will have lost all its momentum of interest for the reader."
>
> Robie Macaulay and George Lanning [29]

No matter how lively or intriguing the content of these stories-within-a-story, their forms of delivery strain the reader's ability to sustain the image of an inactive, inert figure for a length of time.

Whereas a verbatim transcript might describe a conflict, reading about it does not engage the character *in* conflict. If you want to use this device, periodically interrupt the transcript to keep your readers in touch with the sleuth. Don't lose sight of her existence in her own time and space, lest we become aware of our own time and space. Show the character's reactions to what she's reading and occasionally indicate that she's mindful of her surroundings. If she's oblivious to the possibility of being discovered where she doesn't belong, she comes across as clueless— not a desirable trait in a detective.

Break up a transcript so your reader has something to visualize other than a figure sitting and reading. That's what *we* are doing. Being reminded of what we're doing in real time takes us out of the fiction. It's disconcerting, like catching our reflection in a trio of mirrors and having that glimpse of infinite sameness pull our attention away from where we'd been heading.

Not to get too existential about it, this dual awareness reminds us that we exist in real time and space, separate from the fictional characters whose hold on our imaginations is so tenuous. Any time the momentum of a mystery stops and lets our attention falter, the characters we identify with cease to exist. They fade into the illusions they are, flimsier than the printed page.

FUNCTION DETERMINES FORM

Think of Scheherazade and *A Thousand and One Nights.* Recall Chaucer's *The Canterbury Tales.* In the days when mystery fans sat at the feet of oral storytellers—before Gutenberg, before TiVo—the literary format known as the frame story made for great listening. The frame offered a structure (all right, an excuse) for stringing together separate, barely related stories that would keep audiences entertained for many days and nights.

The modern novel is the structural antithesis of the frame story. Today's publishers favor mysteries featuring one central character and one central plot, with every thread an indispensable part of the total fabric. Cut into that fabric and the illusion unravels.

Does this mean you can never include other material? No, not if the material is relevant, entertaining, and blended smoothly with the larger action. It does mean knowing how to make the technique work *for* your story, not against it.

CONTROLLING TIME

As you analyze the next example, bear in mind that I am not recommending the story-within-a-story device. My purpose is to show you how one author makes the transition to a transcript and manages a challenge that all writers of fiction grapple with in one way or another: the need to control time and the reader's perception of it.

George Orwell manipulates our sense of time in the novel *Nineteen Eighty-four.* Published in 1949, this prescient work is a suspenseful political satire about a totalitarian society. In this grim future, Big Brother watches everyone through a telescreen that cannot be turned off. No written history has survived to contradict the government's propaganda—except for one banned book, which an old bookseller makes available to Winston, the protagonist.

We're as curious as Winston is to learn how so many personal liberties could have been lost. But our interest in the *content* of this secret history cannot compensate for a *form* of presentation that involves a lengthy verbatim transcript. This form requires us to sit and read about a character who—you guessed it—is sitting and reading. Orwell manages the problem by artfully slowing the pace and resetting the scene to keep it grounded.

Here's how our image of Winston is first established in time and space.

> With a sort of voluptuous creaking in his joints he climbed
> the stair above Mr. Charrington's shop. He was tired, but not
> sleepy any longer. He opened the window, lit the dirty little
> oilstove, and put on a pan of water for coffee. Julia would arrive
> presently; meanwhile there was the book. He sat down in the
> sluttish armchair and undid the straps of the brief case. [p. 151]

Orwell next shifts our attention to the book and to its worn pages and amateurish printing and binding, which:

> . . . fell apart easily, as though the book had passed through many
> hands. The inscription on the title page ran:
>
>
>
> THE THEORY AND PRACTICE OF
> OLIGARCHICAL COLLECTIVISM
> by
> EMMANUAL GOLDSTEIN
>
>
> *[Winston began reading.]*

The bracketed, italicized phrase "Winston began reading" is not my comment but the author's. It serves as a form of stage direction to keep the reading of the transcript grounded in story time. An overt stage direction is unlikely to appear in novels today, but some form of re-anchoring or grounding is appropriate early in the reading. Its function is similar to the *he said/ she said* tag customarily inserted at the first take-a-breath location in a line of dialogue.

Orwell's bracketed anchor seems to ask readers, "Are you with me?" It acknowledges that we still have one foot in current story time and need easing into the longer transcript before we can jump into it with both feet.

Following this stage direction, Orwell quotes no more than one paragraph from the forbidden history before breaking away, mid-sentence, to drop anchor once again. Notice the concrete details that reinforce the scene's third grounding.

> Winston stopped reading, chiefly in order to appreciate the
> fact that he *was* reading, in comfort and safety. He was alone:
> no telescreen, no ear at the keyhole, no nervous impulse to

glance over his shoulder or cover the page with his hand. The
sweet summer air played against his cheek. From somewhere
far away there floated the faint shouts of children; in the room
itself there was no sound except the insect voice of the clock.
He settled deeper into the armchair and put his feet up on the
fender. It was bliss, it was eternity.   [p. 152]

With time and place firmly under control, Orwell continues the transcript and lets it run for twelve pages before setting time and place once
more. Then the transcript begins again, but not where it left off. There is
no reason to suffocate readers with so much exposition. Instead, we are
told that Winston, knowing he "will ultimately read and reread every word"
of the book, "opened it at a different place and found himself at the third
chapter." Clever, yes?

By making Winston a page-turner, Orwell gets more directly to the secret revealed in the book: how ongoing war and a climate of fear produce
the emotional basis that allows a government to usurp its citizens' privacy.

GROUNDING IN TIME

Please remember that I am not in favor of including any transcript in a
work of fiction if its length breaks the flow of a story, which is true of
Nineteen Eight-four. Nevertheless, Orwell's technique of anchoring, or
grounding, is worth examining because his setting and resetting of the
scene prepares readers for the lengthy transcript to come.

To review, the initial scene-setting is followed only by the title and
author of the forbidden book before Orwell reestablishes that "Winston
began reading."

Next, only one full paragraph is quoted from the secret history before
the author once again grounds Winston in the scene. This start-and-stop
pattern is similar to the reinforcement used in progressive relaxation or
self-hypnosis, in which the subject is deliberately brought out of an early,
light trance for the purpose of being sent into a longer, deeper trance.
Orwell's twice calling attention to the fact that the protagonist is reading
gets us ready for what lies ahead. He does not submerge us in a full-length
transcript all at once.

Also examine how Orwell sets the scene. He increases the distance
between the room at the top of the stairs and the world outside by going

beyond the visual and capturing the feel of the summer air and the sounds of distance: the shouts of children far away and faint; the clock with its insect voice. Time may continue to pass in the outside world, but inside the room, everything is slowing down.

Orwell's techniques give our inner clocks permission to wind down. And his settling Winston deeper into his armchair helps us settle in and be read to.

PARAPHRASING TRANSCRIPTS

If your story involves the discovery of a letter, diary, or other written text, and if its contents are essential to quote, be selective: quote only a few lines at a time, not whole passages. Paraphrase some of it, and splice that paraphrase in with the character's actions—a technique that lets readers visualize the character grounded in current time and place.

Those are the techniques Nancy Pickard uses in *No Body,* her Anthony-nominated sixth mystery novel, third in her Jenny Cain series. The following extract portrays the reading of a lengthy newspaper article. Jenny has asked a reporter, Lew Riss, to find a story in the paper's archives about funeral scams, which she's investigating.

> When he returned, he held up the front page for me to see. "Which story?"
>
> I scanned it, looking for news about the funeral industry.
>
> "This one," I said, and handed it back to him. "Here. Why don't you read it aloud, so we'll both know?"
>
> "Sure." He folded the paper back. "And after that, boys and girls, Uncle Lewis will read to you all about Brer Rabbit and the Three Blind Mice, since Uncle Lewis doesn't have anything better to do on a Sunday afternoon, right? Draw up a rug, kiddies, here goes. . . ."   [pp. 216–17]

This trailing off is the author's, as Pickard switches, without interruption, from dialogue to paraphrase—*not* to a verbatim transcript.

> He read to me the *Journal*'s report that prearrangement salespeople in Texas had been caught skimming off their client's contracts. When customers paid in cash, the salesperson simply falsified the contract and pocketed a little money off the top. . . .

I'm stopping here to call your attention to three references in the paragraph coming up: the *Journal,* the paper, and the story. Each reminds us that we are hearing a paraphrase of a newspaper article.

> They were easy scams, the *Journal* pointed out, and possible
> not just in the funeral industry, but in any business that depends
> to a great extent on the inherent honesty of its salespeople. The
> paper went to some pains to point out that the "vast majority"
> of prearrangement companies dealt honestly with their custom-
> ers. But if the story had an editorial slant, it was "buyer
> beware."   [p. 217]

If Lewis's reading of the article were presented verbatim, it would run considerably longer than this concise paraphrase. It would also pull us out of the scene and into that suspended twilight zone of a story-within-a-story. Instead, Pickard frames her paraphrase with "Uncle" Lewis's pretense of reading to a child. Humor lightens a grim topic and adds to Lew's characterization, getting additional mileage from the scene.

MORE OPTIONS

What if substituting a paraphrase or an abbreviated transcript loses the style of the quoted material? Or calls too much attention to a clue contained within it that you'd prefer to bury among many words? One way to get around these limitations is to interweave pieces of the transcript with other action, which breaks up the material and postpones our discovery of key parts of it. By building our anticipation of what *will* be revealed, writers can intensify suspense and keep audience attention focused on story time—not on the real time in which we are sitting and reading.

Postponing information is not the same as withholding it. If you are playing fair with your readers and planting clues throughout, however obscure, you are withholding only the correct *interpretation* of those clues.

During revision, see where you might:

1. let readers learn only partial information;
2. make them anticipate the rest of it; and
3. delay its fulfillment to increase dramatic tension.

These techniques are effective whether or not you're using a transcript.

FIND & FIX CLUE #5: TOXIC TRANSCRIPTS

- ► Make any transcript that you include as brief as possible.
- ► Break it up with paraphrase, action, description, setting, dialogue, or thought so we don't lose touch with the character who is reading the transcript and reacting to its content.
- ► Gradually slow the pace that leads into a transcript or begin a new scene with the desired pace.
- ► Set and *reset* the scene to keep it grounded in story time and space.
- ► Consider revealing quoted lines from a transcript over several scenes, knowing that postponement builds suspense.

CLUE #6: DECEPTIVE DREAMS

A sinister figure steps from the shadows and begins to chase the sleuth. She tries to run but her legs turn to stone. She feels this presence getting closer. It's right behind her. Now it's reaching for her! She opens her mouth to cry out but there's no sound. Suddenly, she hears a terrifying scream. It's so loud it wakens her, and she realizes she's the one screaming.

Surprise! It's only a bad dream.

Fooled you, right? Not even a little? Good. You recognize the scenario—it's been done often enough to have become its own cliché. This is the deceptive dream, typically placed at the start of a chapter to make readers think the villain is about to inflict actual harm on the character we've come to care about. But today's sophisticated mystery fans wake up to the illusion well before the character does.

A dream that arouses emotion for its own sake is a gimmick—which screeners recognize. Gimmicks can turn an already challenging submission process into a nightmare.

KEEP IT BRIEF

If you intend to mislead, keep dreams and nightmares brief. Readers who catch on by the second or third line quickly tire of the charade and want to get on with the real story.

Often, writers use dreams for the purpose of dumping backstory. You already know how backstory can stop a mystery cold. Some readers skim dreams or skip past them as soon as they recognize the clues, just as they do with prologues, transcripts, and lengthy italicized passages. In their experience, such devices get in the way of the story. They are usually right.

For these reasons, and because dreams are hard to present effectively, I suggest not dramatizing them. To reverse the conventional show-don't-tell wisdom, telling about a dream can often be more effective.

To demonstrate this upended principle, here's a passage from Jan Burke's first mystery novel, *Goodnight, Irene,* an Agatha and an Anthony nominee. The dream scene takes place after the brutal murders of several people known to the series character, investigative reporter Irene Kelly. Irene's sleeping companion, as you might not guess from his name, is a cat.

> As I crawled into bed later that night, I thought about how I
> had made it through two days in a row in a fairly peaceful
> fashion. Cody jumped in with me and I snuggled close to him.
> I felt good all over. I don't know how I could go from feeling so
> good to the nightmare, but that night I dreamed that someone
> was trying to cut off my hands and feet.   [p. 287]

Dramatizing the dream would lengthen it. Burke's paraphrase condenses it and incorporates Irene's comments. Brevity has power. Moreover, the quick ending contrasts sharply with the relaxed pace and feel-good mood leading up to it. A violent image ends the chapter, an ideal place to shake readers awake and keep them from putting the book down for the night.

PARALLEL THINKING

When dramatized effectively, a dream becomes a vehicle for taking us places we could not otherwise go. If steered competently, that vehicle can be made to:

- expand characterization;
- reveal contradictions that the character may be hiding from others or from himself;
- take the story to a deeper level by probing a situation or a character in ways that could not be achieved by other means;
- suggest parallels and symbolize relationships by juxtaposing two or more of the story's themes.

M. Diane Vogt's first mystery novel, *Six Bills,* includes several dreams, each closely related to the story. None is deceptive. Vogt makes clear each time that her protagonist is asleep.

> I didn't realize when my head fell to my chin. I went to sleep in
> the chair with troubled thoughts about life and death spinning in
> my head.   [p. 168]

Those troubled thoughts belong to U. S. District Court Judge Wilhelmina Carson. She is trying to overturn the life sentence of a woman who already served thirty years. If freed, the woman could live her remaining days in the role of grandmother to two little girls who've seen her only in prison.

Parallel to this main plot runs a theme about Willa's unresolved feelings toward the loss of her own mother. Where she confronts those feelings is in her dreams. In one, young Willa stands watch in her mother's sickroom, moving in and out of sleep along with her mother. The technique effectively blurs the line between dream and reality.

> *Tears began to stream down my sixteen-year-old cheeks. I finally realized I would never share so many things with my mother that daughters want to share. My high school graduation, my wedding, perhaps the birth of my own children. The lilac's fragrance was cloying now as hope died in my chest. Grace Harper would never be a grandmother or smell the flowers in her garden again. I began to cry in earnest then. Great gulping sobs.* [p. 170]

The author's abundant sense data slows the pace, reflecting the dying woman's quiet, peaceful slipping away. The dream ends with the merging of two parallel themes: the loss Willa feels as the daughter of Grace Harper, and the loss felt by the family of the prisoner, Billy Jo Steam.

> Now, the dream sobs jerked me awake from my dream world, with tears in my adult eyes and a heavy, knowing heart. I rubbed the ache in my neck, trudged to bed. I spent a restless night thinking about Harris and his tragic family. About a mother's life cut short and how that hurt never goes away. [p. 170]

Despite knowing that facilitating the prisoner's release is not in her own best interests, Willa is motivated to do so by experiencing, through her dream, the tragic parallels between the two families.

ADDING MEANING

In a later scene, Willa has another dream in which elements of the earlier flashback coalesce with her conflicts about the present situation.

> Hours later, I woke up in a cold sweat. I had had the dream
> again. This time, Mom and I were not in her sickroom. We were
> in [the accused's] jail cell. But her bed was there. The acrid,
> hopeless pine scent from the jail replaced the gentle, fragrant
> lilacs. Instead of dying peacefully while my back was turned,
> Mom was thrashing on the bed, crying out, trying to say some-
> thing.   [p. 185]

Dreaming lets Willa release her profoundest emotions, and readers get
to enter her thoughts and know her feelings at a deeper level of consciousness. Skillfully managed, dreams add meaning to memories about the past.
As in Vogt's sickroom scene, a dream can serve as a flashback. It presents
opportunities for symbolism and allegory, drawing relationships between
unrelated experiences. A sequence of dreams can be used to raise tension
and reflect a character's growing anxiety.

Dreams can also foreshadow the future by revealing a character's fears,
conscious or unconscious, as in this early scene from *Six Bills*.

> I came wide awake with a jolt at four o'clock in the morning.
> My heart pounded wildly as I tried to catch my breath. The
> nightmare seemed so real that I didn't realize I was home, in my
> own bed, my husband sleeping beside me.
>
> In the dream, I'd seen Billie Jo Steam on a stretcher, a white
> sheet covering her dead face as the paramedics carried her out
> of her prison cell. For some reason that I couldn't dredge up
> from my subconscious, Billie Jo's dream death was my fault
> and the guilt was overwhelming.   [p. 35]

Once again, telling about a dream instead of showing it keeps it brief,
conveys its emotion, and lets it be smoothly incorporated into the narrative. It diminishes the risk that readers will want to skip over it, and it
doesn't try to fool the reader.

PURPOSEFUL DREAMS

Know what purpose you want a dream or a nightmare to serve. If its
purpose is to foreshadow an upcoming event, give your protagonist a reason to feel anxious, suspicious, or fearful *before* having the nightmare.

Don't use a dream to reveal a missing piece of the puzzle that your central character does not already possess. You want your protagonist to be smart, not psychic—unless you are intentionally writing fiction that contains elements of the paranormal.

More effective and less controversial is the clue revealed in a dream about something the protagonist *already knows but doesn't know she knows.*

For example, if the trauma of witnessing a murder has blocked a character's conscious memory of the killer's identity, the killer's face might gradually become more distinct over the course of several dreams. This scenario has been done before, but when it's done well it becomes fully synthesized with the plot.

Despite my cautions about dreams in fiction, in the right hands the device can be effective. After all, one of the most famous works of literature—a novel that writers themselves often cite as the most well-constructed precursor to the modern mystery—opens with the following line:

> Last night I dreamt I went to Manderley again.
> Daphne du Maurier, *Rebecca*

FIND & FIX CLUE #6: DECEPTIVE DREAMS

- If your manuscript includes a dream scene, do you know what story purpose you want it to serve?
- Determine whether that purpose could be achieved as effectively by paraphrasing the dream instead of dramatizing it.
- Establish a reason for the character's feeling the anxiety that leads to dreaming.
- Select details that add meaning and value to your story and to the character's thoughts and emotions.
- Keep a dramatized dream brief; briefer still if you are attempting to deceive.

Alice Orr, in *No More Rejections,* emphasizes
the need for a positive attitude toward revision.
She writes that revision is where "the richness
of a story comes to life." It's where authors can
take the time to discover previously unrevealed
story layers and elements.   [p. 102]

CLUE #7: CRAZY TIME

The writer's need to handle time effectively is not limited to dreams, transcripts, flashbacks, and prologues. It covers everything in a typical day in the life of the lead character. I've seen manuscripts packed with so much running around by the protagonist, who interviews one suspect after another and chases clues from one end of a big city to the other, that you'd think the thirty-hour day had become reality when you weren't looking. Even Supersleuth can't travel faster than a speeding bullet in Chicago traffic.

Some writers get so caught up in plotting their stories that they lose track of time—story time, that is. (Losing track of mealtime and bedtime is nothing I'm qualified to discuss.) Scenes open with profuse descriptions of the morning sky and the weather—and all awareness of time stops right there. The protagonist takes off and keeps going like the Energizer bunny. If the plot doesn't call for a change in the weather, the day's events progress with no further reference to the environment or to the passage of time.

That's why readers get a jolt when Supersleuth, having driven across town to check out a suspect's reported hideout, conceals his approach by turning off his headlights a block away. Headlights? Nothing about the drive through the city even hinted at the sun's setting or the streetlights coming on. In fact, we realize that nowhere has the writer indicated the month or season, or otherwise prepared us for an early or a late sunset.

This is crazy time.

Writers who disorient readers by suspending the lead character's clock also diminish the busy screener's willingness to suspend disbelief.

TRACKING TIME

As a writer, you control how time passes. That's a nice thing about fiction. Three hours in the life of your crime-fighter might take only five minutes of real time to read, unlike literary fiction, in which five minutes in the life of the main character could take three hours to read. But that's another story.

When you self-edit, observe how you introduce the element of time into the lives of your characters. You might state the day and precise hour at the start of each chapter: Monday, 4:35 P.M. Or you might reverse the process and state how much time remains until an anticipated threat is carried out. This suspense-building countdown is known in crime fiction as a ticking time bomb. Go easy on literal ticking sounds, though. The device is more effective at generating suspense with subtlety, not with a smack on the head.

Perhaps your story lends itself to a technique often found in the subgenre known as the police procedural, in which the story follows the day-to-day investigation. Eleanor Taylor Bland, creator of the first black woman homicide detective, Marti MacAlister, uses the opening line of each chapter to track time and keep her readers oriented. Here are just a few of those chapter openings from her fourth mystery novel, *Done Wrong.*

> *Chap. 3:* Marti decided to take Thursday off.
> *Chap. 4:* It was after nine o'clock Thursday night when Marti parked at a beach in Evanston near the Northwestern University campus.
> *Chap. 5:* After court on Friday, Marti and Vik went to the Barrister, a pub not far from the precinct.
> *Chap. 6:* DaVon was whistling as he parked the van alongside a U-shaped apartment building Saturday morning.
> *Chap. 7:* On Saturday afternoon, Marti met. . . .
> *Chap. 22:* When Marti and Joanna got up, the house was quiet.
> *Chap. 33:* It was still dark when Diablo walked. . . .

The author's method is obvious here because I deliberately stack one example on top of another. In practice, the technique is subtle. Notice how Bland controls the grammatical structure of her opening lines to subordinate all time references to the action. In other words, subject and verb are devoted to the action, while dependent clauses keep the time references in their place.

In the Peaches Dann mystery series, Elizabeth Daniels Squire uses the name of each chapter to let us know when events are taking place. Here's a sampling of those names from the first book in the series, *Who Killed What's-Her-Name?*

> *Chap. 1:* Friday Morning, May 24
> *Chap. 2:* A Few Minutes Later
> *Chap. 3:* That Afternoon
> *Chap. 8:* Monday Afternoon, After the Funeral
> *Chap. 24:* Home from the Hospital, Noon

Squire's time references are unobtrusive enough that readers can skip over them if they wish. As a reader, I value these remedies for crazy time. As an editor, I can tell you that more mysteries would benefit from similar efforts.

SENSING TIME

Without environmental clues to echo real-world rhythms, characters seem stuck in a time warp. Readers experience a disorienting sameness, like that described by S. J. Rozan's private investigator Bill Smith in *Winter and Night.*

> The sun never showed that morning, so I had no real sense of
> the passing of time. In diffuse gray light that was always the
> same. . . .   [p. 138]

Daylight is more than setting in this passage. It functions as a metaphor to emphasize the sameness of the investigators' results:

> The light was the same and the guarded faces of the kids were
> the same and the answer was always the same.   [pp. 138–39]

When you revise, look for opportunities to drop visual clues about changes in light during the course of a day. Perhaps your crime-fighter looks for her sunglasses or adjusts the angle of her car's sun visor. After a long day of detecting, she might notice the lengthening shadows or the coming on of lamps at dusk. Perhaps she has difficulty making out street names or unlit house numbers, as real people do. As I do.

Add sounds and smells to reflect changes in season: the squeals of children under the sprinkler, the scent of new-mown grass or burning leaves. Keep such environmental references brief and subordinate to the action. Genre fiction is better served by one or two deft brush strokes than by a lavishly painted dawnscape over a copiously recreated landscape. Readers of genre fiction pay little attention to elaborate descriptions of settings. They are more interested in what the main character is up to—exactly what you want.

PASSING TIME

The next example is taken from Elizabeth Peters' *Naked Once More,* winner of an Agatha award for best mystery novel. I'd like you to observe both the frequency and the variety of clues that keep readers time-oriented. Your mystery might not need as many, or it might benefit from more. The following lines represent five consecutive scenes spanning twenty-seven pages.

> *Chap. 10, Sc. 1:* Monday morning. Seven glorious empty days ahead. . . .
> There was also the delightful possibility of catching some of them still asleep, blissfully unaware of the fact that it was Monday morning.
> *Chap. 10, Sc. 2:* As she drove back . . . she felt like bursting into song. . . . "Oh what a beautiful morning. . . ."
> It was afternoon, not morning, but she could not think of a song celebrating that time of day. . . .
> On her way through town she stopped at the supermarket to pick up a few supplies. School would be out shortly and she wanted to be prepared.
> As she approached Gondal, the mutter of an engine greeted her and she saw a riding mower lumbering across the lawn. . .
> When she reached the door the child was standing outside. She must have come directly to the cottage after getting off the school bus. . . .
> *Chap. 11, Sc. 1:* The sound of the mower had stopped. Sunlight turned the stubbled grass to gold. . . .

> A chilly finger touched her foot and she looked up to see that the shadows of the surrounding pines were creeping upon her.
>
> *Chap. 11, Sc. 2:* Twilight had fallen by the time she got home, and as she lugged the half-filled carton of books along the shadow-enshrouded path, she found herself moving a little faster than she had intended . . . dusk was not as pleasant a time of day as she had once thought it. Fumbling for the light switch in the dark house. . . .
>
> *Chap. 11, Sc. 3:* Jacqueline was at her desk at nine the following morning. . . .
>
> For the next few days. . . .
>
> On the morning of the third day. . . .
>
> The sun was shining. . . .
>
> After leaving the cottage she stood breathing deeply of the winy autumn air. . . .
>
> A stroll down the sunny street restored her. . . and [she] paused to say good morning.
>
> ". . . and I thought, why not drop in and see if she'll join me for lunch?"   [pp.147–73]

Elizabeth Peters' clues to time's passage range from the specific *it was afternoon* to the metaphorical *chilly finger* of creeping shadows. Her less obvious hints are unrelated to light. Twice she mentions school letting out. Especially effective is the reference in one chapter to the mutter of the riding lawn mower, and in the next, to its sound having stopped.

NATURE CALLS

It's hard to relate to a character who puts in an eighteen-hour day of heavy sleuthing without a break or something more substantial than a cup of coffee.

No more than a detail or an allusion is needed to suggest how anyone in the same situation would react. Yet I've heard some interesting defenses from writers for not mentioning anything so natural as a bathroom break. Supposedly, bathrooms are too "delicate" an issue to acknowledge. They might give offense to genteel readers.

Baloney. Who says the mere mention of a break requires indelicate details? What could be less offensive than the following paragraph? In

P Is for Peril by Sue Grafton, Kinsey Milhone has arrived at a hospital to question an employee.

> On my left, the coffee shop was sparsely occupied by hospital employees and visitors. I inquired at the information desk and was given directions to the office of the Director of Nursing Services. I passed a ladies' restroom and made a brief detour before I continued my quest.   [p. 125]

A brief detour. No fuss, no muss.

In a later scene, after Kinsey has been waiting hours for some sign of the killer, she tells the first person who joins her how hungry she is.

> "I missed dinner. I'm about to eat my arm."   [p. 217]

Perhaps Kinsey's contemplated dinner alternative is indelicate, but not the need that prompts it.

ILLOGICAL SEQUENCE

Frequently I come across manuscripts with a different sort of unnatural behavior that I call *crazy timing.* It's a consequence of the writer's presenting ideas out of sequence.

> Laci decided to leave the stupid party and go home. She could feel Don's warm embrace enveloping her tired body, kissing away all distractions. After an hour of small talk and large drinks, she slipped away and began the long drive home.

In my made-up example, we buy into Laci's decision to leave, aided by the writer's getting us to visualize the warm embrace waiting for her. This sensory data seems to transport Laci to her destination, and our imaginations along with her, when—whoops! Fast rewind. For the next hour she's still at the stupid party. She hasn't even gotten behind the wheel and we're already experiencing whiplash.

Can you fix the order of events? Avoid suggesting that the character's goal has already been realized. For example:

> Laci decided to tolerate the stupid party for no more than an hour of small talk and large drinks, all the while aching for Don's warm embrace to envelop her tired body. As soon as she could, she left for the long drive home.

A small change, but the new sequence keeps our imaginations at the party together with the long-suffering Laci, not leaping ahead of her.

Another typical cause of illogical sequencing comes from delaying a character's reactions to her environment. Visualize someone arriving at a house and taking the time to notice the expensive-looking Queen Anne chairs, tall reading lamps, gold-framed paintings on the wall, and luxurious beige broadloom, *then* mentioning the distinguished-looking host walking toward her with his hand outstretched. She didn't notice this guy among all those tall lamps?

> "Jane Austen managed to put fruit trees in bloom in a scene where her characters are picking strawberries. She had to endure much ribbing from her brothers."
>
> Kim Wilson, author of
> *Tea with Jane Austen*

Or, after treating us to a similarly detailed *House Beautiful* spread, the detective first mentions the dead body sprawled in the middle of that bonnie beige broadloom. Gimme a break.

Examine your manuscript for instances that defy the logical sequence in which a supposedly keen observer would notice obvious things first—unless you have an equally logical reason for defying that sequence. (Like, if your detective is a complete ditz.) If your reason is to shock readers with a corpse by slowly leading up to it, let the slowness precede the entry into the room where the body lies. Don't mess around with crazy timing.

CALENDAR

For your own guidance, always make a calendar of the events taking place in your novel so that all times of day and days of the week make internal sense. Also note the location of every character at key times. When you revise your manuscript, double-check that every entry on your calendar has an actual counterpart in the story, and vice versa. Without such a guide, your use of time can make readers crazy.

When I edit a manuscript I construct my own timeline from the unfolding plot and let the writer know of any discrepancies I find. According to the calendar I produced for one author, the protagonist rose "early the next morning to beat the rush-hour traffic heading downtown."

On Sunday?

FIND & FIX CLUE #7: CRAZY TIME

●◆ When you edit your manuscript, go beyond an initial scene-setting or weather report; suggest time's passage throughout the story.

●◆ Use sensory details that lend authenticity and depth to your story and accurately reflect its timespan.

●◆ Review the ways you keep readers from mistaking when an event is taking place.

●◆ Don't avoid referring to a washroom break or other physical need if its absence would create an unrealistic passage of time over a long day's events.

●◆ Enter every event in your story on an actual calendar, together with the whereabouts of each character, and double-check your manuscript as you self-edit to confirm the chronological accuracy of the days and weeks of your plot.

PART V: THE LINEUP

Lawrence Block said he learned more about writing
while he worked for a literary agency reviewing bad
books, learning things not to do, than he ever learned
from reading the masters. [30]

CLUE #8: DASTARDLY DESCRIPTION

Pretend you're telling a friend about your new coworker. Would you be more likely to mention his height and weight or to tell how he spreads his papers out on the conference table and takes up enough space for three people? Are you more likely to say his hair and eyes are brown or his eyes never seem to meet yours?

Because you know the benefits of capturing the idiosyncrasies of your coworkers, you describe your fictional characters through their behaviors, too, don't you?

Behavioral quirks and habits are not only more interesting than a straightforward physical description but also more revealing of personality and attitude. Behavior creates stronger, more memorable impressions and helps set characters apart from each other.

Regrettably, the majority of submissions confront the busy screener with passages indistinguishable from this one:

> Clyde was six-feet-two, 325 pounds, with brown eyes and brown hair combed straight back. He wore a dark blue suit and a white shirt, wire-rimmed glasses, and he had a thick, brown beard.

This is a description dump. It shows no sign of an author's having selected one or two unique details to make an unforgettable impression on the reader. Instead, the dumper unloads a Hefty bag of unremarkable features from two typical sources: the driver's license and the clothes closet.

Such choices lack purpose, as if a child reached into Barbie and Ken's trunk and pulled out whatever was not already being used.

RELEVANCE

Include a physical detail or an article of clothing if it expands the reader's understanding of a character, but know that readers gain the sharpest impression of characters from what they say, what they want, what they do.

Ask yourself why you select one detail over another. Whim? Impulse? Or to serve a purpose relevant to something in your story? Careless choices can set up expectations that, if unfulfilled, become distracting. One first-time writer populated his manuscript with five blondes and one brunette.

Five blondes? Hmm, must be a clue.

Carla Damron says, "Don't describe a character so much that a movie star couldn't play the role."[31]

As I edited his manuscript I kept watching for the significance of all that blondness to become clear. Nothing did. *Bupkis*. When I queried the writer, he admitted being unaware of his lopsided color selection. He simply liked blondes.

Hair color may be relevant to a story if, for example, a killer disguises himself with a dye job. Or a stalker has a thing for redheads. Hair *style* may be relevant if it indicates a character's tastes or lifestyle. But if one's thatch or lack thereof has no connection with anything in the story and no bearing on our perception of the character, why mention it?

I agree that readers need to visualize your characters. But stats from a driver's license and garments from a clothing closet rarely create lasting, distinct impressions. Readers assume each character is dressed, unless you say otherwise. Fashion reports have value only when their details *add* meaning.

Likewise, don't bother describing facial features if they merit no special attention, because readers assume that every character has a face—well, I can't be certain about *your* characters. The idea is to include only those specifics that matter, that set each cast member apart from all others. Your options are infinite.

Whenever I encounter the usual assemblage of features—this color eyes, that style hair, those kind of pants, or anything else that *could be changed without affecting the story in any way*—I'm reminded of my days of youthful innocence when all creativity was contained in a box of sixty-four Crayolas.

Piling on more colors, features, and details makes a character's appearance harder to visualize, not easier. Tall or short, blond or bald—it's all a grab bag, a Crayola-and-Barbie-doll pastime.

MAKE AN IMPRESSION

In the first mystery novel by Toni L. P. Kelner, *Down Home Murder,* the second chapter opens with this graphic image:

> A short, red-haired nurse with a bosom like the prow of an
> aircraft-carrier strode into the room. [p. 16]

For the brief time that the nurse plays her role, the image of an aircraft carrier remains vivid because Kelner gives us an *impression* rather than a description.

Carla Damron offers a combination of both when she introduces the police captain in *Keeping Silent,* her first mystery novel.

> Captain Frank Bentille leaned against the door jamb and stared
> at them. Gray and black tweed pants and a gray shirt hung
> loosely on his gangly frame, making him look like a greyhound
> long retired from the track. The striped tie had a red spot from
> some recent meal. His close-set eyes were dwarfed by the dense
> brows that nearly met each other over his nose. [p. 46]

Although three articles of clothing and three physical features are mentioned, they are not listed as an inventory. They are presented as part of an impression. After a while, what image of the captain resides in your memory: the wearer of a striped, spotted tie? Or an old greyhound?

Here's another impression from *Keeping Silent:*

> The twenty-something-year-old man standing at the check-in
> desk wore a crisp tie and a huge white smile that advertised the
> fortune his parents must have spent on orthodontics.   [p. 35]

From this passage we learn four of the desk clerk's physical features: sex, approximate age, tie, and smile. If Damron had included the *color* of his tie, that irrelevant piece of information would soon be forgotten. Letting us know the tie is crisp gives us a sense of the desk clerk's *bearing*.

To see what Damron can do with a necktie, compare the above two descriptions. Yet the feature that produces the most memorable impression of the desk clerk is his smile. It is priceless—monetarily and metaphorically—the kind of writing that makes a busy screener smile.

When you revise your manuscript, trim your descriptions to the sharpest, most memorable impressions. Go for quality, not quantity. Less is more.

IMPRESSION VS. INVENTORY

Take a look at this description, which I wrote:

> Sellito gazed at the computer. He weighed about 250 pounds
> and wore a rumpled brown jacket and a graying shirt hanging
> out of wrinkled blue pants.

How memorable is that? Here is the original description written by Jeffery Deaver from *The Coffin Dancer,* his third novel.

> Sellito, who reminded Rhyme of a large unmade bed, gazed at
> the computer. . . .   [p. 14]

Compare Deaver's powerful image of an unmade bed with the description I wrote about Sellito's size and clothing. Is my version stronger because of its greater detail? No. Sharper? No.

Mine is a parody of the uninspired, undistinguished writing I find in most submissions, which misrepresents every grade school English teacher's commandment that thou shalt use specific details. "Be specific" does not mean use all the facts you can think of. It means be precise instead of general. It means don't say *car* if you can say *blue Chevy.*

Details, carefully selected, are essential. They add texture to one's writing. But using too many gets in the way of the story. A single comparison to a large unmade bed is superior to my feature-packed rendition because Deaver summons forth an image more graphic than any wardrobe could.

Notice the specifics James Lee Burke selects for this description from *A Morning for Flamingos:*

> I took out another girl, a carhop from up north who wore hair rollers in public and always seemed to have sweat rings under her arms. [p. 78]

Details like these do more than paint a striking picture. They stir an emotional response, because each of us holds some opinion about similar behavior. Descriptions that pack an emotional punch do double duty.

For the most impact with the fewest words, check out this minimalist description by Pat Browning from her first mystery novel, *Full Circle.*

> Maxie was built for stakeouts—short, wiry, collapsible. [p. 1]

Writing with this economy of style means abandoning the driver's license approach and coming out of the clothes closet.

DESCRIPTION AS METAPHOR

See what Nancy Bartholomew does with the features she selects to describe a race track photographer in *Drag Strip,* her second mystery novel. In the words of the protagonist, Sierra Lavotini:

> He was a short oval of a man, with a belt line that hit him just below the armpits, white socks, black sneakers, and a bald head. He looked like a brown shiny egg, and the closer he came, the more I realized that he smelled much worse than a rotten egg.
>
> [p. 18]

A less imaginative writer might use the identical categories of body type, baldness, and clothing to write:

> He was a short, round man with a bald head. He wore dark trousers, a plaid shirt, white socks, and black sneakers.

This recitation of observable data reflects what I see in manuscripts all the time. Flat. Boring. One-dimensional. Information totally forgettable by the next paragraph. Where's the writer's style? Without style, *anyone* could be writing your mystery. Most submissions sound as if anyone did.

Bartholomew's description is multi-dimensional. She takes baldness and body shape, two features that establish their own literal image, and she likens them to something else—an egg. The payoff is a figurative image—a metaphor. *That's style.*

The egg metaphor creates such a powerful image that it serves a third function: as an epithet or stand-in for the photographer when the author extends the metaphor three pages later.

> I could've told her I'd seen it all before, but I was busy having
> my picture taken by a smelly egg.   [p. 21]

Using a metaphorical egg to take Sierra's picture conjures up a more vivid, entertaining effect than having it taken by (duh) a photographer. An extended metaphor enriches the reading experience, letting readers enjoy the "aha" that comes from recognizing an allusion to something mentioned pages earlier. The technique lets us "get" what amounts to an inside joke.

DESCRIPTION IN ACTION

Don't think of action as mostly car chases and shoot-'em-ups. Action is any behavior that produces a reaction, especially if each action and its reaction intensify conflict or tension. At the opposite end of the conflict continuum, action in its least reaction-driven form is simply movement. Look to the verbs; some movements are more dynamic than others.

Here's a description from *Murder of a Sweet Old Lady* by Denise Swanson, second in her series featuring school psychologist Skye Denison.

> Scumble River High School Principal Homer Knapik was
> seated to her right, and every time she glanced his way, her
> attention was drawn to the hair growing out of his ears. The
> long wiry strands quivered like the curb feelers on a car's
> wheels.   [p. 1]

Quivering like curb feelers—what an imaginative simile. Going beyond this striking image, we can appreciate Swanson's verbs by comparing her sentence with this too-common phrasing:

> Every time she looked at him, she *saw* that hair *was growing* out of his ears.

Or the more awkward but equally unimaginative phrasing:

> His ears had hair growing out of them.

Verbs in a typical description tend to suggest static properties of the things described: ears *had;* hair *was.* But Swanson's verbs show how the things described are experienced by her character: she *glanced;* her attention *was drawn.* The differences are subtle, but the overall effect keeps the busy screener from hearing the same kind of unimaginative, uninspired writing that pervades submission after submission.

I've seen identical verb phrases murdering whole forests of manuscripts for years.

In editing your own writing, stay alert for the verbs *have* and *had* that reflect a feature's properties. Refer to objects in the way your character would experience them, as Swanson does. Also watch out for all forms of the verb *to be* (am, is, are, was, were, be, been, being). Locate them by a computer word search, and where possible replace them with active verbs.

Your efforts can reduce one of the most easily spotted clues to amateur writing: flat, static word choices that suck the life from most submissions and make busy screeners reach for another cup of caffeine.

DESCRIPTION AS EMOTION

In choosing details, favor those that evoke feelings. "She felt very cold" is better than "She was very cold." Better still, use active verbs to show how your character experiences the cold, as Julia Spencer-Fleming does in the opening passage of *To Darkness and to Death.*

> Cold. The cold awoke her, creeping underneath her blanket, spreading like an ache along her hip. She tried to move, to burrow into some warm space, but the cold was beneath her, and then there was a hard hot twinge of pain in her shoulders and she had a panicky moment of *Where? What?*

To *show* feelings, not merely *tell* how a character feels, combine description with action. That's what Beverly Connor does in the following passage from her first mystery novel, *A Rumor of Bones.* Mrs. Greenwood is described as she is being observed by the series protagonist, forensic anthropologist Lindsay Chamberlain.

> Lindsay turned and stared at a thin, haggard woman in a faded housedress. Her mouse-brown hair was streaked with gray and hung in her face. Her frightened brown eyes darted from Lindsay to the sheriff as she absently wiped her hands on her apron.   [p. 105]

Connor presents the woman's appearance in the context of the protagonist's observations: *Lindsay turned and stared.* Active verbs introduce features: hair *hangs,* eyes *dart,* and hands *wipe.* These details are not randomly pulled from a grab bag of stock features. Connor shows the woman's hands and eyes in motion, establishing a specific image of Mrs. Greenwood's emotional response to her visitors. That response, and her attitude toward the evidence Lindsay and the sheriff present in this scene, are relevant to the plot.

Because the descriptive details Connor selects appear so ordinary, they bring a deceptive simplicity to this passage that masks the density of her writing.

DESCRIPTION AS MOTIVATION

From the details Jeffery Deaver uses to describe the character Percey in *The Coffin Dancer,* what do you interpret about her?

> The pug face. Black hair in tight, stubborn curls. (In her tormented adolescence, during a moment of despair, she'd given herself a crew cut. That'll show 'em. Though naturally all this act of defiance did was to give the chahmin' girls of the Lee School in Richmond even more ammunition against her.) Percey had a slight figure and marbles of black eyes that her mother repeatedly said were her finest quality. Meaning her only quality. And a quality that men, of course, didn't give a shit about.   [p. 24]

Deaver artfully works into this description bits of backstory, which contribute to our image of Percey. And instead of black hair and black eyes, we see *tight, stubborn* curls and eyes like *marbles.* Together with hints about Percey's adolescence—rejection by peers, acts of defiance, a crew cut—this description prepares us to more readily accept her reckless behavior and uncompromising motivation. These character traits are significant because they set off a chain of events that drives the plot of *The Coffin Dancer.*

APPEARANCE ISN'T EVERYTHING

Paying too much attention to a character's physical appearance, given the infinite choices fiction offers, suggests a case of arrested development. Observe the limited attention Jeanne Dams pays to appearance in the following description from *The Body in the Transept,* winner of an Agatha award for best first mystery novel. The narrator is Dorothy Martin, the series protagonist.

> My next-door neighbor, Jane Langland, is my only real friend in Sherebury. It's easy to dismiss Jane as just a typical English spinster. She looks and sounds a good deal like Winston Churchill, and dispenses gallons of tea and oceans of gruff sympathy. It took me a while to discover that Jane is typical of no one but herself. Behind the brusque façade is a mind of diamond—and a heart of custard.   [pp. 3–4]

Chances are you get a vivid picture of Jane even though only one brief reference is made to her appearance: a resemblance to one former resident of No. 10 Downing Street. Dams does a fine job of selecting specific behaviors to show the kind of person Jane is— a more important depiction of the character than how she looks.

Analyze the descriptive techniques of the authors you read. Discover how they use impressions to expand characterization and create multi-layered effects. This analytical process will improve your ability to spot one-dimensional, dastardly descriptions in your own writing before a busy screener does.

To prove the low value of unremarkable, undistinguished physical descriptions, here's

"Pick the right essential details to show readers how to complete the non-essential details in their minds that you don't need to tell."

Bruce Holland Rogers, reviewed by Roxanne Aehl[32]

a quick test. In my earlier parody of a description by Jeffery Deaver, was Sellito wearing a blue jacket and brown pants, or a brown jacket and blue pants? Does it matter? Not in the least—not unless a jacket is found at the scene of a crime.

FIND & FIX CLUE #8: DASTARDLY DESCRIPTION

- Double-check that you are creating memorable impressions by selecting the fewest descriptive details and having them serve *some* purpose in the story. (Please review "WITH PURPOSE AFORE-THOUGHT" in PART II.)
- Rewrite your character descriptions so that appearance is subordinate to behavior.
- Determine whether the impressions you strive for stir an emotional response in your readers.
- Be alert for verbs such as *have* and *had* that indicate static properties, and replace them where possible with active verbs associated with a character's behavior.
- Substitute action verbs for verbs of *being* wherever possible.
- Experiment with ways to make your descriptions do double duty.

CLUE #9: POISONOUS PREDICTABILITY

L et's pretend you are reading a murder mystery and a new scene opens with a character who is making her first appearance. The setting shows that she is standing in line at the bank. Suddenly, she hears three shots ring out and a voice yell, "Everyone down on the floor!"

What do you think comes next, how the character reacts to the shooter's demands, or how she looks? Chances are that the next thing you learn has nothing to do with the bank robbery in progress. Chances are it has everything to do with this new character's appearance.

You already know how predictable this *type* of description is. That's bad enough. Now I want to demonstrate how predictable its *placement* is.

TYPICAL PATTERN

In a great many manuscripts, published as well as unpublished, the moment each member of the cast steps on stage for the first time, dialogue and action stop and physical description begins. Never mind that it's too early in the character's dramatic career for anyone but the writer to know whether the new arrival is someone we should care about. Ready or not, here comes a dose of dastardly description administered with poisonous predictability.

Again and again, busy screeners are confronted with intros that go something like this:

> Long after midnight, the bell at the back door broke the
> silence, followed by loud, insistent pounding. Bonnie jumped
> and peered at the figure through the rain-spattered glass. Quickly
> she unbolted the door.
>
> Clyde rushed in, breathless. He was six-feet-two, 325 pounds,
> with brown eyes and brown hair combed straight back. He wore

a dark blue suit and a white shirt, wire-rimmed glasses, and he
had a thick, brown beard.

"Wait," shouts the reader, "get on with the story!"

Stopping the action to describe Clyde sends the message that the situation couldn't be as serious as his middle-of-the-night door-pounding would
have us believe. Putting action on hold contradicts
its urgency, shatters the mood, and undermines the
writer's credibility. Description is supposed to *support* the action that develops characterization, not
overthrow it and establish its own regime.

> "Any time you
> stop to describe
> something, you
> have *stopped*."
>
> Author and
> educator Jack
> M. Bickham[33]

Busy screeners, like jaded readers, have learned
to skip description dumps and scan ahead for the
next sign of dialogue or action. Elmore Leonard says,
"Try to leave out the parts that readers tend to skip."[34]

The writer who has not yet learned the value of Leonard's advice might
write this reaction to Clyde's out-of-breath arrival at Bonnie's back door:

> "At last! I thought you'd never get here," cried Bonnie. She was
> petite and wore her straight blond hair long and loose. Her sweater
> was blue and matched her eyes, and her slacks were black. . . .

Whenever I read Bonnie's stop-action description aloud in a writing
workshop right after reading Clyde's, the class bursts into laughter. The
pattern of poisonous predictability has exposed itself with all the absurdity
of the flasher in socks and shoes and nothing under the raincoat.

By the third and fourth time that the identical pattern occurs in a novel,
what seems laughable at first becomes monotonous and irritating. Predictability is desirable in a weather forecast. In most fiction it's fatal; in a
mystery it's murder.

Delivering a description dump the moment a new character comes along
suspends the action's momentum and forces readers to meet all characters
in the same way. We *have* to stop meeting like this. The busy manuscript
screener stopped long ago.

As the following extracts show, a more effective way to handle description is to slice, dice, and splice a few details in with the continuing action
and dialogue. Both description and action benefit by working together.

ECONOMY OF STYLE

A catalogue of physical features and clothing is just a catalogue, but a skillful dramatization of behavior is a moving picture show. Readers need to see each character in motion, taking up space, like any flesh-and-blood person. Unless you are writing a ghost story, behavior and dialogue cannot float ethereally, with no physical dimension to ground them.

Analyze Karen McCullough's description of Ray in *A Question of Fire,* her sixth mystery novel. Ray is the newspaper editor who sent reporter Cathy Bennett, the protagonist, to cover an event that turned into murder.

> . . . Ray clomped into the room an hour later, in the midst of her second detailed recounting of the events of the evening.
>
> He plopped into a chair in a corner, nodded to her, shut his eyes, and gave a good imitation of falling asleep. Cathy wasn't fooled. Ray might look like a large, sloppy puppy, but the mind behind the unruly brown hair and rounded features was sharp and alert. More than could be said of her at that point.   [p. 4]

McCullough works Ray's description in with the clomping and plopping actions that ground him in the scene, and she expresses his attitude by showing him arriving late and pretending to fall asleep.

We form a picture of Ray from his actions before we come to the simile comparing him to a large, sloppy puppy, and before the first mention of his hair and features. Even these physical details are presented indirectly, as part of another point the protagonist is making, not as direct description—not *he had brown hair that was unruly and his mind was sharp and alert.*

If you furnish no visual evidence about a character, readers fill the vacuum with their own mental images. There's nothing wrong with that, and in many cases it's desirable—except where later events are likely to contradict a reader's initial visualization. Here are some guidelines.

- Include, at first, the fewest attributes that distinguish a character on the basis of gender, age, and maybe skin color—demographic information that is part of most character introductions anyway. For example: "The young white cop grew agitated."
- Bring characters to life through their actions and dialogue. Keep their descriptions subordinate to the action.

- ◆ Show characters interacting with their environment and with others, opening doors, spilling drinks, plopping into chairs, and doing a thousand other things to affect their surroundings and be affected by them.

- ◆ Anticipate any physical abilities or inabilities that may become significant later. Plant the first reference to that ability early, before readers make a faulty assumption and form a contrary image.

Avoiding later contradictions is something all writers have to anticipate and head off anyway, as we discuss next.

UNINTENDED MISCONCEPTIONS

A friend wrote to tell me that her enjoyment of a book was spoiled by the author's placing the character's description too *late.* It seems the protagonist was portrayed as shuffling around the house, leading my friend to visualize an old woman. When the story made clear that the character was much younger but was suffering from a bad cold, my friend said the contradiction took her "completely out of the book, and I had trouble revising my image."

Would a full physical description have been appropriate from the outset? No. But the false image should have been anticipated by the book's editor, who could have suggested the earlier inclusion of some fact, indirectly, of course—such as "every bone in her forty-year-old body ached," or "the flu was making her feel twice her thirty-five years."

Postponing or eliminating a description causes no problem unless later information contradicts a reader's earlier mental image. Supposing the strangler turns out to be a mousy salesclerk who is much stronger than she looks. To avoid the reader's calling "Foul!" when the strangler's identity is later revealed, do not omit the attribute—her strength—but treat it as you would any other clue: plant it early and minimize it. Surround it with other details and show a result of the behavior without explaining it.

If you intend to mislead, do so with a deliberate plot twist, not with contradictions that yank readers out of the story. Yet writers are seldom aware of such contradictions, because the mental images of one's own characters are perfectly clear. Familiarity with one's own story gets in the way of anticipating the interpretations of many different readers.

When jarring contradictions occur in published books, readers blame the authors. I fault the line editors, because it's our job to expect a variety of audience responses and recommend appropriate revisions. (Of course, authors can and do ignore editorial recommendations.)

INTENDED MISCONCEPTIONS

In certain circumstances, describing a character at first sight may be desirable. If two characters meet by phone, letter, or e-mail, one might form an impression of the other that turns out to be false when they come face to face for the first time. A wrong impression can get a point across that would be difficult to express in some other way.

For example, in *An Eye for Murder,* Libby Fischer Hellmann's first mystery novel, Ellie Foreman visualizes someone based on voice only.

> I picked up the letter and dialed Ruth Fleishman's number.
> "Hello?" The voice was somewhere between a bleat and a foghorn. I pictured a woman with too much makeup, dyed hair, and lots of jewelry.   [p. 13]

Three pages later, when Ellie arrives at the woman's house, this is what she sees.

> Ruth Fleishman's face was thick with powder, and her arms jangled with bracelets, but her hair wasn't dyed. A brown bouffant wig in a young Jackie Kennedy style covered a seventy-year-old head. She was either a cancer survivor or an Orthodox Jew who still wore a *sheitel.* Most likely an Orthodox Jew. This part of Rogers Park has replaced Lawndale as the center of *frum* life in Chicago, and she looked too vigorous to have suffered a round of chemo.   [p. 16]

Here, the pace has slowed enough to address the discrepancy between what Ellie had imagined about Ruth Fleishman and what she observes when they meet—an opportunity to add a bit of background about Chicago neighborhoods and an Orthodox Jewish tradition. This taste of regional and ethnic detail enriches Hellmann's writing and effectively flavors her Ellie Foreman mystery series.

TIMED RELEASE

Instead of launching into an immediate description of your own characters, try this alternative:

1. Select one key attribute, physical or not, and slip it in while dramatizing the character's first action.
2. Work other details in with the action a little at a time, keeping the action dominant and the description subordinate.

This timed release approach is easier to apply than you think. See how Anne Underwood Grant describes Fred in the first of her Sydney Teague mysteries, *Multiple Listing.* Our initial impression of Fred comes well before we see him, when Sydney observes that her secretary, Sally, has a self-centered jerk for a brother. Not until Scene 2 of Chapter 2 do we meet Fred in person. He is being held by the police on suspicion of murdering his about-to-be-divorced wife.

> Sally and Fred sat huddled at the far end of a long metal conference table. They looked like both sides of a bipolar personality, she depressed and he manic.
> Fred's voice was strained, a loud, raspy whisper. "I will not stay here any longer. How dare they suggest. . . . "   [p. 18]

This first glimpse of Fred is an impression, not a description of physical features or wearables. Grant offers us the sound of his voice, the words he speaks, the attitude his words reveal, and a clever simile to let us know he is acting manic.

Another four paragraphs of action and dialogue intervene before Grant introduces the first descriptive detail.

> Fred ran a hand through his collar-length black hair as he stood up. He pushed a stray corner of his wrinkled white shirt back into his pants and extended his hand. "Good to see you again, Sydney."   [p. 18]

In addition to postponing these few specifics, Grant shows them through Fred's movements: *ran* a hand, *stood, pushed,* and *extended.* Nothing about the content of this description or its placement is predictable. Delaying it neither risks our forming an earlier, contradictory image of the man nor robs him of substance. When he is shown to us he is sitting in a specific place in a specific way, looking like—don't you love it?—the manic side of a bipolar personality.

DIALOGUE IS PARAMOUNT

More minimalist still are the details Richard Helms selects for the physical description of Hotshot in *Voodoo That You Do,* his second Pat Gallegher mystery.

> Hotshot leaned back in his seat, rubbed his ample belly, and belched once for effect and punctuation. [p. 1]

That Hotshot's belly is ample is made known in the context of an action: he rubbed it. This first physical detail occurs after an opening paragraph of 121 words, most of it dialogue spoken by Hotshot.

Despite delaying that first glimpse of the man's appearance, Helms runs no risk of having readers form an inaccurate image of Hotshot, because those 121 words introduce the character in action.

I'll back up a paragraph to show you how Chapter 1 begins.

> "Man, it ain't so easy being a gangster anymore," Hotshot Spano told me as he refilled his wine glass with the valpolicella he'd ordered to go with his veal piccata. "When I got into the game up in the Bronx, it was a breeze. Some guy got in your face, you took his off for him. Bodda bing, he's toast. You just push the ol' double deuce up behind his ear, pump in a couple of shells, and wait for the lights to go out behind his eyes. Now, it's like you gotta get a fuckin' act of Congress to do a decent whack. Fuckin' families are acting like it's some kind of reunion. Nobody wants to mix it up anymore."
>
> Hotshot leaned back in his seat, rubbed his ample belly, and belched once for effect and punctuation.

These opening elements are worth looking at in sequence. The first line (the hook) is dialogue (a form of action), followed by a line that identifies the speaker and places him in the scene (an anchor or grounding in the context of action). This anchor gives substance to the character, shows his taste in wine and food, and lets us know he is Italian. Next, via a longer speech (dialogue), we learn more of Hotshot's background, values, and feelings.

All this before we see one physical attribute—also presented through action: leaning, rubbing, belching. Nothing predictable in placement.

Note that the opening sentence of *Voodoo That You Do* offers an ideal beginning for a mystery: a change in the status quo, which Hotshot experiences as a threat to his well-being.

RICHER PORTRAYALS

If you have any remaining doubts about breaking the description-first habit, let Margaret Maron's characterization inspire you to renounce the practice for all time. This author furnishes almost *no* physical description, yet she captures each personality so effectively we scarcely realize that the vivid images we "see" are supplied by our own imaginations.

Southern Discomfort is the second title in Maron's award-winning Deborah Knott series. Two characters who play pivotal roles in the mystery are Deborah's brother Herman and his only daughter, Annie Sue. Maron portrays them through their actions, their dialogue, some exposition, and the dialogue of others. Almost no description. Yet we experience their tense parent-teen relationship as if it were our own.

When Maron introduces these two members of Deborah's family, she limits backstory to one specific example of a recent clash between them.

> I was glad to see that Annie Sue and Herman seemed to be speaking to each other today. A lot of days, they didn't.
>
> From infancy, Annie Sue had tested the limits of paternal authority; but she'd turned sixteen this spring and now that she had her driver's license, she wanted more freedom and less accountability than ever. According to Minnie, they'd had a monumental clash last weekend. I didn't get all the details; but I gather it involved a broken curfew and confiscation of car keys. Nothing new there except that both my brother and my niece had lost their tempers and Herman had warned Annie Sue—and in

front of her friends, which made it twice as humiliating—that she
wasn't too big to get a switching if she didn't apologize at once.

"In the same breath as she apologized, she swore she'd never
speak to Herman again as long as she lived," Minnie had
reported with a shake of her head. "Herman's way too strict, but
that child's sure got a talent for pouring kerosene on a hot fire."

I watched her pour Herman a cup of punch with every appearance of daughterly affection and hoped their reconciliation
would last a while this time.   [p. 16]

By now we have a pretty clear picture of this relationship, despite the
fact that the only physical data we are given about Annie Sue is her age,
"sixteen this spring." We have to jump twenty-two pages to observe father
and daughter again, also in action.

He was growling at Annie Sue when I drove into their back-
yard after supper that Thursday evening. Annie Sue was huffed
up and sir-ing him in that snippy-polite way teenagers do when
they want to make sure you know that their respect is only on
their lips, not in their hearts.

"I told Lu Bingham I'd wire our WomenAid house and now
he says I can't," she told me hotly, her Knott-blue eyes flashing
in the late afternoon sunlight. "He never lets me do anything!"

"She never did a circuit box by herself and she don't have a
license," said Herman. From the tone of his voice, I gathered
he'd already said that more than once before I drove up.

"Reese hasn't got a license and you let him wire everything
by himself."

"No, I don't and even if I did—"

"Because I heard you tell Granddaddy and Uncle Seth I know
more about how electricity works than he does."

"Miss Big Ears is liable to hear something she don't want to
hear, she keeps talking back to me," Herman said darkly.

He still had his work clothes on, as if he'd just come in
himself. Hot, tired, dirty and probably hungry, too. There was a
pinched look on his face, and I had a feeling this might not be
the best time to ask him to lend me a hammer.   [pp. 38–39]

Herman's dialogue gives us such a strong impression of the man that we're surprised to discover only three references to his actual appearance: "he still had his work clothes on," he was "hot, tired, dirty," and "there was a pinched look on his face." That's it. And the only new physical data we learn about Annie Sue is the color of her eyes.

From such rich dialogue and believable characterization that mirror our own family experiences, our imaginations fill in whatever else we need to visualize. With no action-stopping description occurring—and certainly not in any predictable way—we run no risk of having those visualizations contradicted in later scenes.

FIND & FIX CLUE #9: POISONOUS PREDICTABILITY

- ➟ Find the places in your manuscript where each character makes a first appearance, and watch for any predictable patterns in where, when, and how you describe them.
- ➟ Introduce characters through their dialogue and action, and hold off on description except where its later occurrence could contradict an earlier assumption.
- ➟ Present the fewest physical details, and work those into the action a little at a time, as you already know.
- ➟ Avoid having description stop the action or sidetrack your story's forward progression.

CLUE #10: DISAPPEARING BODIES

Remember breathless Clyde, whose high-anxiety middle-of-the-night visit to Bonnie stops short for description? Remember how a dastardly description of Bonnie interrupts her reaction to his visit, and how both occur with the same poisonous predictability?

That kind of amateur writing is predictable in one other way: Nothing from all that description relates to anything that comes after. Though the same characters reappear in subsequent scenes, rarely are any details from their opening description mentioned again.

As Gertrude Stein might observe, there is no *there* there.

One-time description dumps are quickly forgotten. If characters who make forgettable first impressions later emerge as people we should have paid more attention to, tough. Nothing from the initial description is even hinted at later to help us visualize the person in action.

Wouldn't petite Bonnie have to look up to carry on a conversation with Clyde, who's a foot taller than she is?

How meaningful is Clyde's body size if we are shown no difference in, say, the way he climbs a flight of stairs, or breathes after doing so, compared to bouncing Bonnie?

When a character's presence fades and his or her actions become indistinct, we become disconnected from the character and lose interest. Readers have three options:

1. Page back and hope to find a memory-refresher.
2. Plod ahead and hope to piece things together from the context.
3. Stop reading.

If the disconnected reader is a busy screener, forget options 1 and 2.

WITHOUT PURPOSE

Why make Bonnie petite and give Clyde 325 pounds to lug around if these details affect nothing the characters do from then on? Writers need to follow through on the features they assign—otherwise, why assign them?

Take clothing. Clyde, we are told, is wearing a dark blue suit when we meet him, but no mention is made of his attire when he shows up again in later scenes. Are we to assume he wears the same thing every day? If he changes clothes, a fashion update would be in order. But that would give more importance to Clyde's wardrobe than it merits.

Think through your details for their use in successive situations.

Here's a dress-for-successive lesson: select details you intend to carry forward. For every choice, you and only you are responsible for its credibility. If you sit a pair of glasses on Clyde's nose, you need to show him wiping them when you bring him in from the rain. That's not all. Endowing him with wire-rimmed glasses carries the additional burden of showing how he takes them off and puts them on again in the singular manner that distinguishes the wearer of wire-rims from the wearer of horned-rims.

ADD ATTITUDE

For continuity, assign features and behaviors that you are prepared to bring to bear on later actions. If Bonnie were one of your characters, what purpose would you have in giving her long hair? How might you integrate that feature in her actions? A commonplace gesture is to show her sweeping her tresses behind her ears. A more telling mannerism would reveal her feelings. Perhaps when reading a disturbing e-mail she pulls at her hair, and while talking with her lover on the phone she winds a strand of it sensuously around her finger.

We're going to say good-by to Bonnie and Clyde now, recalling that at no time did their descriptions give us any reason to remember them or relate to them as real people. Their author's choice of garments, body size, and hair served no story purpose whatsoever. The only function this odd couple served is to illustrate a few dos and don'ts:

- ➤ Do have a purpose for every detail you select.
- ➤ Do select details that contribute to characterization.
- ➤ Don't hand out features if you don't intend to maintain their authenticity—and your credibility.

●◆ Do recharge your powers of observation, especially if you bring a bespectacled character in from the rain.

Most of all, if a descriptive detail is worth mentioning the first time, it's worth mentioning again.

FOLLOW-THROUGH

One author who follows through on the features she assigns to her characters is D. C. Brod. The next example comes from *Error in Judgment,* her second mystery novel featuring Quint McCauley, P. I. Notice how Brod uses body size to effectively sustain the images of her characters.

> I barely had time to run through my story once more before the first squad car pulled up and a man stepped out. I'd only met Chief Carver once before, but I knew, even without the benefit of sunlight, that the tall, lanky figure approaching the office was his. Damn. [p. 24]

When additional characters are introduced a page later, Brod shows each in relation to someone else's size or position.

> [Carver] turned to the scowling policeman who stood in the doorway to the outer office. "Henninger, Barlowe's here. Keep him out." Henninger was a big man—shorter than Carver but with about fifty pounds on him. He responded with the speed of a large snake with a full stomach. Carver regarded him with a mixture of disgust and wariness but kept silent.
> "Who's Barlowe?" I asked Carver.
> "Newspaper," he said like he was talking about rat droppings.
> There was some commotion in the outer office followed by the protest, "Hey, man, I've gotta right to be here."
> I stepped into the office to get a look. The reporter barely came up to the deputy's chin but had stepped right up to him and was using Henninger's discomfort at the proximity the same way Carver had intimidated me with his height. [p. 25]

Two pages later, the author further emphasizes the police chief's position of power by shifting Quint to a one-down position—literally:

> Carver turned on me abruptly and the dog growled. Just as
> quickly, he dropped his gaze to the snarling animal. "If you
> don't shut that mutt up, I'm gonna kick its ass up the river." I
> had to kneel down to do it, but I placed a restraining hand on the
> dog. Carver towered over me. "I'm running the show here, not
> you."   [p. 27]

Later, Quint runs into the reporter again at a tavern. Barlowe's behavior
in relation to his size merits notice by Quint because it is different enough
from the stereotype.

> [T]he night before, I had been impressed with Barlowe's
> aggressiveness. Not just in the way he conducted an interview
> but also in his walk, his posture and the way he left anyone who
> couldn't keep up with him in his wake. He reminded me of a
> small feisty terrier that would take on a dog twice its own size
> because it had never occurred to it that size made a difference.
>   [p. 42]

When the police show up in Quint's sparsely furnished living room, the
author follows through on an earlier mention of Henninger's size.

> Carver and I sat on the couch and there was a moment of
> suspense as Henninger lowered his huge build into the director's
> chair on the other side of the coffee table. It creaked and held.
>   [p. 152]

D. C. Brod keeps her characters from fading away by selecting the fewest physical attributes, using them to show action, relating them to her
characters' personalities, attitudes, and behaviors, and maintaining consistency. That's being accountable for choices made. That's follow-through.

DEEPENING IMPRESSIONS

Carolyn Wheat, two-time Edgar nominee, is another author who knows
how to follow through on descriptions that keep her characters vivid. In
Fresh Kills, Wheat's third mystery novel featuring attorney Cass Jameson,
Cass recognizes another attorney in a courtroom in Brooklyn, N.Y.

"Anyone here a notary?" The voice was unmistakable, though it had been a while since I'd heard it. East Bronx Irish, loud enough to cut through the din of legal chitchat but not so loud as to render the speaker unladylike.

Marla Hennessey. Sometime friend, sometime rival, sometime bitch. Which of her multiple personalities would be out today?

[p. 6]

So far, Marla's voice and a little narrative give us a quick impression of her. Two paragraphs later:

"Can you come out in the hall for a minute?" Marla's green eyes had a calculating look I knew all too well.

"I don't dare miss the first call," I whispered back. "I'll be in this damned courtroom for the rest of my natural life as it is."

. . . .

"Cass, don't bullshit me." Marla was one of the few people I knew who could shout in a whisper. . . .   [p. 6]

Though the visual details of Marla's appearance have yet to be mentioned, Carolyn Wheat creates a stronger, more distinct impression of this character with dialogue and with the sound of her voice than most writers do with pages of description.

Other than one mention of green eyes, readers do not learn what Marla looks like until two paragraphs later. Nothing is lost by delaying that description. In fact, by now we have become so interested in the character from her words and actions that we are ready to absorb the few descriptive details that complete the picture.

. . . she lit a cigarette and began waving it in her hand, her huge hammered-silver bracelet riding up and down on her wrist.

She'd put on weight. She'd colored and cut her hair, wearing it in a platinum pageboy that fitted her head like a cap. Her clothes were silver and mauve, flowing garments that gave an illusion of soft femininity. As I listened, I reminded myself that it was only an illusion. Marla was as armored as if her clothes and hair were made of stainless steel.   [p. 7]

Appreciate the symbolism: Marla's huge hammered bracelet in motion, her armored, stainless steel hair and clothing, her weight—which she keeps throwing around, metaphorically—plus the twice-mentioned *illusion.*

Most of these details live on in later scenes, from Marla's clothing and jewelry to the sound of her voice. Each additional image reinforces and amplifies Marla's character and anchors her in her surroundings.

Take Wheat's continuing references to Marla's shoes, for instance, and how they make an impression—a deep one.

> "Jesus" was all Marla said, but she slammed the car door hard and walked quickly, the heels of her shoes making little holes in the grass as she took the straightest path to the door, disregarding the curved flagstone path.   [p. 16]

> She then swept out of the car in a cloud of expensive perfume. I followed, racing to keep up even though the heels on my shoes were half the height of the bronze pumps Marla wore. Did the woman ever *walk?*   [p. 45]

> She dropped her cigarette to the floor and crushed it with her silver pump. . . . Marla's eyes held a malicious glint as she shot back, "What conversation, Cass? It's your word against mine." Her heels clicked on the pavement, and she swung the courthouse door open with a wide flourish.   [p. 82]

Study Carolyn Wheat's techniques. They present a model for resolving all the issues I raise in CLUES #8 through #10 about the deadly effects of dastardly description, poisonous predictability, and disappearing bodies.

FIND & FIX CLUE #10: DISAPPEARING BODIES

- Review the ways you describe your major characters and evaluate each descriptive detail for its contribution to characterization.
- Replace details mentioned only once with those you intend to carry forward and use again because they relate to your characterizations.
- Track the attributes you assign to each character to see if they continue to be reflected in the individual's actions, where appropriate.
- Select features that:
  - do double duty
  - are worth repeating
  - enrich your writing (please see "WITH PURPOSE AFORE-THOUGHT" in PART II).

In an interview in *Newsweek,* Janet Evanovich calls herself
a slow, "reductive" writer. She uses the cooking term
"reduction" to compare writing to making gravy,
in which a big pot of ingredients is boiled down
to "a little pot of stuff, which is the essence." [35]

PART VI: CHANGE OF VENUE

> "The way manuscripts are thrown into the Rejection
> pile on the basis of early mistakes is a crime."
> Pat Holt, former *San Francisco Chronicle* book reviewer [36]

CLUE #11: SHIFTY EYES

With publishing's continuing emphasis on novels that are more character-driven than plot-driven, selecting an effective point of view (POV) is one of your most important decisions. Anne Underwood Grant cautions that in a mystery, more than in any other literary form, each POV choice offers a different advantage.

If you are still developing your skills for the effective use of this technique, you probably researched the considerable literature on POV before you settled on a choice for the novel you are now revising. This CLUE, like the 23 others, helps you evaluate the results of your choices and understand the POV problems that show up most often in manuscripts.

FIRST-PERSON POV

Let's suppose your story is told from your protagonist's first-person POV. You write: *I parked at the branch office and did a quick check in my rearview mirror: short red hair, green eyes, freckles—*

Oops! For a narrator's self-description, the reflection-in-the-mirror device is a cliché. More imaginative alternatives can be created, as the next few pages demonstrate. Meanwhile, back at the branch. . . .

Before I could knock on the manager's door it flew open, and I found myself face-to-face with a man who glared at me, wanting me to get lost.

Whoa! A first-person narrator cannot know what others want, think, or feel. She knows only what she wants, thinks, or feels with her own five senses. Here are three of them: *He glared at me* (sight), *poked me sharply on the shoulder* (touch), *and growled* (hearing), *"Get out of my way."*

Okay, let's try this once more. *The front of his tee-shirt read "Builders do it with . . ." and the back bore the words—*

No, no! Ms. First Person cannot see what's on someone else's back if they have just come face-to-face.

One manuscript I edited had its first-person narrator eating lunch in a coffee shop and thinking about the two women in the booth behind him. He described what Rhoda, the attorney, looks like, as well as Gladys, her paralegal. Unless this is another mirror trick, no way can he see them.

Then, when Mr. First Person finishes eating, he gets up, says, "Hello, I haven't seen you around before. My name is. . . ."

Uh-oh. If he is first meeting them, how could he know their names and occupations? He couldn't. He's a victim of the writer's shifty eyes.

Review your manuscript for slips like these, which pull observant readers right out of a story. One clumsy slip, slide, or shift in POV is enough to cause a busy screener to shift a submission to the "no" pile.

LOOK MA, NO MIRROR

The clichéd reflection in a store window or mirror is an amateur approach to self-description. Instead, be imaginative and theatrical, as Denise Dietz is in *Footprints in the Butter.* In this first title of Dietz's second mystery series, she subjects Ingrid Beaumont to a fumble at a football game.

> The Broncos blitzed. The Cowboys fumbled. The Broncs recovered. I roared my approval, then performed a high-five with the fat man sitting next to me. He fumbled for my breast, I don't know why. I'm not a ravishing beauty, quite the opposite, yet men always try to ravish me. I've been told I look like Bette Midler. When people tell me this, they usually stare at my bust, then, embarrassed, raise their eyes to my slightly crooked front teeth, which are frequently clenched.   [p. 2]

Or be straightforward and charming, like John D. MacDonald's protagonist in *The Deep Blue Good-By,* the first book actually written in his
long-running Travis McGee series.

> "Mrs. Atkinson? My name is Travis McGee."
> "Yes? Yes? What do you want?"
> I tried to look disarming. Am pretty good at that. I have one
> of those useful faces. Tanned American. Bright eyes and white
> teeth shining amid a broad brown reliable bony visage. The
> proper folk-hero crinkle at the corners of the eyes, and the
> bashful appealing smile, when needed. . . .
> So I looked disarming. When they give you something to use,
> you use it.   [p. 33]

Or be roundabout and defensive, like Cathy Pickens' attorney Avery
Andrews in *Southern Fried,* winner of an Agatha award for best new traditional mystery.

> "So you're defending Donlee? Figured you would. Him bein'
> so sweet on you and everything. He's always been partial to
> that red hair of yours."
> I've always thought it more a burnished gold, but whatever.
> And Donlee developed crushes on any female unwary enough
> to smile at him.   [p. 2]

Or be self-deprecating and confessional, like Lieutenant Jack (Jacqueline)
Daniels, as presented by J. A. Konrath in *Whiskey Sour,* his first mystery
novel, nominated for the Anthony, Macavity, and Gumshoe awards.

> My last sound sleep was sometime during the Reagan
> Administration, and it shows. At forty-six my auburn hair is
> streaked with gray that grows faster than I can dye it, the lines
> on my face shout age rather than character, and even two
> bottles of Visine a month couldn't get all the red out.   [p. 7]

Always, *always* be original, like Kathleen Anne Barrett in *Milwaukee
Winters Can Be Murder,* who lets us know what Beth Hartley looks like
through the words of a friend.

"What are you going to do," Emily said, "wrestle the guy to the ground when you catch him? You don't even weigh enough to donate blood, for Pete's sake. I mean, you're even smaller than my nine-year-old niece. . . . my dog sat on you once and you couldn't even get up, do you remember that?"   [p. 322]

How original is your character's self-description? 'Fess up.

MORE FIRST-PERSON PITFALLS

First-person POV may seem the most natural way to tell a story, but it's not as simple as it looks. Inviting us into your character's consciousness means playing fair—not withholding information he discovers in the course of his investigation. However, nothing prevents you from underplaying a clue, disguising its significance, or diverting attention with a red herring.

Another first-person requirement is that the sleuth-as-narrator must be present in every scene. If your plot makes this impossible, you don't want to discover that problem three-quarters of the way through your first draft. I've seen too many first-person manuscripts that attempt to later accommodate point-of-view issues by awkward maneuvering of the plot or by having the sleuth hear or read about key events after they occur off-stage. Second-hand action is weak and cancels the value of a you-are-there POV. As for plot maneuvers, anything awkward is amateur.

Also, first-person writing tends to ramble, use thoughts more than dialogue, and rehash the same thoughts. One way to use thought effectively is to create self-talk in which your protagonist argues with herself.

In this POV more than any other, your narrator's character must be revealed, and that character needs to be so interesting, quirky, and insightful that readers will want to see the world through her eyes for an entire novel.

If your story exhibits any first-person weakness, fix it or consider using a more flexible POV.

THIRD-PERSON POV

The most versatile, most popular narrative mode is third-person. It comes in two flavors, limited and multiple. *Limited* sticks to one viewpoint character throughout, the same as first-person, and it imposes similar limitations. But it lets readers see a character objectively as well as subjectively, both from the outside and from inside her head.

Multiple expands the number of heads the narrator is able to access, but not more than one head per scene.

Among the plusses of writing from multiple viewpoints is the opportunity to leapfrog: to open a scene from the POV of a character who is *not* the one just smacked by the plot twist at the end of the previous scene.

You can prolong suspense by knowing where readers expect you to take them and not going there—at least not for another scene or two. Leapfrogging is a technique for braiding separate story lines until you are ready to show how they all come together. However, frequent POV switches can lead to a reader's feeling detached from the protagonist.

Remember that caring about one character engages interest more than caring what happens to a group of near strangers.

When you begin a scene from a different viewpoint:

- open with a hook to diminish the potential for a loss of interest;
- let readers know right away whose viewpoint they're in;
- use action and dialogue, not the slower thought mode, to establish the identity of each viewpoint character;
- take a detail from an earlier scene that left readers hanging at its end and refer to it at the start of the later scene that picks up with the same character;
- rotate such scenes according to some consistent pattern that you establish early, so you aren't changing viewpoints for the first time after a hundred pages of going steady with the same person.

In *More Than You Know* by Meg Chittenden, Nick's third-person POV continues to the end of Scene 1 of Chapter 2. It is replaced in Scene 2 by the third-person POV of Maddy, the woman Nick is following. The plot continues as if no change occurred. That's one smooth shift.

The technique of alternating viewpoints lets Chittenden show Nick and Maddy collaborating on a mutual goal while mistrusting the other's personal agenda. Dramatic irony and tension build when characters are attracted to each other but also need to hide their suspicions.

OBJECTIVE DISTANCE

Whether limited or multiple, third-person permits *distance,* as shown by this excerpt from *Blood Lure,* ninth in the Anna Pigeon, park ranger, series by Nevada Barr, an Agatha and an Anthony winner.

"I see you've made yourself at home," Harry said acidly.

"Yeah." Anna was too absorbed to notice the intended reprimand. "So the army jacket Carolyn was wearing wasn't hers?"

Ruick shook his head disgustedly. Since Anna'd not been aware of his implied rebuke, she also missed its annoyed follow-up at her obtuseness and took the headshake as a negative about the jacket.   [p. 178]

Because part of Anna's characterization is her inability to see herself as others see her, she is not a good candidate for first-person narrator. Third-person allows Barr to control how much objectivity and distance to maintain in portraying her series character.

Consider the opening from the first title in the Elderhostel mystery series by Peter Abresch, *Bloody Bonsai.* The protagonist is James P. Dandy (yes, that's Jim Dandy, to his frequent consternation). From the first line he is grousing about going on his first solo junket after his wife's death.

You'll have a really good time, they said.
You'll learn lotsa stuff, they said.
You'll meet people, they said.
Yeah, right.   [p. 8]

Jim brings his anxiety with him, along with a suitcase-sized chip on his shoulder. That attitude immediately introduces a conflict and quickly establishes his character and his voice.

Shouldn't have come.

Uncle George's fault. . . .

Or maybe it was Ceecee's fault.

"Go Dad, you already paid your money." It went on for two months. Getting her brothers to gang up on him. "You need to get away. You haven't gone anywhere since Mom died."

Did any of them ever wonder that maybe he hadn't wanted to go anywhere after Penny died? And on top of it, two to a room, he would be paired up with a stranger for a roommate.

Great, really great.   [pp. 9–10]

These passages suggest a first-person viewpoint—until you glance at a few of the lines I omitted. Directly after Jim's opening grumble *(Yeah, right)*, Abresch orients us in the scene: *Jim's two-year-old blue Lincoln.*

And Jim's sarcastic riff on bunking with a stranger *(Great, really great)* is followed by: *He climbed out of the car, got his bag from the trunk. . . .*

This is third-person limited subjective. Gone are all the usual third-person "he thought-felt-wondered-realized" tags that impose a filter between narrator and character and increase the distance between them. Instead, Jim's thoughts blend seamlessly with the narrative. The form could almost (not quite) be generated by writing in first-person, then changing pronouns.

MULTIPLE SUBJECTIVE

For third-person multiple subjective, look at Nancy Means Wright's *Mad Season.* It's first in the series of Vermont mysteries featuring Ruth Willmarth, who is singlehandedly rearing two children and running a dairy farm. When the elderly couple on the neighboring farm is attacked and robbed, Ruth's ten-year-old son wants to know what happened.

> Vic gazed down at the floor as she spoke, clasping and unclasping his hands. His face was pale for all the freckles. She sensed he was empathizing. She wanted to go to him, hug him, say it was all right: Mom was here, no one could harm him.
> But he was ten years old. Pete was right, she had to let him grow up. Though it was hard not to interfere, hard!   [p. 20]

Vic tells his mother that at one time he accidentally saw where the neighbor kept a wad of money. But the boy had said nothing at the time.

> "I didn't want him to think I saw all that money. There were safety pins, the coat was heavy, like he kept more than showed. Then, then I was afraid—"
> "Afraid of what?" She clasped her knees. She saw how thin Vic was. He'd been losing weight and she was only just aware of it. She was too busy, she was a terrible mother, she couldn't keep up with farm and family. The fear of losing her children crept over her again and she held out a finger to touch Vic. But he shrank away.

Wright's style lets us experience the mother's angst as powerfully as if the narrative were first-person. It almost is; such intimacy is what subjective third-person can do. Ruth's interior voice becomes one with the invisible narrator's and produces an effect known as tight, the opposite of distant.

Whereas dialogue tags would emphasize the gap between character and narrator, Wright diminishes the gap with beats that reflect Ruth's feelings: *She sensed. . . She wanted to. . . She saw. . . .* (I discuss beats more fully in CLUE #17.)

Something else worth noting is that Wright's subjective POV is also third-person multiple. Occasionally the thoughts of a few other characters are presented, but always within strict limits: each has his or her own scene.

In my opinion, Wright's style combines the best of all worlds: the flexibility and control of third-person with the intense closeness of first.

This technique is not to be confused with omniscient POV, which lets the narrator enter the thoughts of any and all characters at any time. That lack of boundaries can keep readers from bonding with important characters. Moreover, omniscient is difficult to pull off effectively, so I don't recommend it for the developing novelist.

THIRD-PERSON PITFALLS

Because third-person offers the freedom to enter the thoughts, feelings, and fields of vision of different characters, a frequent mistake is to present too many viewpoints. Doing so fragments the focus of your readers and keeps them from feeling close to anyone, including the main character. In some novels it's hard to tell who the main character *is*.

Another problem is *head-hopping:* visiting the minds of different characters in the same scene. The result weakens the impact of the scene's events on the character most affected by them. Head-hopping also disorients readers and marks the writer as an amateur.

Phone calls give rise to a special kind of wrong number. If you present a dual sound track for telephone dialogue, don't include actions and mannerisms for both parties. The viewpoint

Lesley Grant-Adamson, in *Writing Crime Fiction*, cautions new writers that the more viewpoints you have to cope with, the more complicated the writing. She adds: "Please think very hard about whether you feel ready to tackle a form that presents extra difficulties."[37]

character cannot see into the receiver. Ellis Vidler avoids this trap in *Haunting Refrain,* her first mystery novel, by limiting Kate McGuire's five senses to the one required for taking a call from her ex-husband: hearing. She does not see him pacing; she intuits it from what she hears when he says:

> "I tried to get you last night, but you didn't answer." His rhythmic steps echoed through the line as he paced the length of the phone cord.   [p. 68]

If you do want your audience to see the party on the other end, begin a new scene in that person's POV. Stay put for a while before switching again so your readers don't feel like spectators at a tennis match.

INTENTIONAL SLIPPAGE

Occasionally, experienced writers serve a purpose by intentionally slipping into another character's point of view in the same scene. *Blood Orchid,* a Holly Barker novel by two-time Edgar-winner Stuart Woods, opens with two brief scenes, each of which has someone getting shot in the head.

The second of those scenes puts us on a golf course in the third-person POV of a con artist, Steinberg. It's the eighteenth hole, and this sandbagger has kept the score tied until now, when his plan is to win big and take the other player's money. At this time the narrative becomes less subjective, more objective, putting distance between Steinberg's opening viewpoint and the POV shift at the end of the scene to Fleischman, the other golfer.

When Fleischman catches on that he's being played for a sucker, we know it through his dialogue. We are not inside his head—yet.

> "So how come, all of a sudden, after seventeen holes, you're outdriving me?"   [p. 3]

Steinberg shrugs, recommends which club Fleischman should use, and takes his final, winning swing. Get ready for the switch in viewpoint. . . .

> Then Steinberg's head exploded.
> For a tiny second before he screamed, Fleischman wondered if cheating at golf could make your head explode.   [p. 4]

Our learning what Fleischman wonders marks an end-of-scene shift in POV. But when the viewpoint character is killed, it's time to shift.

MORE DISTANCE

J. A. Jance makes an equally effective shift at the end of a scene in *Desert Heat*. Joanna Brady's husband has been seriously wounded. During the long ride to the hospital in Tucson, Joanna grieves, then composes herself and handles the admitting procedure with the efficiency of an insurance agent, which she is.

> "One of the forms is missing," Joanna said.
> Annoyed, the clerk peered at her. . . . "Really? Which one?"
> "The organ donor consent form," Joanna answered firmly. "His heart's already stopped once. I want to go ahead and sign the form now, just in case."
> The clerk frowned. "That's not a very positive attitude, Mrs. Brady," she sniffed disapprovingly. "Our surgeons are very skillful here, you know."
> "I'm sure they are, but I still want to sign it, if you don't mind."

After the form is produced, signed, and witnessed, Joanna asks if she could see her husband before surgery.

> "I doubt that," the clerk replied coldly. "I doubt that very much."
> Actually, as far as the clerk was concerned, if it had been left up to her, the very fact that Joanna Brady had insisted on signing the prior-consent organ-donor form would have cinched it. No way would she have allowed that woman to see her husband now, not in a million years.
> Women who were that disloyal didn't deserve to have husbands in the first place.   [p. 34]

At the word "Actually," Jance shifts from Joanna's POV to the clerk's. The narrative takes on the clerk's attitude and thoughts, and exhibits a style of speech that could belong to no one but the clerk. This shift in viewpoint adds a lighter tone following two grim chapters, and it accounts for a plot event—Joanna's not being permitted to see her dying husband.

As skillfully executed as Jance's and Wood's techniques are, shifting viewpoints within a scene is risky. My advice to the still-developing writer? Don't try this at home.

MIXED UP

Over the years, a great many guidelines have been put forth about point of view, all of which have been disregarded at one time or another by well-respected authors. Occasionally a break with tradition is effective; occasionally it bombs.

Consider what's known as *mixed* POV. The writer presents certain scenes in first-person, others in third. Some readers admire the technique; others, citing the very same novels, hate it.

The author with a supportive editor and loyal fans can afford to experiment. Innovation is riskier for midlist writers with borderline sales, who may be thinking of trying a name change and finding a new agent and publisher. For the writer who has yet to find either one, embracing the unconventional could be suicide.

Dawn Cook's debut novel, *First Truth,* originally used first-person for the protagonist, Alissa, and third-person wherever the tension benefitted from the reader's knowing more than Alissa could know.

Cook's agent advised that a consistent POV would more readily meet the preferences of publishers for a first novel. Cook weighed the need to sustain the story's tension against the potential loss of first-person "punch" and began extensive revision. In its published form, *First Truth* is a compelling fantasy, told throughout in third-person.

> "Rewriting is the whole secret to writing."
> Mario Puzo

Despite growing acceptance for mixed POV, even experienced writers get mixed results. One popular author presents the first four chapters of one of his mysteries in the sleuth's first-person POV, then opens Chapter 5 with a jarring third-person "he." We discover we're in backstory, learning about this unnamed individual's first assignment as a cop.

For one and a half pages we don't know if this is still the sleuth talking, reliving his early days on the force. Readers new to the series might think so. Or maybe this no-name rookie is the friend who visits the sleuth in the preceding chapter. Until we learn what's-his-name's identity a page and a half into Chapter 5, we continue wondering who "he" is—a state of limbo that prevents our fully engaging with this fellow's backstory.

Any time a reader wonders, attention wanders. That's when we stop reading.

Famous or not, this author violates two basic principles of technique:

- ❧ to always keep the reader oriented, and
- ❧ to always identify the new POV character right after a switch.

By comparison, in *Whiskey Sour,* J. A. Konrath mixes first and third in a nearly perfect pattern of alternating chapters. Such consistency gets readers quickly adapted to the shift and anticipating it. Verb tense and gender help, too. The "I" of Lt. Jacqueline Daniels' chapters and the traditional use of past tense contrasts with the "he" of the killer's chapters and the present tense—techniques that make the villain's actions appear more immediate and menacing.

Mixing first and third can nevertheless be hazardous to the health of an unsold manuscript. For every choice you make, let your reason be that no other point of view could be as effective.

FIND & FIX CLUE #11: SHIFTY EYES

- ❧ When revising, identify the point(s) of view you use in every scene and review for consistency.
- ❧ Check that whatever POV pattern you select, you establish it early, before readers learn to anticipate some other pattern.
- ❧ Ensure that any character narrating in first-person is physically present in all key scenes.
- ❧ Verify that no viewpoint character knows others' attitudes except through observable sensory experience.
- ❧ Confirm that first-person does not ramble, overuse interior thoughts, or constantly rehash the same thoughts.
- ❧ See that after any shift in POV, the new viewpoint character is promptly identified and the reader is kept oriented.
- ❧ Take care to keep the focus on your main character, and reduce or eliminate other viewpoints that diminish the focus.
- ❧ Resist mixing first- and third-person in the same novel.

CLUE #12: UNSETTLING SETTINGS

What's the first thing a movie or comic book character is expected to say upon coming to after being knocked out? *"Where am I?"* We humans have a primal need to orient ourselves in our surroundings. A story that neglects to instill a sense of place leaves readers feeling unsettled and *dis*-oriented.

Make one editing pass through your manuscript specifically to check that each scene establishes setting right away. This does not mean beginning each scene with a full-blown description; it means letting readers have a quick, general sense of where the action is taking place—downstairs from "that front bedroom where you sleep, Ashley dear," or "out back" in the garden, or at the eighteenth hole.

One manuscript I edited opened with a character watching a public figure smiling for the press. I visualized the narrator standing among the crowd gathered in front of a government building. A paragraph later I discovered that our observer was sitting at home watching the press conference on television.

Sometimes, setting is mere orientation and backdrop; sometimes, just another pretty place. When used expertly, setting reflects a time and a culture and it unifies a story. It can evoke the mood of a story, underscore its theme, and add depth to the characters and their behaviors. In some fiction, setting plays a role as significant as that of a character.

When setting is *not* used effectively, some or all of the following unsettling signs become immediately apparent:

- The story's location is so indistinct that events could be taking place in Anyboro, USA.
- Features are put forth all at once, not interwoven with the unfolding action.

133

- Description is little more than an inventory of commonplace features devoid of the location's uniqueness, with quantity of detail trumping quality.
- Some information is more detailed than necessary: "The path split after five minutes, so I took the right fork, walked about ten yards, and off to my left about a quarter of a mile farther. . . . "
- Once described, setting is not mentioned again, unless a later scene occurs in a different location.
- Mood is established once during the initial scene-setting, but without continued maintenance it fades.
- Nothing about the setting appears related to the story, its theme, its characters, or their actions and emotions.

The usual setting for manuscripts with these qualities is the "no" pile.

In addition to aesthetic value, a novel has potential market value if it offers a fresh locale that depicts a previously untapped regional, ethnic, or interest group. A compelling sense of place rich in local color and history can make a well-written manuscript stand out among the hundreds of others set in faceless places.

FAMILIAR SETTINGS

Even an often-used location, such as Miami, Chicago, the Big Apple, or La-La Land, can make editors take notice of a new writer who presents it with originality. Michael Connelly received an Edgar award for best first mystery for *The Black Echo*, which introduced Harry Bosch, LAPD homicide detective.

In the scene opener that follows, only the first sentence puts forth the type of descriptive detail usually associated with setting. The three sentences after that deepen the relationship between the location and Connelly's theme.

> The setting sun burned the sky pink and orange in the same bright hues as surfers' bathing suits. It was beautiful deception, Bosch thought, as he drove north on the Hollywood Freeway to home. Sunsets did that here. Made you forget it was the smog that made their colors so brilliant, that behind every pretty picture there could be an ugly story. [p. 70]

Would the idea of a beautiful deception resonate with as much meaning if the story were set somewhere other than a city devoted to creating illusion?

A similar theme pervades *Almost Night,* Ann Prospero's first mystery novel. Set on the opposite coast, it opens with Miami homicide detective Susannah Cannon wanting to run away from images of a murdered child. In introducing the locale around Biscayne Bay, Prospero emphasizes its contrasts.

> Miami sparkles. Green leaves spill over the streets from extravagant neotropical plants, and flowers bloom. . . . Passenger ships and cargo ships leave Miami heading toward foreign ports. They glide away from downtown and past the MacArthur Causeway, where cars speed between Miami and Miami Beach. From the causeway, the ships look like moving, massive apartment buildings on their way out to sea.
>
> At downtown's southern edge, a river runs into the bay. Seminole Indians and early settlers once traveled that river, the Miami River. Water pours out from its mouth into the bay—as if the craziness in the city were overflowing.
>
> And there is a madness buried underneath Miami's beauty, a madness that resides below the surface layers of tourism and glamour. The putrid Miami is the one I most often see as a homicide detective. . . .   [pp. 1–2]

Miami's madness is the reality that challenges Susannah in both her professional and personal life. How she reacts to it as the story unfolds brings out the complexity of her character. Further contrasts in the setting parallel incidents and people, who—as in all good mysteries—are not what they seem.

PERVASIVE SETTINGS

A setting is occasionally made to play such an integral role in the lives of a novel's characters that it takes on the importance of a character. A fine example can be seen in *A Place of Execution,* winner of half a dozen awards, including the Barry for best British mystery. Val McDermid infuses everything with the atmosphere and mood of one small English village.

> Scardale wasn't just a different world from the bustling market
> town where Swindells lived and worked; it had the reputation
> of being a law unto itself.   [p. 10]

The details McDermid selects capture the insular quality of this unusual village. Notice that she presents those details in the way that Detective Inspector George Bennett experiences them.

> . . . In the eerie light of the moon, George could see fields of
> rough pasture rising gently from the road that bisected the
> valley floor. Sheep huddled together against the walls, their
> breath brief puffs of steam in the freezing air. Darker patches
> revealed themselves as areas of coppiced woodland as they
> drove past. George had never seen the like. It was a secret
> world, hidden and separate.   [p. 22]

Your setting doesn't have to be as palpable or as pervasive as Scardale, and your presentation of it doesn't have to be as comprehensive. But the details you do present should be no less deliberately chosen for effect.

SMALLER-SCALE SETTINGS

Balance the amount of attention you give to a setting with its importance to your story as a whole. One technique that packs a powerhouse of meaning in a minimum of words is *allusion.* Lynette Hall Hampton uses it to introduce a scene in her first mystery novel, *Jilted by Death.*

> The house, a stately plantation-style mansion, sat at the bend
> of a curved drive on the eastern side of town. As I stopped
> behind Nevis's blue Lexus, I half expected Scarlett O'Hara to
> meet us on the columned front porch.   [p. 25]

The author's naming of one well-known fictional character is all it takes to endow her own setting with the same way of life so richly portrayed in the most popular Southern novel ever published. Because allusion is a highly condensed, efficient device, it can take the place of longer descriptions.

Most any interior—whether a house, room, car, garden, or place of business—can be made to do double duty by not only setting the scene but by also showing what its occupant is like. Be careful not to get carried away, as some writers do, by devoting considerable attention to describing an interior belonging to someone whose role in your story is insignificant.

Besides maintaining a sense of balance, maintain the *perspective* of your main character. I've read more than one description of a four-bedroom ranch, with a family room off the kitchen, from the POV of the sleuth who just rang the front doorbell and is waiting to enter the house for the first time. If you're writing science fiction your characters might describe sights beyond their line of vision. For all other fiction, ixnay on the x-ray.

Instead, weave description into your action, as the next examples show, and present it in a sequence that your viewpoint character would logically experience. As always, be selective. Offer a few well-chosen details and trust your readers' imaginations to fill in the rest.

SETTING AS ACTION

S. J. Rozan creates a vivid impression of both a setting and its occupant in this passage from the Edgar and Macavity award-winning mystery *Winter and Night.* Bill Smith, one of Rozan's two lead characters in the Lydia Chin/Bill Smith P. I. series, drives to an address in search of information.

> . . . I turned in, parked behind a rust-pocked Olds Cutlass that was probably as surprised as anyone every time it found itself running. Mud clutched at my shoes as I walked to the porch, and the steps creaked as I climbed them. . . .   [p. 209]

All description proceeds from Bill's *actions,* from his turning in and parking to walking to the porch and entering the house.

> I wiped my feet on a worn mat, followed Beth Adams and the dog through a dank hall to a sticky-floored kitchen. I took the can of Bud she handed me, and then followed again into a living room sloppy with old magazines and *TV Guides.* . . .
> The cloud of dust I raised when I sat on the broken-down couch danced in the sunlight.   [p. 210]

Nothing about Rozan's setting is static: no yard *was* muddy, mat *was* worn, or floor *was* sticky. The living room did not *have* old magazines.

Another setting presented through action can be found in *Sinister Heights* by Loren Estleman. When Amos Walker, P. I., comes to the home of a wife-abuser, he has to defend himself against its inebriated owner. Chapter 6 ends with Amos knocking his assailant unconscious on the front stoop and dragging him inside; Chapter 7 opens without missing a beat.

> We went down a step into a sunken living room that smelled as if it had gone down with the Armada. It was carpeted in deep pile from which Glendowning's heels dragged up dust and strips of cellophane from cigarette packages past as I hauled him backward toward the nearest chair. This was a fat gray recliner that went into its act when I dumped him into it, stretching its spine and swinging up its footrest. . . . If there was an ashtray under the bent cigarette butts on the end table by the chair, or for that matter an end table under the squat brown beer bottles, I would have needed a shovel to find them.   [p. 53]

Like Rozan, Estleman reveals each detail of this setting in the context of action, having Walker either smell, haul, dump, or mentally shovel it. The result does more than characterize the slob of a homeowner; it also characterizes the protagonist, Amos Walker.

EATING AGAIN?

Now that we are indoors, I want to make you aware of one type of setting that's frequently misused and overused: the restaurant or bar. Granted, crime-fighters have to exchange information with others during the course of their investigations, and logical places for doing so range from a five-star French restaurant to a pancake franchise.

Anything wrong with that? Depends. Action is conflict. Busy manuscript screeners want to see it and feel it. Action is also tension that arises from *anticipated* conflict. But information-sharing is not action. Seating two people at a table to exchange it only weakens a scene already at risk.

Writers often make up for the lack of table action by occupying their characters with sipping a drink, looking at a menu, placing an order, taking a bite, having another sip, stirring, cutting, chewing, and swallowing.

That's activity, not action. At best, such meaningless busyness merits an occasional beat. Activity without conflict or tension does not make a scene *a scene.* Nor does tension come from looking at a menu—unless the prices are criminal.

The information characters exchange might produce a little tension. However, dialogue that tells of an off-stage event rarely has the emotional impact of an on-stage event paraded before the eyes of an audience. Conflict talked about falls flatter than a franchised pancake.

Energize those static, action-deprived "table settings." Create a reason for the information-exchanging characters to experience conflict in the setting you choose. Maybe they disagree over how to interpret the information or how to act on it. Maybe they are trying not to be seen together in public. Maybe they dislike each other. Even best friends argue. They may share the same values and goals but not the same priorities at the same moment. Making sure they don't is up to you.

The friend might have to get to the hardware store before it closes. That's tension. Maybe she has no patience for more than a quick drink and a quicker news briefing—not the discussion that her close friend, the amateur sleuth, wants to pursue. That's conflict.

SWITCH SETTINGS

If an interaction lacks tension, consider changing the setting to one that offers conflict of its own. A hockey game might set your characters to arguing about the time Ohio State beat Michigan.

Plant some earlier mention of your characters' interest in the alternate activity, hockey, so their meeting place becomes a logical choice. Different settings offer different possibilities for cranking up conflict.

Suppose your amateur sleuth wants to sound out her theory of the crime with her best friend. Best Friend plans to spend a quiet Saturday fishing. So your sleuth invites herself along, and their day on the water proves anything but quiet. While one focuses on catching a carp, the other keeps harping on catching a killer. When a whopper of a fish gets away, Best Friend blames the amateur sleuth and retaliates by poking holes in her theory of the crime. The sleuth begrudgingly revises her thinking, and the plot goes in a new direction.

Any time feelings run high, nearly any setting will do. Use one that doesn't appear in everyone else's novel.

True, everyone has to eat, and people do arrange to meet for dinner and drinks when they want to talk. Yet too many fictional tête-à-têtes are staged in restaurants and bars for no reason other than the setting's having come easily to mind and needing no research. Convenience food.

If you want to use a restaurant or bar setting but don't want to instigate a conflict between your characters, make those action-deficient exchanges extremely brief. Don't prolong a scene once it serves its purpose.

Some writers make an eatery or night club part of their fiction, giving the setting a continuing role to play in the lives of the main characters. Tamar Myers sets the first of her two mystery series at a Mennonite bed and breakfast in Hernia, Pennsylvania. From the recipes in her first novel, *Too Many Crooks Spoil the Broth,* to well beyond her later *Assault and Pepper,* Myers makes the interactions around Magdalena Yoder's big oak dining table a significant part of the action and characterization.

Nancy Bartholomew's first mystery series features Sierra Lavotini, an exotic dancer at the Tiffany. Her second stars Maggie Reid, a country western singer who performs at the Golden Stallion. Staging a conversation in one of these establishments is as natural as its protagonist's reporting to work.

Alex Matthews makes going out to dinner the source of an ongoing conflict for her series character, psychotherapist Cassidy McCabe. Cass is always reacting to her husband's capacity for hard liquor. The way in which drinking creates tension between the two reflects the couple's ever-evolving relationship. Even meeting a friend for lunch at Eric's in Oak Park represents a fundamental part of Cass's belief system: she doesn't believe in cooking.

RELEVANCE

For a character who does not work around food and drink or who has no issues relating to them, what are some other ways that a restaurant or bar might make a logical, relevant setting? Perhaps. . .

- ● if the weapon of choice is poison or knockout drops administered in a Shirley Temple. . .
- ● if the plot establishes that a suspect or witness is known to hang out at Wookie's Nook. . .
- ● if a clumsy waitperson spills the soup, causing Eliza Dewmore to make an unscheduled trip home to change clothes, where she walks in on. . . .

You get the picture. After all, you don't have your characters meet at the airport if no one is taking a trip or opening a storage locker. So instead of staging a meaningless meal, think about having your characters rendez-vous at a racetrack, dialogue at a dog park, or kibitz at the car wash.

I'm not saying put your characters on a diet and keep them out of the bars. I *am* saying don't pick a place from force of habit or lack of imagination. Choose each setting for its relevance to your characters and plot, or for its potential in heightening tension and conflict.

Is a racetrack or dog park where I recommend your characters exchange their information? Only if it works for your story. If Chez Café is the one best spot for the action you have in mind, of course take everyone out to eat. But please, put a lid on all that sipping and chewing. After a while it's hard to swallow.

FIND & FIX CLUE #12: UNSETTLING SETTINGS

- Identify how you establish and maintain a sense of place.
- Analyze how you use sensory details in setting your scenes.
- Review the ways your characters are shown being affected by their environment.
- Verify that the elements in your settings are presented as part of the action.
- Evaluate how your interiors characterize their occupants.
- Balance the amount of attention you give to describing a setting with its importance to the story.
- Experiment by changing the location of a scene that has little tension to one that adds its own conflict.
- Don't prolong scenes after they serve their purpose.

"Mystery writers never write 'setting for setting's sake'
—it's always *in support* of story and character."
Hallie Ephron,
*Writing and Selling Your
Mystery Novel*, p. 147

CLUE #13: INSUFFICIENT GROUNDS

New writers, like new parents, record every detail of their novel's first setting but neglect the settings that follow. When a later scene opens in a previously described place, the writer adds a meanwhile-back-at-the-ranch kind of reference but makes no effort to reinforce the location's unique imagery or reestablish the desired mood.

Sorry, Charlie, characters and their actions need grounding from time to time. Once is not enough. Though your fictional people and places are real to you, they are mere illusions to the reader. Their substance depends on an occasional visual prop or other sensory data to keep them grounded in their place in space. Fictional folk who are not periodically reconnected to their surroundings revert to the illusions they are, their actions and dialogue drifting and breaking up like cell phones in the Smokies.

When you self-edit, look for ways to keep the spatial dimensions of your scenes alive and your characters grounded. From time to time, repeat a reference to some tangible aspect of the setting—like Estleman's bent cigarette butts and squat brown beer bottles (CLUE #12).

In the same way that a story without a sense of place can make us feel unsettled, a scene with insufficient grounding can make us feel adrift.

SPATIAL GROUNDING

In *Lethal Genes* by Linda Grant, one scene takes place on a ferry crossing San Francisco Bay. The protagonist, Catherine Sayler, P. I., had agreed to go to dinner with a colleague, Kyle, in exchange for his getting information she wants. Tension comes from Catherine's trying to figure out the significance of what he tells her—and from rebuffing Kyle's advances.

Periodically, Grant repeats details of the setting to ground her characters in the scene. To emphasize those grounding or re-anchoring techniques, I'm omitting from the following examples all talk of the investigation as well as all sexual innuendos. (Disappointed? Read the book.)

"Can I get you wine or something harder?" he asked as the
ferry pulled away from the dock.

"White wine would be nice," I said. "I'll be out on deck."

It was a mild evening, but the wind was still brisk and cold.
I was glad I had on a warm jacket. Still, the view was worth
the discomfort. San Francisco was a city of lights, the buildings
just dark shapes against the darker sky, their lit windows like
cutout peepholes into a hidden shining world.

Near the dock they loomed over us, close enough that you
could actually make out some of the features of the lighted
rooms. As we pulled out into the bay, they shrank and became
a spectacular backdrop.

Kyle joined me at the rail. . . .   [p. 177]

We know exactly where we are, what time of day it is, what the air feels
like, and what the eye can see. All this establishes a vivid setting capable of
sustaining a full page of dialogue about the case—after which Grant grounds
the scene again by briefly reestablishing the setting.

. . . We were far enough out into the bay so that the wind was
stronger and I shivered inside my jacket. But looking back at
the sparkling city and the strings of lights that outlined the Bay
and Golden Gate bridges, I wasn't about to go inside. [p. 179]

Next comes another page of Catherine's thoughts about the case before
the next grounding.

We were past Alcatraz now, and the water seemed choppier.
A gust of wind peppered my face with drops of briny sea spray.
                                                             [p. 180]

Each reference to the setting becomes progressively briefer while sup-
porting an increasing amount of dialogue and action. After another full
page about the case, one final grounding takes place while the characters
are still aboard the ferry.

Kyle straightened up, turned, and leaned his back against the
rail.   [p. 181]

Overall, the most striking feature of this ferry scene is its strong sense of place. However, what I want to call your attention to is not the richness of the setting but the pattern of Grant's technique for reestablishing that setting. Here are five lines of nearly inconspicuous business that keep the characters positioned in relation to their surroundings and to each other.

1. he asked as the ferry pulled away from the dock.
2. "I'll be out on deck."
3. Kyle joined me at the rail and handed me. . . .
4. looking back at the sparkling city and the strings of lights that outlined the Bay and Golden Gate bridges. . . .
5. Kyle straightened up, turned, and leaned his back against the rail.

Try a little experiment. When you revise your manuscript, take the five lines above, change the nouns to fit your own story, and see how you might incorporate those amended locational references into your own scenes.

Also compare your scenes with the next six anchors to see if your sensory details are as clear and strong as Linda Grant's, though not necessarily as abundant.

6. wind was still brisk and cold. I was glad I had on a warm jacket.
7. the view was worth the discomfort.
8. Near the dock they loomed over us, close enough that you could actually make out some of the features of the lighted rooms. As we pulled out into the bay, they shrank.
9. the wind was stronger and I shivered inside my jacket.
10. But looking back . . . I wasn't about to go inside.
11. A gust of wind peppered my face with drops of briny sea spray.

Strong sensory data like this lets readers experience a setting subjectively, as the character experiences it. Therefore, instead of the author's objectively reporting that the wind covered the deck with drops of sea spray, she has Catherine say that the wind peppered her face with it. Who doesn't feel *that?*

And who never watched a building "shrink"? Physically impossible, of course, but having Catherine observe the phenomenon puts readers inside her perspective, exactly where we should be.

SATISFYING NEEDS

Become aware of the ways you keep your own characters grounded. Whether your setting is a castle or a cave, choose descriptive details you can mention again as your action unfolds. Don't depend on dropping anchor once and assuming it will hold throughout the ups and downs of the scene's action. Readers have a hankering for anchoring.

How often anchoring or grounding should occur varies with the tempo or pace you desire and the kind of action involved. Grant's leisurely paced ferry scene uses all eleven of the above-listed anchors within four pages.

From the manuscripts I receive, some writers appear unaware of pacing. Some practice random *action interruptus:* inserting beats haphazardly. Some do the opposite: using beats with numbing regularity. One manuscript I edited showed one gesture for every two lines of dialogue. The pattern produced a tiresome, predictable rhythm that flattened momentum and prevented the building of tension.

Unlike a soap opera's installments, there's no written formula. In general, place your first anchor shortly after the initial scene-setting. Make each subsequent regrounding briefer and farther apart. As the action builds, sentences become shorter and the interval between anchors grows. To slow the pace, interrupt the action and dialogue with increasing frequency.

Timing or pacing is an inner sense that novelists refine by practicing their writing and getting reliable feedback on it. Especially instructive is reading the work of others to analyze their techniques and to enjoy the sound of their rhythms.

ANALYZE THIS

For another grounding pattern, take a look at Ruth Birmingham's technique in the following scene from *Atlanta Graves*. The situation is a staple in the genre: an interview of a suspect. The setting is the home of the suspect, an art dealer. A painting has been stolen, and the series character, P. I. Sunny Childs, is about to question the gallery owner for the second time.

> Charlie Biddle was wearing sweat pants and had her hair up in a ponytail when I got to her house, an ugly brick ranch in the not-especially-swank Atlanta suburb of Doraville. I'd expected her in some charming Inman Park Victorian—but I guess Doraville's cheaper. The inside of the house, though, was

> pleasant and warm and lived-in, with books scattered around
> the living room and nice paintings on the walls.
>   She gestured wordlessly to a chair, then flopped down on a
> big white couch and lit a cigarette.   [p. 196]

The scene is set. The author shows us where the two characters are seated before the dialogue begins. Sunny opens with a question to Charlie about the case. That is followed by one paragraph of Sunny's thoughts and four paragraphs of dialogue between them. Then comes the first re-anchoring.

> She stood up. "Can you hold on a second?"
>   She was gone for a minute or two and I could hear noises
> coming out of the kitchen. She came back with a bowl of Froot
> Loops, started eating them with relish, cigarette held in one
> hand, spoon in the other.   [p. 197]

Sunny brings the subject back to the crime and states one theory of how Charlie might've done it, to which Charlie replies:

> "Speaking hypothetically, that's exactly what I'd do." She
> dug into the bowl of cereal. When she was done, she stubbed
> out her Marlboro in the film of milk in the bottom of her bowl.
>   [p. 197]

That anchor sustains two pages of primarily dialogue about the case, accompanied by a few unobtrusive *she saids* or gesture-type beats. The next regrounding is, "She lay back on the couch and looked up in the air through the cloud of smoke over her head." That sustains three more pages of dialogue, until a disclosure surprises Sunny and winds up the seven-page scene.

> . . . I sat there in a stupor for a while.
>   "So am I going to lounge around here smoking all morning
> while you meditate?" Charlie said after a while. I noticed she
> was on her third Marlboro.
>   "Nope," I said. "I think this will get me started."
>   I left her to her lounging and her Froot Loops, and walked
> out without saying another word.   [p. 202]

Here's an overview of Birmingham's pattern, which keeps the characters grounded in their space while it builds a steadily increasing pace:

- 1 paragraph of detailed scene setting, then 3 paragraphs of dialogue.
- 1 brief reference to setting, then 4 paragraphs of dialogue.
- 1 reference to the kitchen and to 2 props (cigarette, cereal), then 1 paragraph of dialogue.
- 1 reference to cereal, then 21 short paragraphs of dialogue.
- 1 reference to the couch, then 38 short paragraphs of dialogue, then 1 final reference to cereal.

The third mention of Froot Loops unifies the imagery. In every art form, unity is valued.

STATIC SETTINGS

When you self-edit your work, review how you anchor or ground your characters in their setting. Notice whether those references to the setting are separate from the action or part of it. To illustrate the difference, here is a description I wrote using (more like abusing) the bookshop scene from George Orwell's *Nineteen Eighty-four.*

> As Winston went up the stairs to the room above Mr.
> Charrington's shop, in his hand he carried a brief case. The
> room had a window, which he opened. There was also a dirty
> little oilstove and an old armchair.

My parody intentionally separates the descriptive details from Winston's relationship to or interaction with those details. The result is wordy, uninteresting, and static, typical of the writing in the majority of submissions.

- *There was also* has to be the dullest, least imaginative verb form.
- *In his hand he carried* makes an awkward connection between the character and the brief case he carried.
- *He went up* and *he opened* offer the only movement in all this description.

Yuck. Adolescent exposition. Static properties. Monotonous constructions. This is the style that drags most writing to its death. If you think I'm exaggerating, I regret to say that phrasing identical to this overpowers the majority of unedited, unpublishable manuscripts.

By comparing my parody with the scene as Orwell wrote it (CLUE #5), you'll see that the author's verb forms reflect what the character *does:* Winston climbed, opened, lit, put, and sat.

You'll also see that Orwell's first re-anchoring occurs after only one paragraph of the transcript. He uses it to add four new details that reinforce Winston's sense of distance and detachment from the world outside the room:

- the air *played* against his cheek
- the shouts of children *floated*
- Winston *settled deeper* into the armchair
- and *put* his feet up on the fender.

Each detail is presented with a verb of motion. *That's* sufficient grounds.

FIND & FIX CLUE #13: INSUFFICIENT GROUNDS

- Select scenes from your manuscript at random and highlight all instances of scene-setting and grounding of the characters in that setting.
- Look for patterns in the frequency, length, and spacing of references to the setting, and see whether those patterns enhance the pace you desire or get in its way.
- Review the sensory details that help readers feel they are experiencing the setting along with the characters.
- Examine your verbs and seek to integrate description with action in time and place.
- Be sure every page offers something to visualize.

"One of the first things you learn about writing is that if you come across a passage that you've written and you're struck by how wonderful it is, you cut it, leave it on the cutting-room floor because (writing) is not self-indulgence."

Fred Chappell, Poet Laureate of North Carolina 1997–2002 [38]

D.O.A.

PART VII: THE USUAL SUSPECTS

Norman Mailer observes that the sole virtue of losing short-term memory is that it frees you to be your own editor.[39]

CLUE #14: SLOW DEATH

When details are too few, a mystery is hard to follow. Occasionally missing are some of the key steps the sleuth takes that lead to solving the mystery. A solution should never be so obvious or predictable that readers can put the pieces together without benefit of the lead character's superior detecting skills. Readers need to see them.

Also in the too-few-details department is the effect that has no cause. That is, we witness the character's reaction, but the action that produces it is missing. Jack Bickham says to show an immediate, physical cause for what a character does, not "merely a thought inside his head."[40]

On the other hand, when details are too numerous, the weight of it all drags the story to a slow, agonizing death. If your manuscript suffers from overwriting, don't worry about what's missing. The busy screener won't read far enough to notice.

Luckily, the condition I call *wordiarrea* is easy to find and fix.

New writers tend to connect every dot in a sequence of steps, even when the sequence is familiar or obvious—such as leaving one location, driving to another, arriving, and walking to the door. Don't underestimate your readers' capacity for anticipating the familiar and the routine. Over-explaining is irritating.

More leaving, walking, and arriving goes on in fiction manuscripts than at Los Angeles International Airport. Slow death.

TRANSITIONS AWAY

Think about the steps Patricia Highsmith omits from this passage in an early mystery novel, *The Blunderer.* Walter Stackhouse, the central character, has telephoned a woman he wants to see again.

> . . ."Maybe I can help you," he said. "Can I come over? I'm not far away."
>
> "Well—if you can stand a mess."
>
> "What's the address?"
>
> "Brooklyn Street, one eighty-seven. The bell's under Mays. M-a-y-s."
>
> He rang the bell under Mays. . . .   [p. 76]

Are you confused because the scene shifts without a break, and Walter is not shown hanging up the phone, driving to Brooklyn Street, and walking into the apartment building? Surprised, maybe; confused, no. The author's omissions are understood because the connections for the leap in time and place are routine. What she omits is not action, it's housekeeping.

One way to see the difference is by reading a great many works of fiction and noting the techniques of others. Look for examples of transitions without wordiness. You know the old saw: If in doubt, leave it out.

A clear leap in time and place occurs at the end of the ferry scene in *Lethal Genes,* by Linda Grant. When last we saw the lights of San Francisco from the ferry (CLUE #13), Kyle had just:

> . . . turned, and leaned his back against the rail. "Doesn't make sense," he said. After a couple of minutes of silent thought, he added, "I need more fuel. You want another glass of wine?"
>
> We had a wonderful dinner of mesquite-grilled shrimp at Guaymas in Tiburon. The restaurant sits on the water, near the dock, and we had a table next to the window so that we looked out across the dark bay at the lights of San Francisco in the distance.

> Anyone watching us would have seen a couple so intensely involved in conversation that they seemed unaware of food, wine, and even the shimmering beauty of the view. They would probably have assumed that a great love was flowering. They'd have been wrong. What animated our passion that night was not romance but murder.   [p. 181]

End of chapter. Do you feel on edge because Kyle isn't shown returning with the wine? Maybe you'd hoped to watch the ferry tie up at the dock. Nice touches, but unnecessary, because the scene does all it needs to. There's no reason to prolong it once Catherine's goal is met. The information she learns from Kyle influences the direction of the investigation from this point forward. All scenes should produce some new development.

With Catherine and Kyle at dinner looking "out across the dark bay at the lights of San Francisco in the distance," the author brings full circle the imagery that runs through the scene from its beginning. The resulting unity brings closure and evokes a theme inherent in all mysteries: things are not as they appear.

More manuscripts would benefit from scenes as purposeful, unified, and grounded as these examples. However, if you're uncomfortable omitting routine transitions from your own writing and long for a bridge to cross small gaps, here's a technique made for you. Before the transition, end the scene, skip a line, and open a new scene in the new location. On the skipped line, center the symbol for a scene break, like this:

(or this: * * *)

One contribution a transition makes is to slow a story's pace and provide a breather after a fast-moving action scene. If you remain aware of pacing, you can use the driving or walking time between scenes for your protagonist to ponder the latest developments and strategize the next step. These pursuits keep the plot moving forward.

Usually, admonitions about transitions have to do with their absence, which can disorient readers when there's a change in time or place. So if you are uneasy with a quick change to "He rang the bell under Mays" or "We had a wonderful dinner . . . in Tiburon," many situations can be taken care of with just a few words, such as: "An hour later he rang the bell. . . ."

Or start a new scene, as you would do when changing to a different viewpoint character.

My transition admonitions concern the more pervasive though less-mentioned issue of superfluous, wordy bridges, as if the writer felt compelled to record the character's every thought, word, and deed en route to the next action. That compulsion drags a manuscript to a slow and painful death.

BLOAT

There are many ways to effectively slow a novel's pace. Wordiness is not one of them. A writer in control draws out a scene to produce a planned effect. A writer not in control connects every step, unaware of the effect.

What moments would you cut from the following?

> Wally Bloat put down the phone and noticed the clock on the wall showing a quarter to five. He walked to the coat rack in the corner of his office, put on his brown overcoat, and picked up his briefcase with his right hand. He was finished for the day.
>
> As he walked through the outer office he called to his secretary, Lotta Thyme, "I'm leaving now, Mrs. Thyme."
>
> "Looks like you're taking work home again, Mr. Bloat," she said.
>
> "Yes, I am, Mrs. Thyme. Goodnight."
>
> "Goodnight," she replied.
>
> Arriving at the elevator, Bloat punched the down button to go to the underground garage where his car was parked. While waiting for the familiar "ding" he took his car keys from his pants pocket. When the doors opened he. . . .

Okay, okay, I'm exaggerating, but not as much as you think. Plenty of writers seem to have learned little from reading other authors. Unsure of what to include to aid their readers' understanding, they connect every dot as a form of insurance. I call it malpractice.

Showing someone grabbing his coat at a quarter to five sends a pretty clear message that he is "finished for the day" and is "leaving." Whether the coat is brown or the briefcase is carried in the right hand doesn't matter unless it matters to the *story.*

Mentioning every step in an ordinary, familiar sequence is different from the legitimate need to account for every step in the solution to a crime.

Anything as plodding as Wally's leaving his office is itself a crime.

When I point out unnecessary details to writers, a few defend their method as adding realism. Careful here, because realism is a means to an end, not an end in itself. Busy screeners have plowed through enough submissions to know that overwriting on page 1 foretells overwriting throughout. They don't have to witness a manuscript's brain death before pulling the plug.

PURPOSE OF DETAIL

If advancing the plot were a scene's only function, entire books could be written in thirty pages. They'd read exactly like a synopsis.

As you revise, be guided by your purpose for each scene. You may be justified in drawing out the wait for an elevator if that slowing of the pace sets up the reader for a surprise—such as a stranger's stepping out of the shadows and joining Mr. Bloat just as the doors close.

What about the set of keys Mr. B. takes from his pocket? Superfluous detail or legitimate clue? Again, be guided by your purpose. Let's say this fellow's body is found the next morning floating in the Gowanus Canal, as bloated as some writers' prose.

If your protagonist is also the victim, your mystery is dead in the water anyway—not the first to self-destruct by killing off its lead character.

Should the keys serve no purpose, lose them. But what if they turn up in someone's bureau tucked under the pink panties? That could be a red herring. (Later, be sure to expose all false clues for the misdirection they are.)

However, if finding the keys represents real evidence, readers should definitely observe the keys in the victim's possession before he disappears—without your drawing undue attention to them. Plant them in the waiting-for-the-elevator scene as you would plant any clue: subtly.

To plant an object, show it among other objects. To disguise a behavior, show it with other behaviors. Thus, Mr. Bloat needs to be seen doing more with his hands than reaching for his keys. Perhaps he repeatedly pokes the "down" button or jiggles his pocket change. In deciding which details to show and which to omit, consider how your choices affect the scene's purpose and pace.

The reason for planting an object early, before its significance as a clue is realized, is to avoid making its later discovery seem overly convenient. Be sure you don't get your character out of an awkward situation with a coincidence. Whereas an opening predicament might be set in motion with a twist of fate—as in someone's picking up the wrong briefcase—a coincidence should never *resolve* a mystery. The solution should come from the crime-fighter's superior investigative abilities.

What's more, unless a paranormal element is present from the start, never, for heaven's sake, have a solution materialize from divine intervention.

REPETITION

Assuming there's no purpose in dramatizing Mr. B's elevator scene, how many unnecessary lines can you slice from his leaving-the-office extravaganza? Here's one stripped-down version.

> Wally Bloat hung up, grabbed his coat and briefcase, and called goodnight to his secretary. As he stepped off the elevator at the underground garage. . . .

The object of editing is not shorter but sharper. Now analyze the sharpness of this next passage.

> She was brutally murdered, her face and neck stabbed ten times with a butcher knife.

Ouch. Stabbed ten times seems sharp indeed. The image is specific and graphic, though a second look reveals that the words "brutally murdered" summarize the more graphic stabbing. Redundant. Not so sharp after all. However, repetition may be forgiven in this case because it reinforces a dramatic effect and is brief enough not to annoy.

Redundancies like the following, which I adapted from an otherwise well-written manuscript are not as easily forgiven.

> When the detective told us how the mine owner had been murdered, Evan and I exchanged glances, remembering that the brother of the trapped mineworker swore he would find and kill the owner. Evan turned to the detective and said, "I didn't take this seriously at the time because it was right after the accident, but the brother of one of the miners threatened to kill the owner."

Repeating information adds nothing but extra words. Which of the above repetitions should be cut? Keep the dramatic action *(exchanged glances)* and the dialogue *("the brother . . . threatened")*. Dump the exposition that explains why they exchanged glances *(remembering that the brother . . . swore)*. The "why" becomes evident from the context.

When an earlier scene dramatizes an event recently enough for readers to easily recall having seen it, an efficient way of referring to old news is to paraphrase it.

> Evan and I exchanged glances. Then he told the detective about the brother's threat to kill the mine owner.
> "I didn't take it seriously at the time because it was right after the accident."

However, when the original dramatization occurs so early in a story that readers might not remember its details, have the paraphrase remind us of the *setting* in which it occurred.

> Evan and I exchanged glances, remembering our run-in at the hospital with the brother of the trapped mineworker. Evan told the detective about the brother's threat to. . . .

Looking at old events in a new way is itself new information. Repeating the same information is not, unless the repetition serves a useful purpose.

PARAPHRASE

The most succinct paraphrase I've ever seen occurs in *Killer.app* by Barbara D'Amato. Detective Jesus Delgado is being asked to tell the police superintendent about events that readers already witnessed in earlier scenes. D'Amato writes:

> Rendell said, "Tell the superintendent."
> Jesus told.
> When Jesus had finished with the details. . . . "   [pp. 179–80]

D'Amato does not subject her readers to a recap of familiar information. Instead, she focuses on the superintendent's reaction to it—which takes the investigation forward in a new direction.

In *An Eye for Murder* by Libby Fischer Hellmann, Ellie Foreman tells the police of incidents that we read about in recent chapters; namely, Ellie's receiving a letter and visiting its sender, now dead. Notice what new material Hellmann dramatizes and what she paraphrases.

> When the cops arrived, I was on the porch steps taking big gulps of fresh air. One of the cops was young, with a leather jacket, crisp uniform shirt, and a pencil-thin mustache that looked pasted on. His partner, older and more rumpled, wore an expression that said he'd seen it all.

After Ellie is asked a few questions. . . .

> The younger cop dug out a cell phone and started tapping in numbers.
> The older cop grabbed it away from his partner. "Don't waste your minutes." He yanked his thumb toward the house. "Use hers. She won't be needing it."
> The younger cop slipped his phone into a pocket and headed inside.
> "Is she. . . ?" I asked shakily.
> The older cop, whose shield read Mahoney, nodded.
> I gripped a stake on the porch railing. "But I was just with her an hour ago, and she was fine. What happened?"
> Interest flickered on Mahoney's face. "You were here earlier?"
> "I left around three."
> "Powers. Get back out here." The younger cop reappeared. "Why don't you tell us about it?"
> Midway through my first sentence, the older cop raised a hand, cutting me off. "Notes, Powers. You gotta take notes."
> Powers lowered his chin and pulled out a notepad. He wrote furiously as I told them how I'd come down to Rogers Park at Mrs. Fleishman's request. How we went through Ben Sinclair's things. How she persuaded me to take the boxes and how, when I came back, she was on the floor.   [pp. 29–30]

Two things are dramatized in this scene: Ellie's reaction to finding the body, and the cynical cop's interactions with her and with his rookie. Here are the benefits of Hellmann's combining them in the same scene:

- ◆ Ellie's emotional reactions build our empathy with her, because we would feel the same way in the same situation.
- ◆ The darkness of Ellie's distress is offset by the cop's manner, which adds light humor.
- ◆ Conflict comes from the cop's actions, which are confrontational and unpredictable, as well as from Ellie's struggle to deal with her emotions.
- ◆ Paraphrasing reminds us of earlier events that we might not have realized the importance of at the time.

Although a recording of the actual dialogue would capture all of Ellie's words, its playback would be insufferably repetitive. Paraphrase minimizes, summarizes, and reminds without repeating.

- ◆ I told them how I'd. . .
- ◆ How we went through. . .
- ◆ How she persuaded me to. . .
- ◆ and how, when I came back. . . .

Hellmann's techniques emphasize both the humorous and the humanizing, producing a well-balanced, multi-purposed scene.

DIGRESSION AND DISCOURSE

Patricia Highsmith admits to occasional digressions. In her classic *Plotting and Writing Suspense Fiction,* she describes it as "writing elaborately about small matters." By stepping back and looking at the whole, she could see when a book of hers was no longer in proportion.[41]

Isabel Zuber, author of the historical novel *Salt,* explains what throws a story off balance:

> An author has learned so much in the search for information
> on a particular topic, often about how to do or make something,
> that an obsession sets in and all that has been collected gets

included instead of parts being integrated into the plot, or only summarized or suggested. For readers who do not necessarily share the obsession, the action of a story can easily slow to a crawl." [42]

Suppose you decide to do away with a certain Mr. Throckmorton. Your weapon of choice is poison. You spend weeks researching every potent possibility before deciding which one the killer shall stir into Mr. T.'s tea. How do you include all that fascinating information?

You don't.

As a fiction writer you have an obligation to entertain, and that supersedes a desire to educate or persuade. If you supply more information than your story needs, you can interfere with its dramatic flow. Whether you call it digressing, obsessing, or going off on a tangent, it's self-indulgent, and self-indulgence rarely entertains.

"Thou shall not fall in love with thine own words."

Ellen M. Kozak, literary arts attorney and author [43]

If a digression offers data that readers need for understanding some technical aspect of the crime, you have options for presenting it without knocking your story off balance. One is to slice, dice, and splice the essentials in with the dramatic action a little at a time.

Another is to invent a character whom the protagonist contacts for specialized information, someone who functions as a subject matter expert (what tech writers call an SME). Beware of the expert who so loves to discourse on his favorite topic that he's delighted to help. The result is not dialogue, it's *lecturing,* slow death for sure.

Talk designed to educate runs the risk of talking down to readers or going over their heads. It can take on a moral tone, offending some, making others yawn. Besides, lecturing lacks action. What some writers think of as action is closer to mannerism or gesture, which is no more action than the taking-another-bite and having-another-sip busyness that goes on in poorly conceived restaurant scenes—themselves thinly disguised data dumps.

I've seen manuscripts in which the sleuth's role is reduced to one of passive listener ("Do go on"), mere questioner ("What happens after that?"), and helpful summarizer ("I see, so what you're saying is Colonel Mustard couldn't possibly have been in the conservatory with a knife").

Action, which is conflict or perceived conflict (tension), emerges from resistance and opposition. Dialogue with a cooperative expert offers little opportunity for conflict to raise its argumentative little head. Consider giving your sleuth one more hurdle to overcome by making your expert less obliging. Turn the dialogue into a verbal fencing match, and include essential bits of information with each thrust and parry.

And if the two characters already have a feud going about something else? That gives you another source of conflict. Think of the opportunity for lively dialogue.

SHORTCUTS

If you don't have an ear for condensing your writing and ridding it of excess, read more page-turners and analyze the ways that skilled writers create their effects. Or have an editor show you how your manuscript can be tightened and sharpened, a process that helps you develop a keen eye and ear for your own writing habits. By studying your editor's notations you can learn to *self*-edit more effectively.

Eavesdrop in public and listen for the shortcuts people take when they assume, rightly or wrongly, that they know what the other person is about to say. Shortcuts help you construct dialogue that leaps from one speaker's assumptions to another's, leaving out the easily understood connections. Once you become comfortable taking shortcuts from A to C, you can avoid passing B and collecting 200 extra words.

Watch how Janet Evanovich uses assumptions to shortcut the following dialogue from *One for the Money,* her first Stephanie Plum mystery. Both Stephanie and her mother assume, correctly, that each knows what the other is thinking. Assumptions suggest that similar dialogues have occurred between these two before.

> "I hear Loretta Buzick's boy is separated from his wife," my mother said. "You remember him? Ronald Buzick?"
>
> I knew where she was heading, and I didn't want to go there.
> "I'm not going out with Ronald Buzick," I told her. "Don't even think about it."
>
> "So what's wrong with Ronald Buzick?"   [p. 9]

As rapidly as this passage moves, it would speed up more without the line: "I knew where she was heading, and I didn't want to go there." But I relish that line because it expresses a principle I'd like you to remember when you self-edit:

"Readers know where I'm heading and don't need to go there."

I nominate these words as the mantra for writers who like to write too much.

FIND & FIX CLUE #14: SLOW DEATH

- List the purpose of every scene and verify that each one achieves the purpose you intend it to.
- Get rid of unnecessary repetition and decide what material is better presented by paraphrasing.
- Sharpen, tighten, and delete overwriting, whether that means killing words, sentences, paragraphs, or whole scenes.
- Omit or condense transitions and routines that are familiar to the average reader, except where drawing out a transition achieves a deliberate benefit, such as slowing the pace.
- End a scene once it serves its purpose.
- Consider getting a pro to show you how to sharpen and tighten your writing—even if you can have that done only one time.
- Don't lecture.

CLUE #15: BURIED AGENDA

Mention "motivation" in the context of "mystery" and most people think of the whydunit behind the whodunit. Yet motivation goes well beyond the bad guy's reason for doing bad things. In any well-written novel, as in life, every character wants something (a goal), has a reason for wanting it (a motive), and harbors some notion, realistic or not, of how to get it (a strategy). In short, everyone has an agenda.

Compared with the life-and-death issues that drive your two primary characters, protagonist and antagonist, the agendas of secondary characters are of little importance. *But not to them.* Treating characters as if they have no wants and needs of their own robs their actions of purpose and direction.

A buried agenda steals the potential within every role for obstructing the agenda of another character. Obstructions are good; they spread conflict and incite rebellion. Some lead to character development.

Only when readers are made aware of what each character wants can they anticipate the *potential* for conflict. Anticipation creates tension, builds suspense, and maintains a reader's addiction to adrenalin, all of which keep mystery readers turning pages. Without an agenda in play there is no conflict, no tension. Without conflict there is neither progress nor setback; consequently, no *scene*. A manuscript without a sequence of goal-obstacle-outcome scenes does not a mystery make.

EXPLICIT AGENDAS

You may have heard that a mystery should have conflict on every page. That doesn't mean constant fighting and chasing. At the high-powered end of the conflict continuum are the high-stakes, life-and-death issues that pit your two primary characters against each other and drive your main plot. At the low end of the conflict continuum are any issues, irritations, or doubts that worry your characters and make readers tense. At every point in between, conflict idles, ready to accelerate and shift into high gear.

If the idea of putting conflict on every page overwhelms you, think instead of putting *tension* on every page. Tension comes from the ever-present potential for conflict that readers feel when the writer keeps them aware of competing goals, motives, and strategies.

Make your characters' agendas known by what they do and say, and by what others say about them. Lonnie Cruse does all this in the opening scene to *Murder in Metropolis,* her first full-length mystery novel.

> Sheriff Joe Dalton plunked his boots on top of his desk, leaned back in the protesting chair, snapped open the newspaper, and reached for his coffee.
>
> Before he could down a swig, the intercom buzzed, forcing him to wade under a stack of files and push a button.
>
> "Yes, George?"
>
> "We've got a situation outside on Market Street, Sheriff. Guess you'll have to handle it," the elderly dispatcher informed him. "Morning shift hasn't arrived yet, and the night deputies are still at that big accident scene over on Highway 145."
>
> "Would the situation outside be Big Ed Simmons?"
>
> "Yes sir, drunk as they come and singing fair to wake the dead."
>
> "Where is he? On the courthouse steps again?"
>
> "Nope, this time he's on the steps at Lipinski's Appliances. Miz Lipinski says if we don't shut him up, she will, with that old pistol her husband kept in the store. Though what an eighty-year-old woman with crippling arthritis is doing with. . . ."
>
> "I'll get right on it, George. We don't need Mrs. Lipinski shooting up Market Street at day break."   [pp. 1–2]

How many individual agendas can you find in this opening scene? The sheriff's newspaper, coffee, and boots on desk are unmistakable clues to his immediate objective, which takes precedence over the piles of files on his desk. Yet as soon as he learns of a situation, his priorities shift, and his longer-range goal of serving the public good reasserts itself at the top of his to-do list.

How about George, the elderly dispatcher? His agenda, what we see of it, is to perform his job by promptly handing off every new assignment to the work detail next in line.

Based on what George and the sheriff say *about* the shopkeeper, we understand that her objective is to get the drunk away from her store. An old pistol affords a clear and present strategy. We can guess her motivation, but the sheriff's actions suggest we shall learn it soon enough.

From what is said about Big Ed Simmons, though we don't know *why* he keeps doing what he does, we're sure we'll learn that, too.

All told, Cruse's opening scene is brimming with explicit, overt actions and implicit possibilities. The immediate agendas of four characters set us up to anticipate several collisions ahead.

WHAT'S AT STAKE?

You may be thinking, "How do I maintain suspense if I let readers know what every character is thinking and planning?" The more useful answer comes from asking yourself a different question: "What part of each character's agenda must I conceal for the time being?"

Suspense depends on anticipation—the expectation of something about to happen. For readers to feel anticipation, they need information, not its absence. If we are unaware of the relentless descent of a razor-sharp pendulum, we have no reason to feel anxiety for the condemned man strapped directly beneath it.[44]

Anxiety increases in relation to our awareness of how improbable escape seems, how drawn out the approaching danger is, and how high the stakes are. Suspense comes not from ignorance but from knowledge: the certainty that something bad is going to happen.

To illustrate the value of letting readers in on all or part of a character's agenda, imagine this scenario. Time and place: early one morning on a city street. Action: a young woman is searching for a place to park. We'll call her, oh . . . I dunno, Ms. Parker. We watch her battered Ford Pinto starting to circle the area for the third time. Do we care? Not really. Not until the writer lets us know she will be fired if she's late to work again.

By learning what she has at stake, we share some of her anxiety and begin to care about her—a little.

For us to care a little more, we have to know what losing her job means to *her.* So the writer revises the scene and discloses Ms. Parker's fervent desire to remain independent of her father, who keeps badgering her to stop all this career nonsense and come home to the farm in Cornville.

If the writer chooses to develop this scenario further, we could be let in on Ms. Parker's longer-range goals. We might learn, for instance, that the job in jeopardy is with a publishing house *(hmm, this could be interesting)*, and that she's working toward a promotion to acquisitions editor *(how 'bout that?)*. We discover that her ambition is to nurture new writers *(about time someone did)*, and that her specialty is the erotic mystery *(no kidding!)*.

Knowing what a character has at stake makes a difference, doesn't it? Now we're actually rooting for her to park that Pinto, pronto.

TANGIBLE AND EXPLICIT

When you revise your manuscript, see whether you make the goals of your characters tangible and their agendas as explicit as the plot allows. Give your audience an emotional stake in your characters' wins and losses by letting us know what penalties they face if their strategies fail. Most strategies *should* fail, because setbacks are what let you intensify your crime-fighter's desperation and raise her motivation to take greater risks.

Perhaps one of Ms. Parker's initial strategies is to set her alarm an hour earlier. When that fails to resolve her problem, she becomes ready for a bigger step. Maybe she decides to change publishing houses. Or pay higher rent to live closer to work. Maybe she eventually gives up her goal and returns to the farm, where she produces corn, not porn.[45]

You don't need to pursue every agenda to its completion. Characters seldom think beyond their immediate objectives. A brief mention of a minor character's fate should be sufficient to put closure on his role—which you want to do only after each character serves your purpose.

What might that purpose be? To create obstacles, of course. To complicate and frustrate the goals of other characters. The more frequently you put one agenda in direct opposition to another's, the higher your novel's conflict quotient. Your antagonist's goal may be to upset the status quo. *Your* goal is to keep tension on every page.

HIGHER STAKES

For a primary character, the stakes must be considerably higher than failing to find a parking place and getting fired. Losing or winning should be of life and death magnitude. That's why most mysteries are murder mysteries. (Never mind that drivers have been killed over contested parking spots.)

The submissions I see do a fairly good job of revealing the agendas of their primary characters, although some writers make the mistake of treating the killer as a minor character. The antagonist is at least as important as the protagonist—often more so, for without the villain's motivation for doing evil, your hero has nothing to react to and become heroic about.

Examine your story to see how you make your killer's agenda known. Some writers reveal it in early scenes that show him justifying his crime *as he sees it.* For the killer whose thoughts are not revealed until the climax, his agenda can be made known in other ways. Ever wonder why so many mysteries involve anonymous threats left on a victim's answering machine or cryptic words scrawled in blood at the crime scene?

As for making your protagonist's agenda known, if she is a professional crime-fighter, such as a cop or a P. I., her motivation is built into the job description.

To make your story even more compelling, add to that motivation. How? By raising the stakes. Add a personal ingredient. Create some complication that forces your crime-fighter to struggle with her *feelings.* Get her to make decisions that risk compromising her professionalism, that force her to wrestle with her inner impulses at the same time as she's fighting an external opponent.

> Gary Provost's writings point out that once writers understand the concept of character goals and the value of letting readers in on them as soon as possible, "it's surprising how easily some boring scenes can be made compelling."[46]

If your sleuth is an amateur, with neither a cop's job description nor a P. I.'s need for paying clients, her motivation must be extra-convincing. For instance, you might give her a strong commitment to justice and world peace—except that ideals are too broad and generalized to produce a measurable victory by the penultimate chapter. A winnable goal is one that's specific and measurable, such as catching the ski-masked sniper who shot Cousin Amelia as she led Sunday's demonstration for world peace in front of the county war memorial.

You probably endow your sleuth with certain traits: a streak of stubbornness here, an independent lifestyle there, here a quirk, there a quirk.

Yet personality traits are *preconditions* for an amateur sleuth's getting involved in crime-solving; they do not convince readers that an ordinary citizen would choose to pursue a cold-blooded killer. How do you build that kind of motivation?

By raising the stakes, of course—a technique missing from a number of first-time submissions. When you edit your manuscript, identify where and how your manuscript satisfies these motivating factors:

- emphasizing *l'ingrédient personel:* the conviction that she, or someone she knows and cares about, will be grievously harmed if the killer isn't stopped before he strikes again;
- establishing the amateur sleuth's initial reluctance to get involved;
- showing her exhausting all logical alternatives, such as trying but failing to convince the authorities to take her suspicions seriously;
- continuing to dramatize events that keep ratcheting up her desperation.

Wasn't it the need for this sort of compelling motivation that put so many personal friends and family members of TV's Jessica Fletcher in harm's way week after week?

GO SCHIZO

The goals of minor players may be insignificant compared to the life-and-death issues of the primary players, but don't let those goals be invisible. Determine how each member of your cast behaves when his desires are thwarted. Does he become more subtle and cunning? Or angrier and vindictive? Examine the profiles you developed for your characters and identify the following a, b, c's for each one:

- a. what *specifically* the individual wants;
- b. how far she or he is willing to go to get it; and
- c. what it takes for the individual to adjust her or his priorities and shift strategies.

Verify that your manuscript includes a, b, and c for each character. Color-code everyone's script, starting with the killer's, and highlight his part from beginning to end as you live his role—and only his role. Repeat the process with your hero.[47] Take her role to its end before starting on the neglected agendas of the secondary characters.

As you trace one complete script at a time, want what each character wants and is desperate to get from someone else. Go beyond knowing someone's motivation to *feeling* it, both the all-consuming compulsions and the momentary whims. One at a time, take on each cast member's beliefs, attitudes, incentives, and insecurities as if they were your own. Let their feelings guide you as you milk every role for its adversarial potential.

In strengthening each character's script one at a time, also revise the words of the other party to the same confrontation. Later, when you take on the role of that other party, revise again. Make all words and actions sharper and more representative of *each* character's true feelings.

And if you intend someone's words or actions to mislead, be sure to present the false agenda with the same degree of clarity.

As all-powerful creator, you naturally want everyone's actions to serve the goals of your story. But characters cannot exist solely for your convenience. They need to behave as if they are advancing their own agendas. Keep tightening and sharpening each one's actions and reactions as if *your* self-interest were at stake. It *is*.

INTERNAL CONFLICT

Conflict in a genre novel must be externalized so readers can see the characters acting out their opposition to each other. Whereas early pulp fiction may have taken conflict no further than physical encounters, today's editors expect to also see a more profound form of conflict: internal.

The struggle within a character's psyche is the source of character development. If your crime-fighter is to work through a dilemma and emerge a better person, you need to show her confronting her own internal demons in addition to having a face-to-face confrontation with her antagonist.

A dilemma is not simply a problem; it is a fork in the road that leads to trouble regardless of which path is taken. The dilemma's motto is, "You can't have it both ways, and you can't have either one without some negative consequence."

Mystery's most consistently conflicted hero is Parnell Hall's luckless Stanley Hastings. Stanley's job is to sign up accident victims for an ambulance-chasing attorney—a job that ensures many close encounters of the unsavory kind.

In *Murder,* the second of Hall's more than a dozen mysteries featuring this unlikely hero, here's what happens when Stanley stumbles across a body.

> On TV, private detectives . . . examine the body and search
> the apartment for clues. Yeah, that's what a TV detective would
> have done.
> What I did was throw up.   [p. 45]

Does this weakness cause our hero inner turmoil and interfere with his work? Does it provoke a struggle between his cowardly feelings and his knowledge of the right thing to do? You bet it does.

> I was in a hell of a mood as I pulled off the Grand Central
> and took the Interboro down into Brooklyn.
> Coward, I told myself. You big, dumb, fucking coward. This
> is your chance, your one chance to get out from under. . . . You
> ought to walk right up to him and tell him you know he's slime
> and a murderer. Look him in the eye and say, "I know you
> popped Darryl Jackson."
> As I envisioned myself doing this, I got so paranoid I started
> shaking all over. I had to pull the car over to the side and stop.
> Jesus Christ. If just the *thought* of doing it does this to me,
> what would *doing* it be like?
> Not that bad, I told myself. He couldn't touch you in a
> crowded bar. There's nothing he could do. You'd be perfectly
> safe.
> Yeah, sure. Safe. I'd be safe.
> But so what? What did it matter?
> The question was academic, anyway.
> 'Cause I was a bloody fucking coward, and I wasn't going to
> do it.   [pp. 183–84]

Does Stanley do it? We know he manages to solve crimes in spite of himself . . . but how?

INTERNALIZING OPPOSITION

Three-time award-winner Vicki Hinze opens her second mystery romance, *Duplicity,* with an external conflict that transforms itself into an internal one within the first few pages. Captain Tracy Keener, a staff judge advocate in the Air Force, learns from her colonel that she's been assigned as defense counsel to a case no one wants. Observe that Hinze is explicit in presenting Tracy's motivation and conflict.

> . . . Only a sadist would be elated at hearing they'd been assigned to defend Adam Burke. . . .
>
> She had to get out of this assignment. That, or kiss off her career.   [pp. 1–3]

With the same clarity, Hinze reinforces Tracy's agenda by raising her hopes and revealing the agenda of the military, as expressed by the colonel.

> . . ."The Burke case has tempers running hot and hard up the chain of command and the local media is nearly out of control. Between the two of them, they're nailing our asses to the proverbial wall."
>
> Hope flared in Tracy. If he could see that, then surely he would see reason and assign someone else to the case. "I'm up for major, sir," Tracy interjected. "My promotion board meets in about a month."
>
> . . . This was her fifth year in the Air Force. Her first and . . . last shot at selection. If not selected, she'd promptly be issued an invitation to practice law elsewhere, outside of the military.
>
> This was not a pleasing prospect to an officer bent on making the military a career.   [pp. 4–5]

Colonel Jackson adds another objective to the mix: the need to show that the accused receives the defense he's entitled to. Tracy agrees, but she presses for answers to further questions:

> ". . . can't an attorney who already has Career Status defend him? If I lose this case—and we both know I will lose this case—then that's a huge strike against me with the boards. Competition is stiff and losses bury you. I'll be passed over for promotion and for Career Status selection. If that happens, my military career abruptly ends."   [p. 5]

When Colonel Jackson explains that Tracy is the military's asset with the media, she begins to grasp the complex, contradictory nature of her position—symbolized by a paperweight.

> . . . She stared at the eagle paperweight, at the dark shadows between the glints of light reflecting off it. As much as she hated admitting it, Jackson and Nestler's rationale made sense. As a senior officer in the same situation, she'd use whatever assets she found available to defuse the situation. Could she fault them for doing what in their position she would do herself?   [pp. 7–8]

Once Tracy understands this, she *internalizes the motivation of her opposition.* Conflict moves from the opposing agendas of two people to one person's inner struggle between her own loyalties, suddenly incompatible.

> . . . Burke was guilty. Everyone knew it. And while she might be media-attractive, she wouldn't get him off. She didn't want to get him off. But even F. Lee Bailey couldn't get Burke off, or come out of this case unscathed.
>
> Yet the man was entitled to the best possible defense. Would any other JAG officer make a genuine attempt to give it to him, knowing personal disaster was damn near inevitable?
>
> Probably not. And Tracy couldn't condemn them for it. Given the sliver of a chance, she too would have avoided this case as if it carried plague. But she couldn't avoid it, and that made only one attitude tenable. She had to handle the case and give Burke her best. Not so much for him, but because it was right. When this was over, she had to be able to look in the mirror and feel comfortable with what she'd done and the way she'd handled the case, and herself.   [p. 8]

Hinze's technique shifts the conflict from an external power over which Tracy has no control to an internal struggle that forces her to choose between her principles and her career desires. Demonizing an external power is easy; resolving a dilemma when the power rests in one's own hands is agonizing. In this, Hinze expertly continues raising the stakes.

IMPROBABLE CAUSE

Because every character in every work of fiction wants something and no two want precisely the same thing at the same time, *all* interactions, including those between friends, are ripe for conflict. In your self-editing, make certain that every scene puts forth the agenda of at least one character and presents at least one hurdle to overcome.

Also verify that your scenes end with some change in the situation that existed when the scene began. Things might improve a little for your protagonist; preferably, things get worse for a while—a lot worse. Either way, let the outcome cause some readjustment in the agenda of the main character. Perhaps a new intermediate objective emerges, and with it a shift in strategy.

> "When anticipation ends, the story is over."
>
> "Suspense,"
> *Mystery Writer's Handbook,* 1956[48]

If nothing changes, examine your reason for maintaining the status quo. Progression in any story requires change of some kind.

Beware the motiveless character—one who floats through the story causing no conflict, getting in no one's way. The symptoms are weak dialogue and aimless action. Probable cause: no agenda. The character exists for your convenience only, without wants or needs of his own.

Test your writing skills through continued revision. If you cannot embrace the desires and sense of purpose of each character, you'll know it's not an agenda that needs corrective surgery, it's the character.

FIND & FIX CLUE #15: BURIED AGENDA

- Review each character's agenda and make it explicit as early as the story permits.
- Confirm that your characters' objectives are shown in their dialogue, actions, and reactions.
- Verify that for each scene you make the agenda of at least one character clear and raise at least one obstacle to it.
- Maximize your story's tension potential by placing characters with opposing agendas in encounters with each other.
- Identify where and how you keep raising the stakes that increase your characters' desperation and justify their willingness to take greater risks.
- Play the role of each character from beginning to end, one at a time, and revise each script as if you were that character and wanted the same thing for the same reason.
- Confirm that your story builds anticipation and produces tension on every page.
- Find the internal conflict that forces your protagonist to make difficult choices.

CLUE #16: DYING DIALOGUE

D ialogue in a mystery is not whatever a couple of characters happen to say to each other. That's conversation, not dialogue. Talking that offers no resistance, no characterization, and no meaningful interactions to move the story forward is not dialogue. Neither is a lecture, discussion, or data dump.

Dialogue is a form of action, a potent technique for expressing conflict. It is the mightiest power tool on the writer's workbench for making characters come alive. Instead of your stepping in like an overbearing parent to tell us *about* your characters, dialogue lets you let *them* reveal their feelings, attitudes, and personalities through their own words.

Passages of dialogue look different enough from other narrative forms to let a busy screener skim a few pages of manuscript and form a quick opinion of the writing based on dialogue alone. If the dialogue is snappy, adversarial, and oblique (more on that soon), the screener reads on. If the dialogue sounds dead or dying, the screener has no reason to postpone the funeral. The submission is unceremoniously buried.

Sadly, much of what passes for dialogue in the typical submission is little more than chitchat and data dumping.

Just because you put quotation marks around exposition, don't think you're writing dialogue. Effective dialogue is purposeful—the means by which characters strive to realize their objectives, act on their strategies, and incite reactions from others.

Before you edit your characters' scripts, unearth their buried agendas (CLUE #15). Once their wants and motives are paramount in your mind and theirs, let *them* go at it. But don't let a word be spoken without your having a reason for including it.

To give your novel a fair chance of surviving its quickest screen test, raise your dialogue's conflict quotient.

RELATIONSHIPS

Dialogue is especially effective in revealing relationships. The ripest for conflict are family relationships, as in this extract from Jill Churchill's *The Merchant of Menace,* part of her Jane Jeffry series. Jane's future mother-in-law is visiting for the first time. What attitudes do you sense from their dialogue?

> "I thought you might like a little snack after your trip, Mrs. VanDyne. We're having quite a big dinner later."
> She expected Mel's mom to insist on being called Addie, but instead she said, "How thoughtful, Mrs. Jeffry." Was there a little emphasis on the "Mrs." or did Jane only imagine it?
> Jane asked a few inane questions about Mrs. VanDyne's flight to which she got pleasant, innocuous replies. Mel tried to help. "Mom, tell Jane about the man with the dog in a carrier," he said rather desperately.
> Mrs. VanDyne waved this away. "It wasn't that interesting, dear." She glanced around the room. "What a very nice little house you have, Mrs. Jeffry. I suppose these holiday decorations have some family significance."
> *In other words, they look like shit but must mean something to me, otherwise I wouldn't let them see the light of day,* Jane thought.   [pp. 62–63]

Mrs. VanDyne's attitude toward her son's fiancée is revealed by her formality and "innocuous replies." Her veiled criticisms are conveyed by her words "nice little house" and "I suppose these . . . have some family significance." Mel's relationship with his mother and with Jane is shown through his unsuccessful effort to help the conversation along.

Whatever your characters' relationships, you can increase the tension in your dialogue with the same techniques Churchill uses: innuendo, unmet expectation, suppressed resistance, and negative interpretation of another's meaning.

Good-natured teasing can also arouse tension, as demonstrated in the scene from *Snipe Hunt* by Sarah Shaber excerpted earlier (CLUE #3).

A mystery is no place for a mutual admiration society.

TIP: USING DOTS & DASHES

Interruptions in dialogue are shown by a dash—known as a 1-em dash. It is simulated in a manuscript by typing two hyphens--no spaces. If you don't like the way the hyphens separate at the end of a typed line, make the first one a nonbreaking hyphen:

in Windows, Control+Shift+Hyphen;
in Word for the Mac, Command+Shift+Hyphen.

Do not use an ellipsis for interruptions. An ellipsis (three dots) shows the speaker's letting a line of dialogue trail off . . . incomplete. When an ellipsis occurs at the end of a sentence, add a fourth dot to represent the period. . . .

Some word processing programs convert three dots in a row to one tightly spaced representation of an ellipsis. Turn off the keyboard shortcut for that feature, because the size and spacing of the dots do not match the rest of your punctuation, especially when you have to add the terminal period.

SOWING DISSENSION

Any ordinary, amiable question-and-answer sequence can be given an adversarial flavor by having characters interrupt each other, answer a question with a question, give an unexpected response, and change the subject. Kill the words "yes," "okay," and "I agree," even when no disagreement exists. Merely the sound of an affirmative can breed a congenial, agreeable tone that takes the steam out of any encounter.

Where possible, create disagreement and suspicion among your characters. Invent misunderstanding. Encourage misinterpretation. Add distraction. Use snappy dialogue. All of the above.

Eliminate direct replies to questions; they make dialogue *symmetrical,* a pattern that itself suggests cooperation. If symmetry is continued too long, it puts the reader to sleep.

The passages below come from *Gone, Baby, Gone,* Dennis Lehane's fourth mystery novel. Private investigators Patrick Kenzie and Angie Gennaro are about to visit a wounded cop in the hospital when they encounter special agent Neal Ryerson in the parking garage.

"He's dead."

We stopped, and I turned back and looked at the guy. . . . He tapped some ash from the cigar, put it back in his mouth, and looked at me.

"This is the part where you say, 'Who's dead?'" He looked down at his boots.

"Who's dead?" I said.

"Nick Raftopoulous," he said.

That's symmetrical dialogue. Every question receives an answer. Short bursts can be effective, especially if it sets up a contrast for the asymmetrical dialogue that comes soon after it, as in the next set of lines.

Angie turned fully around on her crutches. "Excuse me?"

"That's who you came to see, right?" He held out his hands, shrugged. "Well you can't, because he died an hour ago. . . .

He smiled. "Your next line is, 'How do you know who we're here to see?'" he said. "Take it, either one of you."

"Who are you?" I said.   [p. 334]

Kenzie's "Who are you?" changes the subject, breaking the pattern of seemingly cooperative responses and taking control of the conversation away from Ryerson.

A page later Angie asks the special agent a question.

"So who killed Mullen and Gutierrez?"

Ryerson looked up at the garage ceiling. "Who took the money out of the hills? Who was the first person found in the vicinity of the victims?"

"Wait a sec," Angie said. "Poole? You think Poole was the shooter?"   [p. 336]

Notice Lehane's technique in once again breaking the expected Q and A sequence. Ryerson responds to Angie's question with a series of rhetorical questions. Angie, instead of replying, asks another question that interprets the meaning behind Ryerson's replies. Jumping ahead to confront what someone else *implies* is another form of asymmetrical or oblique dialogue, and it makes events move at a vigorous pace.

Hal Glatzer uses similar techniques in this extract from *A Fugue in Hell's Kitchen,* a mystery set in the neighborhood of the same name in New York City, 1939. Violinist Katy Green, investigating a crime at a classical music conservatory, is questioning a reporter. He replies:

> ". . . Yeah. I wrote about that. Good local angle, too: she died in the house she was born in. Did you see my story?"
> "No, I was out of town."
> "Did you know her?"
> "What happened, exactly?"
> "Nobody's saying your friend murdered her, if that's what you're thinking."
> *"Was* it murder?"   [p. 163]

Katy's reply in line 2 is symmetrical; after that, she takes control of the questioning. When she gets to her purpose for the interview, the dialogue jumps ahead. The reporter interprets the *implication* in Katy's asking "What happened, exactly," and he becomes defensive, which further advances her agenda.

To strengthen your own dialogue, revise it line by line to increase the number of indirect, unexpected replies that make dialogue asymmetrical.

INFORMATIONAL DIALOGUE

In a genre that relies on gathering clues and deducing meaning, characters have to exchange information. They cannot be shown acting on information they had no opportunity to learn. Therefore, the writer needs to show or otherwise account for *who* knows *what* and *when.*

Don't let data appear to be the primary reason for a dialogue. If the only interaction is an exchange of information, that exchange is not itself a conflict, even though the dialogue might tell *about* a conflict. Have readers feel tension by seeing the cause of a character's tension.

When you revise, confirm that each scene has been built around opposing agendas. Use some dialogue and some paraphrase to work a limited amount of information into the scene, but be careful not to dilute the tension. Too much exchanging of data leads to a tension deficit disorder.

To add tension, put your characters in situations that produce anxiety—like sending best friends fishing (CLUE #12). Then pump up the pressure.

Maybe the sleuth gets seasick. Or falls overboard. If your protagonist wants something from the other character, he has to play nice and not rock the boat, so to speak—an effort that itself adds another tension dimension.

Making characters focus on different priorities lets you write *bypass dialogue:* two people talking but not communicating.

Transforming allies into temporary adversaries not only increases tension but also builds the reader's empathy with your protagonist, whose suspicions are pooh-poohed by others. The desire to be proven right in the eyes of a disbeliever can add to your protagonist's determination to pursue a solution. Remember to establish a reason for a friend's resistance, impatience, or skepticism.

PARALLEL CONVERGENCE

When dialogue cannot turn argumentative, should the scene be left to sputter and die from lack of conflict? No. If readers are kept aware of your characters' agendas, you can make the tension from unsatisfied goals felt from one scene to the next. Also, you can borrow tension from an unrelated source, such as a minor character who sets off a short-term conflict. Or invent some other business that offers its own action.

What do I mean by "other business"? Here's a scene from the Agatha-nominated *Blues in the Night* by Rochelle Krich, the first title in her third mystery series. Molly Blume, reporter, is seeking background about the victim of a mysterious hit-and-run. Among those she interviews are the managers of the building where the victim lived. Because this interaction is not an adversarial confrontation, Krich borrows conflict from a tennis match taking place on TV.

> "We were shocked when her mother told us Lenore died," Marie said, her voice rising to compete with the droning of a former tennis champion turned commentator. . . . "Just shocked. Weren't we, Tom?". . .
>
> "Shocked," he agreed. "She was a nice gal. Pretty." He fixed his eyes on the television screen.
>
> ". . . It's just so sad what happened, isn't it, Tom?"
>
> "Rotten shame."
>
> "How long was she living here?" I asked, sipping the iced tea Marie had insisted on serving me.

"Seven months," Marie said.

"Did you ever meet her ex-husband?"

"Son of a bitch," Tom muttered.

I turned to him. "Why do you say that, Mr. O'Day?"

He looked at me and blinked. "What?"

"Mr. Saunders was a son of a bitch?"

"Was he?" He shrugged. "I wouldn't know. Never met him."

He returned his attention to the screen. "That ball was on the line, you imbecile!" he shouted.   [p. 82]

Tricked by Krich! First, she has Tom respond to his wife's comments about the deceased, then the author switches his response, without warning, and has Tom respond to the televised event. Where his two scripts converge, Tom's remarks make sense in both contexts.

Molly is fooled, and so are we.

Krich has created a moment of dramatic irony in addition to injecting borrowed conflict into an ordinary fact-finding mission. Tom's emotional outbursts continue to punctuate the scene to its end.

SIMULATED DISAGREEMENT

Borrowed tension also features in Cynthia Riggs' *Deadly Nightshade,* the first of her Martha's Vineyard mystery novels. Victoria Trumbull, ninety-two, is a possible witness to a murder. As she and her granddaughter, Elizabeth, drive home late one night, a car follows them. When they see the lights still on at the home of Domingo, a former New York cop-turned-harbormaster, they drop in to tell him what's been happening.

Nothing the women tell Domingo is news to us, because these events are dramatized in previous scenes. So where's the conflict in *this* scene? It begins with Elizabeth telling of her encounter with a "weird, creepy man," which prompts Domingo to tell a gruesome story of his own.

In these extracts, follow the role played by his wife, Noreen.

"Christ!" Noreen sat up straight in her chair. "You're making that up."

Domingo shook his head. "His name means 'dead.'"

"Where do you get this stuff?" Elizabeth said.

"He's full of it." Noreen turned to Elizabeth. . . .   [p. 52]

When Victoria and Elizabeth begin to talk of being followed, Domingo keeps interrupting them—a tension-producer in itself. Noreen berates her husband for not letting the women tell the story in their own way. As the scene progresses, her scolding increases and her language grows more abusive. The ex-cop pays no attention.

Domingo then becomes interested in some water-soaked papers the women found on the beach that morning, and he prepares to separate the papers so they can dry.

> "Get me a knife, honey." He reached out his hand without looking at Noreen, and she went back into the kitchen. She returned with a thin-bladed knife, making a gesture for Victoria's benefit, as if she were going to impale her husband with it before she put it in his outstretched hand.
>
> "Thank you," he said, eyes bright.
>
> Noreen went back into the kitchen and returned with a clear plastic cutting board and a handful of paper towels. Domingo looked up at her. Their eyes met. There was a faint smile on his face. Victoria felt a touch of electricity in the air. Noreen gave him a soft slap on his cheek. . . .
>
> Noreen left the room again and came back with a clear piece of glass, a small windowpane. Domingo made a kissing sound in her direction, and Noreen punched him on the shoulder.
>
> [pp. 55–56]

Riggs could have paraphrased all the incidents that her characters retell, but in dramatizing this scene she reveals the special relationship between Domingo and Noreen. Because conflict *seems* the norm at first, it does the job of adding tension. Characterization expands, the plot advances, and readers get a new development to anticipate once the wet papers dry.

BREVITY, PLEASE

Not every development merits its own scene. Instead of inventing a situation solely to bring tension to an informational exchange, try paring the information to its essentials and merging those essentials into another scene.

The next example shows the benefits of a just-the-facts approach applied to one of dialogue's worst offenders: the phone call. Telephone conversations in fiction often furnish low conflict and little to visualize.

You already know, I'm sure, not to reproduce every *um* and *ah* of actual speech, but you might not realize how much other garbage builds up from all the routine hello-how-are-you chatter. Misguided efforts to simulate realistic conversation serve no useful purpose, so please—take out the garbage.

> "[W]hat is said is not always what is meant and what is not said is often just as important, if not more so, as what actually is said. . . ."
>
> Brett Jocelyn Epstein, in the Mensa magazine [49]

To help you practice doing precisely that, I invite you to edit a passage I wrote based on an effective, extremely brief phone conversation that takes place in Chapter 20 of *Death's Domain,* the sixth Cassidy McCabe mystery from Alex Matthews. Cass is in her car when she thinks of one other person she should be interviewing. To learn the man's name and address, she phones her husband, Zach, at work.

Here's the paragraph that sets up the purpose of the call just as Matthews wrote it:

> He'd mentioned the name of his company but the corporate title was unfamiliar to her and had failed to lodge itself in her memory. Zach, however, would have it written down. Fishing her cell phone and a spiral pad out of her tote, she called him.

Next is my talkative version of the call itself, which begins immediately after the words "she called him." Edit it by drawing a line through every unnecessary word. No rewriting is needed.

> "Hi Zach, it's me. How y'doing?"
>
> "Oh, hi Cass. Not bad. What's up?"
>
> "Well, I forgot to ask you something. Do you have a couple of minutes?"
>
> "Sure, I just filed today's story."
>
> "Remember that man we wanted to question," she asked, "the one who worked for the company on the other side of town?"
>
> "Yeah, I do," he replied.
>
> "Well, I can't think of the company's name. I figured you wrote it down. Do you have it?" she asked.
>
> "Yeah, I can get it," he said. "Just give me a minute." She sat

on hold for a while. Half a minute later Zach was on the line
again. "Got a pencil?" he asked.

"Yes," she answered.

"Escovar is the name you're looking for. I've got the address
right here on the screen. . . ."

Obviously, my deliberate wordiness ruined Matthews' original dialogue,
the same way I've seen thousands of writers ruin theirs.

Before you look ahead at the professionally written lines on which I
base this exercise, notice that nothing about the phone call involves conflict, drama, or tension. Nor is there any reason it should. The call serves
only to show how Cass gets a tiny piece of information. Because there's no
value in turning this kind of situation into a conflict, it can be kept as brief
as possible.

So go back and take out more words. Go on. See if you can reduce my
bloated passage to one paragraph. Then compare your version to the author's,
which follows.

With apologies to the award-winning Alex Matthews for my parody,
here is the phone call as she wrote it, beginning immediately after the words,
"she called him."

"Yeah, I can get it," he said. "Just give me a minute." She sat
on hold for a while. "Escovar is the name you're looking for.
I've got the address right here on the screen. . . ."   [p. 182]

That's it. No need to hear Cass telling Zach why she's phoning; we
learn why just before she calls him. Zach's "Yeah, I can get it," follows
immediately. No filler, no gabby chitchat, no transition.

Since readers would be well aware by Chapter 20 that Cass's husband is
a reporter, the reference to Zach's filing a story is unnecessary, the kind of
background an insecure writer repeats for insurance. Chitchat this far into
the story would undermine the pace and serve no purpose. Once dialogue
serves its purpose, nothing is gained by prolonging it.

The information exchange written by Matthews is crisp, compressed,
and clear. It moves like an express train. Mine derails, like a train wreck.
The original reaches its destination in only thirty-two words, no excess
baggage. Mine runs over the action with more than four times the freight.

PACING DIALOGUE

It's a fact that dialogue moves faster than narrative. Even the "look" of dialogue, with lots of white space, encourages more rapid reading than solid blocks of text. Lean, well-written lines and bursts of incomplete sentences move faster still.

Is there such a thing as a too-rapid tempo? We know that reading a series of high-speed chase scenes can leave us emotionally out of breath, wanting a break before the next action scene hands our emotions another speeding ticket. Yet dialogue can move rapidly without ill effect, provided it is not so abbreviated that the meaning gets muddled.

Duration is a factor along with speed: rapid-fire dialogue that goes on for more than two pages might lose its punch.

Once you take out the meaningless chatter and routine steps that clutter your scenes, you'll notice how everything accelerates. If you find a tightly self-edited scene moving faster than you want it to, here are some techniques to help you restore a slower pace. *Do not restore the clutter.*

- Break up dialogue with exposition.
- Turn some dialogue *into* exposition.
- Make sentences and paragraphs a little longer.
- Add some description.
- Change the setting.

To see how a change in setting can affect pace, imagine a couple sitting and talking on a porch swing in the moonlight. Next, imagine the same couple shouting the identical words over the roar of city traffic while they try to flag a cab. In the rain. At rush hour.

To speed up the pace of your dialogue try these methods:

- Determine whether the road from A to B to C is within the experience of most adults, so that leaping from A to C will be understood.
- Eliminate words, sentences, and gestures that are non-essential and offer no conflict, characterization, or plot advancement.
- Compress what's left, except where a good reason justifies spelling out each statement made by each character.
- Continue to revise, striving for rapid-fire confrontation.

Also review the phone call from *Death's Domain* as Alex Matthews wrote it to appreciate how easily dialogue can be understood even when it leaps tall buildings in a single bound.

With practice, you, too, can produce super dialogue.

FIND & FIX CLUE #16: DYING DIALOGUE

- When self-editing, verify that you reveal your characters' buried agendas through what they say and do, and what others say about them.
- Make dialogue as goal-oriented and adversarial as your story permits.
- Be sure your dialogue moves the story forward.
- Rewrite exchanges that fail to evoke tension, create conflict, or expand characterization.
- Invigorate dialogue with interruptions, interrogation, asymmetry, and the unexpected.
- Don't prolong a dialogue beyond the point where it serves a useful purpose.
- Keep informational exchanges extremely brief or splice them into other tension-producing action.
- Say farewell to good-bys, greetings, chitchat, and other filler.

D.O.A.

CLUE #17: TREACHEROUS TAGS

The usual method for attributing words to the character who speaks them is by hanging a little *he asked/she replied* tag from the line of dialogue. Sometimes the dialogue tag is like a forgotten price tag hanging from a sleeve: awkward, distracting, unnecessary.

To prepare for your manuscript's debut, cut unnecessary attributions.

> "Tom, you got one helluva nerve!" Dick bellowed angrily.
> "I told you to stay outta my office," Tom retorted.

Start by deleting adverbs. "Angrily" is redundant when the dialogue itself conveys its speaker's feelings—no authorial interpretation needed. Dialogue *shows;* adverbs *tell.* Wordiness weakens your writing, especially the wordiness I call *adverbosity.*

Next, delete tags such as "he bellowed" and "Tom retorted." Verbs that tell how a line is delivered are rarely needed with strong dialogue, because the dialogue itself reveals how its speaker is behaving. Often, a line can stand by itself, without the crutch that a tag offers.

> "Tom, you got one helluva nerve!"
> "I told you to stay outta my office."

Attention-getting verbs like "bellowed" and "retorted" don't add meaning; they add distraction. If you want to add meaning, use action and body language.

- ❧ Action anchors spoken lines in their setting, giving readers something to visualize other than talking heads.
- ❧ Body language authenticates the dialogue's content, offering a physical parallel to the speaker's emotions.
- ❧ Body language *shows* how a line is delivered, whereas adverbs *tell* how.

For example:

> "Tom, you got one helluva nerve!" Dick said, bursting in.
> "I told you to stay outta my office," Tom said as he jumped
> up, knocking over his chair.

Acceptable, but instead of adding action to a tag, as in "Tom said as he jumped up," see what happens when you use action to *replace* a tag.

> "Tom, you got one helluva nerve!" Dick slammed the door
> he'd just burst through.
> "I told you to stay outta my office." Tom jumped up, knock-
> ing over his chair.

Each of these action statements takes the form of a *beat:* a sentence that furnishes its own attribution. Compare:

- ❧ Tag: "I told you to stay outta my office," Tom said as he jumped up, knocking over his chair.
- ❧ Beat: "I told you to stay outta my office." Tom jumped up, knocking over his chair.

The same chair hits the floor each time, but the standalone beat is more effective, because it replaces a tag that burdens the spoken line with the wordy "said as he." Where dialogue erupts under its own power, get out of the way and let it flow. But don't give every line of dialogue its own beat; the resulting rhythm and pattern will overpower everything else.

When dialogue is triggered by an action, be faithful to the sequence of cause and effect. Show the action first.

> Dick burst open the door. "Tom, you got one helluva nerve!"
> Tom jumped up, knocking over his chair. "I told you to stay
> outta my office."

When self-editing, scrutinize your dialogue. You'll find all sorts of treacherous tags to exorcise. You'll also spot adverbosity and other redundancies, like those that haunt this line from *The Murder of Roger Ackroyd:*

> "I'm not very sure," I said doubtfully. [50]

Even the great Agatha Christie could have used some line editing.

DISSONANT TAGS

Sometimes characters use humor or sarcasm to disguise the meaning behind their words. Sometimes they lie about their feelings to themselves and others. And sometimes they just lie. In those instances where you want your readers to see a discrepancy between the spoken word and the hidden feeling, don't use an adverb; use a gesture, body language, or other action.

> Dick chuckled and wagged a finger at his partner. "Tom, you've got one helluva nerve."

However, writers don't always select the gesture that successfully conveys the emotion. The result is vague, its meaning ambiguous.

> Dick frowned and stammered, "Tom, you've got one helluva nerve."

Something is off. Discrepancies between dialogue and body language suggest the need for sharper people-watching skills. Consider revising the body language to suggest the character's real feelings, whatever those may be, or changing his spoken words to reflect what a frowning, stammering person is likely to say.

The next example shows an intentional discrepancy between a character's words and her body language. It's from the Edgar-nominated *Sunrise,* the first title in a series featuring Leigh Ann Warren, a D. C. cop—though far from the first novel by the prolific, award-winning Chassie West.

> . . . An expert at going for the jugular with a Teflon-coated stiletto, she oohed and aahed over me, patted my cheek and gazed in mock sympathy at Nunna. "Such a shame," she said. Her beady eyes flitted between us like a fly undecided about where to light. "All that money spent on your education and you wind up directin' traffic and writin' tickets. Couldn't pass the lawyer's exam, I reckon?"   [p. 77]

West's portrayal of this chatty, catty neighbor, with her gaze of mock sympathy and beady, flitting eyes, reveals the speaker's feelings beneath her oohing, aahing, and superficially innocent remarks. In the context of *Sunrise,* this episode serves a purpose more important than characterizing a minor player. Among other things, the neighbor's condescension triggers Leigh Ann's renewed pride in her profession as an officer of the law, and that change in attitude takes the plot in a new direction.

YOU DON'T SAY

In a mystery, originality is valued in everything but tags. The plain vanilla *said* is preferred over any of the fancy synonyms Mr. Roget tempts you with: alleged, averred, declared, rejoined, retorted, stated—and so on. While *bellowed* is out there calling attention to the writer's efforts, *said* remains nearly invisible. It lets the dialogue flow, which is why it's preferred by experienced writers (and by the ubiquitous nine out of ten doctors—book doctors, that is).

In small doses, *insisted* and *repeated* are useful, as are *asked, answered, echoed, replied, told, observed,* and *pointed out.* Also effective is the occasional *complained, cried, muttered, mumbled, murmured, screamed, shouted, shrieked, wailed,* and *whispered.* The operative word is "occasional." More than one *thundered* per book is overdoing it.

How often do thesaurus-style verbs pop up in your own speech?

> "So I stated to my boss that I wouldn't dream of retorting in
> such a manner to a customer, and he rejoined, 'That's what
> Ellen declared to me that she heard you utter.'"

If you wouldn't talk like that, don't write like that. Reaching for unlikely verbs is reaching for rejection.

Put tags in their place by recognizing that they are mere mechanics. An invisible tag like *said* lets readers skim over it on the way to hearing what the dialogue has to say. Dialogue is the portrait; tags are the thumbtacks that hold it to the wall.

Okay, you're convinced that *said* is a perfectly fine tag, but it's so . . . so ordinary. Surely readers get bored with the same old same old?

Consider this: If *said* strikes you as boring, the problem is not with the tag, it's with the dialogue. Chances are, whatever your characters are feeling strongly about isn't coming through in the words and actions you are writing for them. Bring their agendas out in the open. When dialogue puts forth a desire, opinion, or attitude, that may be sufficient to identify the speaker. No tag needed.

TIP: DO YOU KNOW YOUR TAG HABITS?

Examine the ways you write dialogue tags by using the search feature in your word processing program.

1. Write with the "smart quotes" feature in "Preferences" turned on. Or turn it on now, type a quote mark into the FIND option and also into REPLACE, and hit "All." Your computer will produce the correct open or close quotes throughout your text. (Do the same for the apostrophe.)

2. To search for only those quote marks that *follow* dialogue (and thereby control the total number of "hits" your computer makes):

   a) Copy or cut a "smart" or "curly" close quote mark " from your text and paste it into the FIND option.

   b) Press FIND to review each hit one at a time.

3. This method lets you analyze the tags you now write.

4. Observe their frequency and the pattern of occurrence.

5. Evaluate all verbs other than "said," and decide:

   a) would "said" be equally appropriate and less obtrusive?

   b) is the dialogue meaningful enough to need *no* crutch—that is, no verb, no adverb, no tag?

6. Armed with this insight, strengthen your dialogue and avoid impeding its flow with unnecessary or ineffective tags.

SELF-IDENTIFYING SPEECH

To keep dialogue moving, a question-and-answer structure is the next best thing to an argument. Alternating lines mirror an adversarial pattern and leave little doubt who is speaking.

With such a pattern, the need for tags becomes minimal or non-existent, as in this dialogue from *There Was a Little Girl,* by Ed McBain. Presented as a remembered conversation from the past, McBain omits even the quotation marks, and the dialogue works fine without them.

> . . . It was Warren Chambers, instead, who'd given her the first job she'd had since her nosedive two years earlier.

Tell me about the job, okay? she'd said.

First tell me you're clean, Warren had said.

Why? Do I look like I'm not?

You look suntanned and healthy. But that doesn't preclude
coke.

I like that word. Preclude. Did you make it up?

How do you like the other word? Coke?

I used to like it just fine. I still think of it every now and then.
But the thought passes. I'm clean, Mr. Chambers.

How long has it been?

Almost two years. Since right after Otto fired me.

And now you're clean.

Now I'm clean.   [pp. 71–72]

After a series of tagless statements it's a good idea to insert an occasional attribution or beat to reinforce the identity of the speaker, which
McBain does in the line, "I'm clean, Mr. Chambers."

DIRECT ADDRESS

This brings us to the method of direct address, in which speakers address each other by name, a device for clarifying who's who. Like any
other technique, this one must not be overdone or it becomes more conspicuous than the content it supports. In actual conversation, how often do
you speak the name of the person you're talking to?

"Hi, Larry. The coroner's report just came in."

"What's it say, Corinne?"

"Well, Larry, the news isn't good."

Pete looked up from the next desk. "I'm on my way to lunch
but I'd rather listen in on this. Larry, what if I have Selma hold
all calls?"

Selma's voice called from the reception room, "Okay, Pete."

Awful writing! But surprisingly common. Before you read ahead, use
your pencil to perform major surgery on the passage above. Anything will
be an improvement.

Here's one rewrite; many others are possible.

"Hey, Larry, I just got the coroner's report." Corinne handed the file to her boss. "Bad news."

Pete decided this wasn't the time to go to lunch. He buzzed the receptionist to hold all calls and edged his chair closer to Larry's desk.

Compare this rewrite with yours. See if you are using surgical techniques similar to these, by:

- slicing words that fail to expand characterization or advance the scene ("~~What's it say, Corinne?~~");
- splicing lines where exposition is wordy (~~she replied, handing~~ . . .);
- condensing or eliminating characters and their spoken lines (~~Pete looked up~~ . . . "~~I'm on my way~~ . . .");
- paraphrasing for economy (Pete decided . . . and edged).

When you self-edit, read your dialogue aloud and note awkward-sounding, artificial phrasing. Revise, then ask someone to read it to you. If your buddy is agreeable, tape record the reading, make notes, and replay later. Listen for any tripping or stumbling.

BY THE NUMBERS

In revising, review the value of each scene in advancing your plot. Know the specific contribution each character makes in furthering the purpose of every scene. Keep readers aware of the agendas being pursued.

Scenes with two characters are stronger than those with more. For a two-person dialogue, use tags with only one of the speakers, none with the other.

As the number of roles expands, drama and conflict become diluted and the need for identification grows exponentially. So thin your crowds, especially those in which several characters fill similar functions or share similar agendas.

Ask yourself, does this scene really need separate speaking parts for five police officers? Combine roles where you can. Where you cannot, think about having someone else speak for a character who gets called away from the meeting or gets stuck in traffic and can't make the meeting.

Be sure to plant a reason for this absence in advance and keep it plausible.

When a number of characters must be present, control how often each gets to speak. I've seen manuscripts in which lines of dialogue are apportioned in perfect rotation among three or more speakers, as if the writer were dealing a hand of poker. Such "dealings," I suspect, come less from an innate sense of fairness than from sensing the dialogue's blandness and need for action, which the writer attempts to compensate for by adding more characters.

Perversely, rotation increases the need for speaker attribution, and it produces a rhythm that itself is a source of monotony.

If reducing the number of characters doesn't do justice to the different ideas you need to put forth in a given scene, you have other options.

- Focus on only two speakers at a time instead of bouncing back and forth among all of them.
- When a third character speaks, have one of the original two remain silent for a few exchanges so that no more than two speakers are in the spotlight at one time.
- Identify the third speaker as soon as her dialogue begins, so her words aren't mistakenly heard as coming from one of the first two. For instance:

    > "I wonder," said Carmen, who'd been quietly knitting and listening, "if you two considered that Marco might have gone to the roadhouse because. . . ."

- Or introduce the new speaker with a beat that precedes her dialogue:

    > Carmen, who'd been quietly listening, put down her knitting. "I wonder if you two considered. . . ."

- Not every comment needs dialogue to present it. Some comments can be paraphrased and put forth as exposition:

    > Carmen, who'd been quietly listening, put down her knitting and reminded everyone that Marco might have. . . .

For a "town hall" or crowd scene, limit speaking parts to the fewest named characters. Have additional remarks come from unnamed onlookers. Walk-ons don't need names; epithets will do: *said a woman in red; the teacher announced;* and so on.

What to do with superfluous characters after they serve their purpose? More than one author I know kills them off.

CROWD CONTROL

I'm not suggesting that you use a structure as complex as the next example, but I would like you to analyze the techniques its author uses for managing multiple speaking parts so identification is clear. This is the interrogation scene from *The Alibi* by Sandra Brown. It involves five roles, each of which serves a different function in the scene.

One character, Frank Perkins, is new; readers of *The Alibi* already met the other four. Hammond Cross, the protagonist, is secretly smitten with the mysterious Dr. Alex Ladd, who is fast becoming the prime murder suspect. She is about to be interrogated by homicide detective Rory Smilow. Also present for the questioning is Hammond's associate in the D.A.'s office, Steffi, who is suspicious of Alex.

> Frank Perkins spoke first. "Hammond, this is a complete waste of my client's time."
>
> "Very possibly it is, Frank, but I would like to make that determination for myself. Detective Smilow seems to think that what Dr. Ladd can tell us warrants my hearing it."
>
> The lawyer consulted his client. "Do you mind going through it again, Alex?"
>
> "Not if it means that I can go home sooner rather than later."
>
> "We'll see."
>
> That comment had come from Steffi, and it made Hammond want to slap her. Turning the Q and A over to Smilow, he propped himself against the closed door, where he had an unrestricted view of Alex's profile.
>
> Smilow restarted the tape recorder and added Hammond's name to those present. "Did you know Lute Pettijohn, Dr. Ladd?"
>
> She sighed as though she had already answered that question a thousand times. "No, Detective, I did not."   [pp. 196–97]

Let's analyze Brown's method for handling multiple speakers. The passage begins by naming the newest character, whose role as attorney is made clear by his own words, "my client's time." Other lines of dialogue are identified either by direct address or by the action that precedes them.

One line, "We'll see," is identified after it is spoken, and not as a tag or beat accompanying the spoken words. Its I.D. appears in the next line as part of Hammond's reaction to the "We'll see"—a line so brief that as soon as we start to wonder who said it, the answer appears: *That comment had come from Steffi.*

The line that begins *Turning the Q and A over to Smilow* re-anchors Hammond and Smilow in the scene and builds a bridge to the interrogation. Once the first question establishes who is asking and who is answering, Brown is able to keep their dialogue going for twelve more paragraphs without a single tag, beat, or other form of address.

Selective content and form make identifiers unnecessary.

CONTENT AND FORM

I've listened to writers spend more time discussing how to attribute dialogue than how to write it.

Dialogue's *content* is what a character says that no other character is likely to know or say. Content that's purposeful and agenda-specific is able to stand on its own, needing little support from attributions, adverbs, or attention-getting verbs that tell readers who the speaker is and how he feels.

Here is a challenge to help you practice making your dialogue more effective. Up to now I've been suggesting that tags be seen as an option to cut *if* you revise your dialogue to stand alone. Now I'd like you to pretend your year's supply of tags is used up and your dialogue *must* stand on its own. In this way, content becomes the only source of speaker I.D. This belief forces you to strengthen what your characters say.

> Asked what editors would be looking for in the future, literary agent Donald Maass replied: "Quality writing, by which I mean beautiful prose and flawless storytelling, regardless of category. The bar is so much higher now than it was ten years ago."
>
> Sisters in Crime-Internet Chapter newsletter, 3rd quarter 2005

Unlike content, dialogue's *form* deals with how speaking parts are presented. When form obeys certain conventions, most readers understand what's meant by your use of quotation marks, alternating lines, gestures, beats, direct address, and idiosyncrasies of speech.

One convention I want to call your attention to is the punctuation mark that's *not* there: the close quote. Traditionally, this is dropped from the end of a paragraph whenever a speaker's words runneth over to the first line of the next paragraph.

Used correctly, quotation marks for uninterrupted speeches should reflect the following pattern:

> "Blah, blah, blah," Gabby said. "Blah, blah, and much more blah.
> "Furthermore," he continued, "blah, blah, blah."

Note the missing mark at the end of the first paragraph and the presence of another open quotation mark at the start of the next paragraph *for the same speaker.* This convention is worth recognizing for more than mechanics. It's a clue that the writer is letting the speaker make a speech.

Only you, the writer, can keep your characters from running off at the mouth. Loose lips sink scripts.

Typically, people speak in short sentences and fragments, and they interrupt each other, especially when disagreeing. To maintain the "di" in dialogue, break up a too-long speech for the other character's reaction, even if that reaction is a silent gesture. Shorten lengthy speeches and make all passages sharper, less symmetrical, and less like oratory.

If for some reason you decide to stretch a script beyond one paragraph, interrupt it yourself, even if you have to insert a beat, like this:

> When Dick didn't respond right away, Tom continued.

The most effective identifiers come from content: *what* is said that's unique to the character and the situation. Tags and other mechanics are the Wizard's manipulations behind the curtain, seldom needed for dialogue that possesses heart and brains.

Bottom line: Any time readers could be confused about who says what, dialogue needs attribution. More likely its content needs strengthening.

FIND & FIX CLUE #17: TREACHEROUS TAGS

- Use the search feature of your word processor (or a highlighter on the printout) to get a visual picture of your tag habits and other forms of attribution. (See the TIP on page 191.)
- Evaluate all tags for their contribution to clarity and see how many can be simplified with "said," or eliminated altogether, or replaced by a beat that adds meaning, .
- Delete adverbs; show how a speaker feels through action and dialogue.
- Rewrite action and dialogue to make a character's feelings evident, except where the plot requires hidden feelings.
- Make dialogue specific to its speaker and capable of standing alone.
- Verify that your scenes involve the fewest characters who can achieve the scene's purpose.
- Read dialogue aloud and listen for awkward pauses and breaths, unnatural or difficult phrasing, and long speeches that need repairing, rewriting, or slicing.

PART VIII: ROGUES GALLERY

Popular author and syndicated columnist Ellen Goodman has said that she enjoys rewriting. Her first draft is for getting her ideas and theme clear. She compares her next pass through the manuscript to cleaning house: getting rid of all the junk and putting things in the right order.

CLUE #18: MULTIPLE IDENTITIES

When you are introduced to a group of strangers at a party, how many names do you remember? Some of us feel lucky to recall *one* name—possible only because we learned something interesting about the person. Meeting strangers in a book is similar. Too many new names introduced too soon makes all of them forgettable.

One novel I began to read named twenty characters in the first chapter. If I hadn't been looking forward to reading that author, I would have viewed the family tree on the flyleaf as the omen it was. Still, I stuck with this population explosion through six chapters, until the effort of keeping track of who was who outweighed the pleasure of reading for relaxation.

Eventually, my $14.95 purchase went into my donate-to-the-library pile, and my interest in reading anything else by that author vanished.

In a mystery that plays fair with readers, characters who make up the pool of suspects cannot be introduced in the last half of the book. But stuffing them and all their relatives into Chapter one is counterproductive. It's hard to care about one character among many. First chapters are hooks, and the ultimate hook is giving readers one character they can really care about.

When I next browsed the fiction section of a bookstore, I saw one novel that mentioned six names in the first *paragraph.* Despite my belief that this naming frenzy couldn't continue, encountering it in the opening killed any curiosity to find out. When I read to relax I don't want it to seem like work.

Editing is different. I expect to take notes about every character when I edit. Readers don't take written notes, nor should they have to. A roster of names that continues rolling, like credits at the end of a film, holds about as much interest for readers as it does for the average moviegoer. What have audiences been conditioned to do upon seeing a long list of names roll past? Get up and leave. Don't let your submission cause busy screeners to wish they could do the same.

Review your manuscript to see that you bring on only one or two characters at a time, and that each arrives in the context of action or dialogue.

ONE NAME, TWO

Madonna, Cher, and Oprah notwithstanding, real people need two names. Fictional people do not, unless they are main characters—although Spenser is an exception. He's been single-namedly solving crimes for more than thirty of Robert B. Parker's novels.

In general, limit first and last names to your major characters, because double names are subtly interpreted in the same way that overly detailed descriptions are: as a signal that certain characters are more important than others. Given that all roles are not created equal, avoid sending misleading signals.

Characters with secondary roles can usually manage quite nicely with a single moniker, especially if it's catchy. And bit players can spend their moment in the limelight identified by function only: cab driver, bag lady, kid on a bike.

Even for the players worthy of two names, their full monikers do not need announcing the instant they appear. Behavior is more meaningful. A full I.D. can be added *after* the actions of a Johnnie-One-Name capture our interest. First, make readers care enough about him to learn who he is.

Watch how Kathy Reichs introduces names in the next extract. It's from *Death du Jour,* second in the series that became the television series *Bones,* featuring Temperance Brennan, forensic anthropologist.

> I'd worked with Claude Martineau before. The other tech
> was new to me. We introduced ourselves as they set up the
> screen and portable light.
>   "It's going to take some time to process this," I said, indicat-
> ing the staked-out square. "I want to locate any teeth that might
> have survived, and stabilize them if necessary. I may also have
> to treat the pubes and rib ends if I find any. Who's going to
> shoot pics?"
>   "Halloran is coming," said Sincennes, the second tech.
>
> [p. 37]

The first tech's name is mentioned as part of Tempe's statement that she had worked with him before. The second tech's name comes two paragraphs later, slipped in as part of a tag. A third name is mentioned in advance of the character's appearance.

Notice Reich's technique of having three characters introduce *themselves* while setting up their equipment.

REPEAT OFFENDERS

Does repeating the same name and pronoun for a character seem monotonous to you? Some writers make such an effort to avoid the "he-he-he" effect that they have different characters use different names for the same individual. A detective named Robert Smith might sometimes be addressed as Robert, Rob, Bob, Bobby, Detective, Detective Smith, Smitty, or just plain Smith.

Okay, I'm exaggerating again, but not by much. I see more bizarre efforts at variety than that, and not only in unpublished manuscripts. One best-selling author of legal thrillers applies what I call the Muddle maneuver: having the protagonist use different names to refer to the same character.

Here's an example, details changed to protect the blameworthy.

> I didn't trust Muddle. I suspected he'd change his story the
> next time the subject came up.
>   When the supervisor brought in my mail, I noticed Stuart
> sorting through it, apparently looking for something. What
> is Muddle up to now, I wondered.

Is Muddle the surname of Stuart? Or of the supervisor? The narrator could be referring to two different characters, or three. Or one. Maybe we should keep reading and hope the next paragraph clarifies the confusion. Or we could stop and flip back a few pages to see how the character was originally introduced. When confusion profusion occurs in the submission process, the busy screener may flip all the pages—onto the "no" pile.

Any time that readers stop, even for a moment, to wonder who's on first and what's on second, their immersion in the world of the story is interrupted. Illusion vaporizes. Attention drifts.

Don't worry about repeating the same pronoun. Worry about ambiguity and its cause. If you feel a need for variety in how you refer to a character, you might be sensing your own flagging interest in that character. Engender greater interest by showing a well-drawn, empathy-inducing character caught up in a tension-filled predicament.

LIMITED CONSISTENCY

Unlike the Stuart Muddle muddle, in which different names for the same character are used by one individual—the narrator—the next example shows different forms of address for the same character used by different speakers. The secret to this technique's clarity and effectiveness is consistency.

Hurricane Party is Steve Brown's fifth Susan Chase mystery, this one a tribute to Agatha Christie's locked-room puzzles. By the time the following scene occurs, readers know the characters and their relationships. Six are named: Susan Chase, formerly a lifeguard; her fiancé, Chad; Sarge, a military man now working as a security guard; and two other guests, Jeremy and Reynolds. Oh—and Helen. She's the corpse.

> Sarge shouldered his way past my fiancé, reached down, and put fingers against Helen's throat. He straightened up and nodded. "Dead for sure." Sarge looked at me. "Was it you that done it, Chase?"
>
> "She was dead when I found her."
>
> "Or after you killed her," accused Jeremy.
>
> I stepped back, readying myself as I do when confronted with any prick. "Why would I kill Helen?"
>
> "I don't know," Sarge said. "That's for the authorities to find out."
>
> "I agree. Not some rent-a-cop."

"Now, Suze. . ." started Chad as he got to his feet.

"Miss Chase, it doesn't help to call people names."

Reynolds Pearce finally came to life, speaking from the entrance to the living room. "A lifeguard is supposed to trump a security guard? You've got to be kidding."

"I can't believe. . . ." Jeremy stood, then shook his head. "Susan, how could you do something like this?"

"You didn't see anything, Jeremy," said Chad, "so watch your mouth."   [pp. 92–93]

Suze is a nickname used only by Chad, her fiancé, as both a term of endearment and an attempt to appease Susan when she behaves like . . . well, like Susan. Those who call her *Susan* include friends and those who pretend to be. *Chase* is what she's called by those who dislike her smart attitude, such as law enforcement types and the suspects she hounds.

Sarge, trained in the military, addresses her as *Miss Chase* or *Miss,* except for one moment when the author has him let down his guard, literally, and address her as *Chase.* This dropping of the courtesy title signals a slight but meaningful change in Sarge's customarily respectful demeanor as he attempts to shift suspicion onto Susan for the murder. He immediately recovers his formal style in the line, "Miss Chase, it doesn't help to call people names," which is understood as his response to Susan's rent-a-cop insult two lines earlier.

As the hurricane outside the Victorian house by the sea escalates, so does the tension inside. In a later scene when a thump on the porch is heard, Susan is about to open one of the barricaded doors.

"Miss Chase, I can't allow you to do that." The former soldier put a hand on my shoulder.

"Sarge," I said, turning my head, "do you want me to break something?"

He did not smile. He did not grin. He only stared at me in disbelief.

"Take your hand off my fiancée."

"Stay out of this, Chad." I never looked at Chad but continued to stare at the pockmarked face.

"But, Suze—"

"This is between the Sarge and me."

We never got a chance to settle the matter. Beyond the door anyone who wasn't deaf could hear the voice.

"Hey, in the house! Let me in."

I pulled out of Sarge's grasp and put my ear against the door.

"Who is it?" I screamed.

"It's me, babe. Kenny Mashburn."

"You're right," I said, leaving the door. "There's no one out there."   [p. 174]

Kenny is a low-life dope dealer who adds a comic element. His role introduces yet another name for Susan: *babe.*

Notice that each form of address is consistent for its speaker. None is ambiguous when read in context. Also note that in addition to identifying who's who, each form of address communicates information about:

- ●◆ the character who is being addressed (such as *Sarge* for a former military man);
- ●◆ the character who is addressing another in a unique way (only Kenny calls Susan *babe*);
- ●◆ one character's relationship with another (Susan is *Suze* only to her fiancé);
- ●◆ a character's change in attitude (Sarge's switch from *Miss Chase* to *Chase*).

Steve Brown uses names to effectively convey relationships and attitudes, and all without a single *angrily, rudely,* or *bellowed.*

VARIETY AS RELATIONSHIP

As with any technique, examine your purpose. If you are using different names to conceal a character's identity, the technique has a plot-related purpose. If those different names signify relationships and attitudes, the technique has a character-related purpose. If the primary purpose is variety for its own sake, that's the Muddle maneuver.

Return for a moment to our fictional Detective Robert Smith. His captain might consistently call him Smith; his partner, Smitty. His wife might call him Robert or Dear; strangers would address him as Mr. Smith or Detective Smith; and the narrator might alternate between Smith and the detective. Chances are his grandmother still calls him Bobby.

These variations may seem less confusing now than they did earlier, because each name is a consistent expression of the speaker's relationship to the character.

TIP: SWAPPING NAMES

Your computer makes swapping words easy; sometimes too easy. Be careful when using the global search-and-replace feature to change your characters' names. If you are replacing the nickname "Art" with "Arthur," for example, choose "replace whole word" to avoid peculiar results such as "He drew a carthuroon." Much safer is the "find next" command that lets you check each occurrence individually before changing it, thereby avoiding oddities such as "It hung in an arthur gallery."

If you expect to switch the order of your scenes, beware of the naming problem that led to this book review in *The Nation:*

"On more than one occasion, the authors mention someone either just by first or last name whom I had not remembered, causing me to flip back through the pages in a futile search to find what I missed. Then I would move on and find the person introduced pages later. In this and myriad other ways, the authors turned the cut-and-paste function of their word processors into tools of torture."[51]

HURLING EPITHETS

Extremely minor characters who don't need names do need some form of reference, often a function, like the bag lady or the kid on a bike; or a nickname, like Smitty; or a short phrase that stands in for a name, like the "smelly egg" in Nancy Bartholomew's *Drag Strip* (CLUE #8). A stand-in for a name is known as an *epithet.*

Here's an epithet from *Retribution,* Jilliane Hoffman's first crime novel.

Behind him in the hall stood two other Miami Beach cops in uniform. On one shoulder she recognized sergeant stripes.

"We're here for our prefiles," said the striped shoulder as he pushed his way past Chavez. . . .   [p. 202]

Here's another. It's from Jack M. Bickham's *Dropshot,* and it refers to a tennis player.

As I watched, big Jerry served a fireball and lumbered netward, but the opposing jock in a headband handled it easily, returning it to Jerry's feet. Jerry awkwardly got it back, almost falling down, and Headband brought his racket up from the pavement in a huge loop.   [p. 6]

An effective epithet is often descriptive and usually clever. The shorter the better. A long, complex phrase, like "the man who knew too much" or "our partner in crime," is effective one time but becomes strained with repetition.

In *What a Woman's Gotta Do,* Evelyn Coleman has her protagonist, Patricia Conley, invent a pair of epithets to characterize a couple sitting next to her in the waiting room of a marriage license bureau. Patricia, afraid she's been stood up by her fiancé, is attempting to distract herself by speculating about the unnamed couple.

The woman who sat next to me squirmed, her short jet-black hair sprouting blond roots. She had walked in with black manicured nails with white pelicans painted in the center. But at the rate she was chewing on them, the lower halves of the pelicans were surely crippled by now. . . .

The tattooed man with her, his shoulder-length hair also dyed jet black, kept saying, "Damn, you gone bite your hand off before we even get in there."

The engagement ring on her finger made me wonder if Tattoo Man might have a pocket full of bubble gum, since I was reasonably sure the ring didn't pop out on the first try.

By 4:10 P.M. when Kenneth still hadn't shown, I asked Tattoo Man and Biting Nails, "Excuse me. Got any chewing gum?"

Despite the tears stinging the corners of my eyes, I almost burst into laughter when he pulled out a handful of colorful balls.

[pp. 11–12]

Since few waiting room encounters include an exchange of names, Coleman's use of epithets is logical. It's also creative: Tattoo Man and Biting Nails are more artful than "the man and the woman."

NAMING JUST FOR FUN

In the first mystery by Deb Baker, *Murder Passes the Buck,* naming is a running joke. It's also a source of conflict between Gertie, wannabe sleuth, and her son, Blaze, the sheriff. Gertie had named her three offspring to remind her of the horses she never had and her husband refused to own. But the sheriff wants his mother to call him Brian, a "real" name.

His sister Star takes up his cause:

"Ma, nobody takes him seriously. Sometimes they call him Bucky or Bronco to tease him. But he's tried to change it to Brian for years. Where have you been?"

"I've been busy."

My other kids never complained about the names I chose for them. Star and Heather were happy, so I couldn't figure Blaze out. Blaze is a nice name—original, manly. "He has a John Wayne name," I said.

"He has John Wayne's horse's name," Star said.

SOUNDS LIKE?

A sure way to confuse readers is to assign names that begin with the same letter, look similar in print, or have sounds in common, like Barton and Baxter, or Megan, Marilyn, and Margaret. Three that I kept tripping over in one best-seller are Jackie, Richie, and Teddy. Better to use only one of a sound-alike set per book and save the others until each can have a book of one's own. (Apologies to Virginia Woolf.)

Also avoid hard-to-pronounce names. Or do as Shelly Reuben does in her Fritillary Quilter mystery series: limit the unusual name to an attention-grabbing introduction, then switch to a simple form of it throughout: Tilly.

In some manuscripts, names tend to sound alike because they call up

> [U]ntil I was 20 or so, all the characters I invented had WASP names—names like Mitch Mitchell, Robert Robertson, Elizabeth Anderson, Bob Briggs. . . . None of the kids I grew up with had such names. They were all Weinbergers and Hamburgers and Blotniks and Briskins and Friskins. There were even some Singhs and Tsongs. . . . The Mitchells in my high school class could be counted on the digits of one severely frostbitten foot, or one leprous hand. But they were in all my stories.
>
> Erica Jong, "The Artist as Housewife"[52]

images that look alike. I'm referring to the novels in which every character bears an Anglo-Saxon name. Acquisitions editors value diversity. A steady diet of white bread could suggest that the writer's outlook and range of experience in the real world are a tad narrow.

Let's distinguish between two kinds of ethnic naming in American fiction. One is based on the write-what-you-know axiom; the other, on the melting pot phenomenon. When you write from what you know, your characterizations are authentic, and the names you assign represent individuals whose cultural heritage permeates their values, actions, and interactions.

A good example of ethnic authenticity is seen in Lydia Chin, one of S. J. Rozan's two alternating lead characters. Rozan's portrayal of Lydia's family and community goes much deeper than the mother's addressing her daughter by her Chinese name, Ling Wan-ju. The following passage is from *A Bitter Feast,* fifth in Rozan's award-winning series.

> "Yang Hao-Bing thought I was a very well brought up young lady," I said, following her and the food.
>
> "He did?" She sniffed, but I could see she'd felt the compliment. Emptying the grocery bag, she said, "Perhaps, as wise as he is, he can see the great effort even when the results are poor."
>
> I suddenly realized how I could make a gold mine out of this.
>
> "What he wanted, Ma," I said while I dumped the tofu into the brine-filled container we keep for it in the fridge, "was to tell me he's been following my career. He wanted to express his satisfaction at how well I'm doing. He's very pleased at the fact that my work keeps me in Chinatown."

> Her eyes widened involuntarily; otherwise, she kept her
> attention on the bok choy as she peeled off its outer leaves. "If
> Yan Hao-Bing has been following your activities, Ling Wan-ju,
> you have drawn too much attention to yourself."
>
> "He said Chinatown's future was in young people like me.
> Also like Lee Bi-Da." I thought I'd haul Peter in under H. B.
> Yang's umbrella while I could. "Young people who stay here,
> who put our talents into helping the community. The way we
> would if this were our village in China."
>
> "If this were our village in China your future would be with
> the husband from the next village I would have found for you
> by now. . . ."   [pp. 98–99]

Rozan does her homework. She reads widely, has many Chinese friends, and spends much time in lower Manhattan's Chinatown.[53] Her award-winning books are populated with interesting, credible, three-dimensional characters. Some, like Lydia, reflect the outlook of the ABC generation: American-born Chinese. Others, like Lydia's mother, are infused with old world values.

If either your heritage or your research does not measure up to Rozan's level of authenticity, don't fake it. Editors and other readers know stereotypes when we see them. However, if you lack specialized knowledge of another culture does not mean you have to purge all traces of diversity from your manuscript. That's where the second type of ethnic naming comes in. It is based on a reality that touches the daily lives of all but the most reclusive writer.

RAINBOW COALITION

The reality of America's melting pot is that people of color and folks with ethnic surnames fill nearly every role in society. This means you could name secondary characters Felipe Ricardo and Lucia Campanello just as easily as naming them Phil Richards and Lucy Bell, even though you would portray their friends and coworkers calling them Phil and Lucy anyway.

If minor characters are not fully developed major players, their cultural heritage and family background are not expected to be relevant to the story.

Tokenism? Yes. Superficial? Absolutely. Seeding your manuscript with an ethnic-sounding name or two is admittedly a form of tokenism. But think about the alternative. Considering America's multicultural history, the *absence* of ethnic surnames from a contemporary novel is unrealistic. So is a monochromatic cast of characters.

Please don't misunderstand; token name-dropping is *not* acceptable for primary characters. Someone whose life is unaffected by his or her upbringing and cultural values is ill-suited for the role of a well-rounded major character.

Minor roles, on the other hand, can be filled by almost anyone, just as in real life. You won't need to adjust the role to "fit" the name, either, provided you don't go beyond writing what you know—or what you can accurately research and have verified by someone knowledgeable.

A computer search-and-replace that substitutes "Anatole Smolansky" for "Nate Smith" won't convince anyone you're a sensitive soul. But substitution will add a little diversity to a WASP monopoly that itself misrepresents the realism for which the aware, observant writer strives.

FIND & FIX CLUE #18: MULTIPLE IDENTITIES

- Review your character list to see who does not need both a first and a last name.
- Introduce characters one at a time, preferably as part of an action that makes a memorable impression.
- Prevent confusion; avoid names with similar letter combinations or sounds.
- Explore the possibilities for distinctive nicknames and catchy epithets.
- Double-check that characters are consistent in how they address each other, and that variations occur for a reason, such as to suggest a special relationship or a changing attitude.
- Evaluate the ways your manuscript reflects the ethnic and racial diversity of the story's universe.

D.O.A.

CLUE #19: STRANGLED SPEECH

Writers often prepare multi-page profiles to help keep their characters from looking alike, yet many of those profiles are silent when it comes to keeping those characters from sounding alike. Entire populations of fictional characters seem endowed by their creators with the same vocabulary, grammar, and phrasing.

In editing one mystery manuscript, I sensed the same three-word expression occurring a little too often: "Why don't you—." I pursued my hunch with a computer search and found the identical expression coming from the mouths of three different characters. A minor point, surely, but it signals a pervasive problem: a writer who creates all roles in her or his own voice, and fails to think of characters as individuals with their own voices. Strangled speech.

How many of us are conscious of our own speaking habits? It's hard enough to express *what* we mean without thinking about the *how*. As a writer of fiction, you need to do both, distinguishing your characters from each other by their grammar, syntax, idioms, regional expressions, and level of formality or informality.

> "Technique is the ability to reproduce what your ear wants to hear."
>
> Barry Weinberg, pianist and teacher, stating a variation on a theme of Leon Fleisher

Read your dialogue aloud and listen for the sounds your readers will hear. Subtle, individualized speaking styles help establish your characters' authenticity, demonstrate their personalities, and occasionally furnish comic relief. Not having all the folks in a novel sound alike adds interest, reflects their places of origin, suggests educational levels, and shows relationships. Authenticity is good for your characters and for the ears of your readers— especially your first reader, the busy screener-outer.

SUBTLETY IN SPEECH

In a scene from John D. MacDonald's *The Deep Blue Good-by,* his first-written Travis McGee novel, Travis uses a minor ruse to get a boatyard employee to look up an order placed by a suspect. Tension is minimal and conflict non-existent. Sounds dull, doesn't it? But MacDonald gives the employee habits of speech that expand her characterization and add humor.

> "We're not really open," she said.
> "I just wanted to check on a generator that was ordered, find out if it has come in yet."
> She sighed as though I had asked her to hike to Duluth. "Who placed the order?" Sigh.
>
> . . . .
>
> She took the card out and frowned at it. . . . "Goodness, it should be in by now."
> "Doesn't it say on the card?"
> "No, it doesn't say on the card." Sigh. "All I can tell from the card is that it hasn't been delivered or installed." Sigh.
> "Does the card say who handled the order?"
> "Of course the card says who handled the order." Sigh. "Mr. Wicker. He isn't here today."
> "Joe Wicker?"
> "No. Howard Wicker. But people call him Hack."
> "Do you keep a running list of the boats you have in?"
> "Of course we keep a running list of the boats we have in." Sigh. "Down at the dock office."
> "Of course you keep a running list of the boats you have in. Down at the dock office. Thanks a lot."
> She looked momentarily disconcerted.   [p. 95]

Not only does the office worker have two habits, sighing and echoing, but Travis gently mimics one of them, and it produces a reaction that unsettles her. That final exchange adds a fresh dimension to this scene.

In your own fiction, have your main character speak normally—a technique that helps readers identify with the protagonist. Use slightly distinctive voices for your other characters.

Beware of presenting too many idiosyncrasies at a time, repeating them too often, or making them too noticeable. Limit the number of characters in a scene with noticeable speech habits. If one person is a source of colorful regionalisms, another might exhibit lapses in grammar appropriate to his background. Make those roles brief or keep the habit's frequency to a minimum.

Use moderation —a little flavoring goes a long way.

A small amount of conspicuous is . . . er, conspicuous. Here's why.

When we talk with someone face to face, all kinds of stimuli compete for our attention, and we tend not to listen closely. We're distracted by background activity. We're thinking of what we want to say next. We're watching the speaker's gestures. And we're noticing the other's touched-up hair, turned-up nose, turned-down hose.

When we *read* dialogue, especially when it's well written, our attention is focused. Eccentricities on the page are magnified. Bizarre speech habits applied with a heavy hand become absurd; at best, they annoy. For this reason, unless you are writing comedy, limit how often any one character exhibits a noticeable speech pattern.

SPEECH AS SPICE

Whereas Travis McGee encounters sighing and echoing with one very minor character in one scene, the next example presents a secondary character who appears in several scenes and repeats several different expressions, but his appearances are occasional and brief, and not one repetition is overdone.

The book is *Doctored Evidence,* first in Michael Biehl's medical mysteries featuring hospital attorney Karen Hayes. Karen is married to a musician whose easygoing, laid-back approach to life is conveyed through an occasional "No problema" and "No importa." He answers the phone "Y-y-y-ello"—a melody that can be heard from the spelling alone. Distinctive, yet infrequent enough for effect.

Another type of distinctive speech can be seen in *Bad Luck,* Suzanne Proulx's second mystery featuring Victoria Lucci. The name of the series character is pronounced "Lucky"—something Victoria is not. A hospital risk manager, she has just taken the risk of offering a ride to the talkative street urchin whose cat she accidentally hit with a borrowed SUV.

The girl tells Victoria she's a witch.

Right. "I guess you're psychic, too."

"Only a little bit, sometimes, yeah. I mean, like, I can't
tell you what the Lotto numbers are gonna be."

More's the pity. "So that's how you knew I was a lawyer?" I
glance at her as I say this. She looks puzzled.

"Well, no, you know, like, I thought you told me that."

"I don't think so."

"One way or another," she says, "you told me. So, like, yeah,
I'm psychic, I know I am, some other things have happened.
Like. . . . "   [p. 14]

Proulx showcases Victoria's sardonic style by having her react to what
the girl says and how she says it. The technique expands the author's characterization of her protagonist.

Be cautious using slang and other contemporary expressions because
they could date your writing, although "I mean, like" could be safe to use;
it has been around for the past fifteen years or so and might continue for,
like, the next fifteen. More's the pity.

EAVESDROP

To make the dialogue you write sound original and credible, not stereotyped, start by reviewing your character profiles. Know how you want an
individual's speech to reflect place of birth, social class, education, job-
related jargon, and gender. Instead of telling readers about a character's
background, show the influence of that background through his or her style
of speech. Fit grammar to education and fit slang to age and lifestyle. Tiny
details add authenticity.

To gather those details, eavesdrop in places you might ordinarily over-
look. Sit next to families in the waiting room at the Social Security office
and the hospital emergency room. Listen for the vernacular—regional expressions, idioms, and everyday colloquialisms. Tune in to call-in radio.
Hang around the Kmart exit. Stand in line at the symphony and the Stop &
Shop—or should I say *on* line? Depends where you grew up. South Boston
doesn't sound like South Dakota or South L.A., and no place on earth sounds
like the South Bronx or South M'waukee.

Here's an expression I saw in a newspaper that quoted a North Carolina
cable television provider discussing costs:

"[P]rogramming kept going up every year and it put a hurtin'
on us."

Cindy Daniel keeps her Hannah Fogarty mystery series lively with expressions of the fictional folk of Destiny, Texas. In *Death Warmed Over,*
the first book of the series, Hannah says of her sister:

> . . . and before you could blink an eye Ruth was in deeper than
> a rancher's boot in a full pasture.   [p. 1]

The idea is not to scatter expressions throughout your story like
wildflower seeds, but to select specimen plants for deliberate effect in
choice locations.

In *Lavender Lies,* Susan Wittig Albert has her protagonist, China
Bayles, observe that the mayor of her small Texas town had "looked a
little hot under the collar," to which a local lawyer replies:

> "Hot as a ten-dollar whore on the Fourth of July."   [p. 53]

Here's the voice of one of the locals in Vicki Lane's first Elizabeth
Goodweather mystery, *Signs in the Blood:*

> A gaunt chain-smoking woman, just off her factory shift, set
> down a cardboard tub of fried chicken with a dismissive wave
> of her cigarette. "It ain't but Colonel Sanders but I reckon
> someone kin worry it down."   [p. 1]

You won't use all your field research, and you won't use it verbatim, but
eavesdropping will help you hear voices in your head other than your own.

DIALECT

In the late nineteenth century, the writings of Bret Harte and Mark Twain
popularized the trend toward local color, but these literary giants went too
far. Today it's a chore to read the authors of a century ago who tried to
reproduce what the ear seemed to hear. That's because written dialect, though
intended for the ear, is seen first with the eyes, which perceive strange
spellings and prolific apostrophes as obstacles to reading.

Inexperienced writers who represent dialect phonetically always overdo
it. Use restraint with pronunciation—great restraint. To simulate a character's

habit of dropping the final letter of -*ing* words, do so only rarely to give readers the general idea without burdening them with a faithful rendering.

Much more original and effective than dropped letters and other efforts to reproduce pronunciation are the colorful idioms and expressions that perceptive writers put in the mouths of their characters. The examples you see here merely suggest the range of possible techniques.

The regional speech of New Orleans was captured by John Kennedy Toole in his mainstream novel, *A Confederacy of Dunces.*

> "Oh, Miss Inez," Mrs. Reilly called in that accent that occurs south of New Jersey only in New Orleans, that Hoboken near the Gulf of Mexico. "Over here, babe."
>
> "Hey, how you making?" Miss Inez asked. "How you feeling, darling?"
>
> "Not so hot," Mrs. Reilly answered truthfully.
>
> "Ain't that a shame." Miss Inez leaned over the glass case and forgot about her cakes. "I don't feel so hot myself. It's my feet."
>
> "Lord, I wisht I was that lucky. I got arthuritis in my elbow."
>
> "Aw, no!" Miss Inez said with genuine sympathy. "My poor old poppa's got that. We make him go set himself in a hot tub fulla berling water."   [p. 16]

Only a few odd spellings occur to simulate pronunciation. Instead, Toole's book is flavored with the idiosyncratic sounds of New Orleans' expressions, grammar, word choices, and content.

The following anecdote has been told many times, but if it inspires one writer who hasn't heard it before, the repetition is worth it.

John Kennedy Toole was thirty-two when he killed himself in despair over constant rejection of his novel. For the next ten years his mother persisted in circulating his manuscript. Eventually she succeeded in finding a publisher.[54] Shortly after *A Confederacy of Dunces* was published in 1980, it won a Pulitzer.

Patrick Bone reflects the dialect of the backwoods of Appalachia in his first crime novel for adults, *A Melungeon Winter.* Set in the 1950s, the novel shows friendship rising above the racial prejudices of the times.

> "Best be to your manners," my grandmother warned us when she came to visit us from Texas. "Old dark man's gonna come for you lessen you mind your elders and pay attention. Best be to your manners, now."
> The worst part of the warning? The consequences. "He gonna put you in a gunnysack and tote you off. Old dark man gets hungry, he eats you." [p. v]

With only two spelling variants, "gonna" and "lessen," Bone gets his most powerful effects from expressions, grammar, syntax, and that all-important element, content.

In the mysteries of Charles Todd, a Scottish burr distinguishes the speech of Hamish, a voice of conscience that invades the thoughts of a Scotland Yard inspector returned from the hell of World War I. Beginning with *A Test of Wills,* the first title in the Inspector Ian Rutledge series, Hamish's voice is a continual source of conflict and anxiety for Rutledge.

> "Ye'll no' triumph over me!" Hamish said. "I'm a scar on your bluidy soul." [p. 328]

Because readers experience Hamish entirely through his speech, his voice has to be distinctive. *It is.*

The Southern expressions found in Margaret Maron's Judge Deborah Knott series, which is set in a fictional county in North Carolina, are infrequent and subtle. Take this line from *Bootlegger's Daughter,* Maron's first mystery novel, and the first novel ever to win the "big four" in mystery awards: the Edgar, Agatha, Anthony, and Macavity.

> "Your brothers: both free to come and go without punching time cards or anybody keeping tabs on them. They alibied each other for Wednesday, which we might could question. . . ." [p. 62]

To the non-Southerner, the "might could" construction is so unexpected that a New York editor would be remiss in not querying whether the usage

is intentional or accidental. Intentional it is, because Maron excels in characterization (and because New Yorkers, of which I'm one, have much to
learn about Southern dialect).

Tamar Myers uses the same idiom in *The Ming and I,* the third mystery
in her Den of Antiquity series. She also has her narrator, South Carolina
antique dealer Abigail Timberlake, comment on that distinctive usage.

> "Well, Gloria, you certainly have a point. But we might could
> squeeze a little extra out of petty cash, if we tried really hard."
> Please don't misunderstand. "Might could" is a perfectly proper
> speech construct in Rock Hill.   [p. 47]

For your own characters, your comfort level might lie somewhere between the rare *might coulds* and *gonnas,* and the more vigorous *arthuritis*
and *berling water.* Whichever styles work for you, representing believable
voices takes astute listening, judicious selecting, and restrained writing.
And, of course, scrupulous self-editing.

GRAMMAR, ETC.

Depending on how you use it, ungrammatical language can make a character sound like an average Joe or an unqualified jerk. In *Final Jeopardy,* a
Macavity award nominee, Linda Fairstein uses grammar as part of her characterization of the good-looking stud who'd been sleeping with Isabella,
now deceased. This novel is first in the series featuring Alexandra Cooper,
sex crimes prosecutor for the Manhattan D.A.'s office.

> "So did Iz talk about me a lot?"
> "She told me a lot about you, yes."
> "Good things, mostly?" he said jokingly. "We had some
> kinda good times together, her and me."
> The English major in me winced. He may have been great
> in bed, but his syntax was as atrocious as his manners. He was
> shoving the bread in his mouth each time he came up for air,
> rinsing it down with the vodka.
> "Did Isabella tell you how we met and everything? We was
> a hot ticket for a while."
> Enough about me, now talk about what Iz thought about me.
> This was going to be a long evening.   [p. 229]

The reader's impression of this murder suspect evolves not only by hearing how he speaks but also by observing a total complex of behaviors, from his egotism in what he says to the repulsiveness of his table manners—a visual image to parallel the spoken image.

> "What sense is it we use for writing? It's hearing. Writing is listening, and reading is listening, too."
>
> Margaret Edson, Pulitzer prize-winning playwright

As you revise, use your growing awareness of speaking styles to differentiate your characters—in moderation. Naturally, all dialogue should sound . . . well, natural. If this seems like a lot of work, it *is*. You are attempting to create human-like beings who don't sound like clones of each other. That's about as difficult to do on paper as in a petri dish.

SOCIAL COMMENTARY

A brief scene in *My Sweet Untraceable You,* Sandra Scoppettone's third novel featuring P. I. Lauren Laurano, shows Lauren forming an opinion about a couple sitting behind her in a SoHo coffeehouse. An overheard speech habit says a lot to her about the couple's relationship, insight Lauren has gotten from the observations of Kip, her lesbian partner, a psychotherapist.

> "You've never seen film noir, that's what you're telling me? Is that right, Chasilee?"
> "What I'm telling you is that I don't know?"
> "How can you not know? Either you have or you haven't."
> "The thing is, if I have seen it, I wouldn't know I'd seen it?"
> She is one of these women who end every sentence like a question even when it's a statement. Kip's reading on this is total insecurity. I hope she's wrong because if she's right then many people under thirty are insecure. And it's mostly women. Sigh.
> He says, "They're black-and-white films."
> "I've seen those?"
> "Yes, but they're not just black-and-white, I mean there are lots of B-and-W films that aren't noir. Noir is a style. . . .
>
> [p. 127]

Lauren's observation is tempered by sardonic humor.

> I sense the people behind me stand, hear their chairs scrape
> against the tile floor. I look to my right, stalling and curious.
>   She looks sixteen, but is probably in her early twenties, long
> blond hair, pretty; and predictably, he's in his fifties, shorts,
> Gap T-shirt, paunch. Why? What does she want from this guy?
> And isn't he bored? He does what they all do, encircles her
> waist with a possessive arm: I am virile man and give her a
> good time, even though I'm old enough to be her father.
>
> [p. 129]

Lauren's commentary on people who choose unequal relationships, based
on an overheard conversation and a characteristic speech inflection, serves
to deepen Scoppettone's portrayal of her series character.

Sometimes, despite your efforts, the dialogue you write comes across as
weak and ineffectual, and no technique manages to differentiate one character from another. The problem might not lie in a speaking style but in the
characters themselves. They might not be fully materialized for you as individuals—each with his or her own agenda.

It takes a while to reach the state that authors refer to as their characters
taking over and speaking for themselves. Face it, some characters never
do. They need more than a good talking to; they need rubbing out.

FIND & FIX CLUE #19: STRANGLED SPEECH

➡ Review your character profiles to "hear" how each character sounds and to reflect that character's background in his or her speech.

➡ Have someone read snatches of your dialogue aloud to you in random order, without any identifying tags, to see if you can tell your characters apart by the tone, grammar, vocabulary, sentence structure, and expressions you give them.

➡ Cultivate your ear for speech patterns by eavesdropping and picking up the different ways that ordinary people express themselves.

➡ Use the barest minimum of phonetic spellings, *if any,* to merely suggest a character's pronunciation.

➡ Avoid unusual punctuation and dropped letters.

➡ Use contractions that reflect common usage and a natural conversational style.

"In composing, as a general rule, run your pen through
every other word you have written; you
have no idea what vigor it will give your style."

Sydney Smith, founder in the early 19th century of
The Edinburgh Review [55]

CLUE #20: KILLED BY CLICHÉ

Dull as dishwater. That's both a cliché and a style of writing that litters manuscripts with expressions that lost their freshness and originality a long time ago. Sleuths are always waiting for minutes that seem like an hour, or for hours that seem like an eternity. One character is sure to be described as having hooded eyelids. And at least once per book, a frown creases somebody's brow.

Unfortunately, hackneyed expressions are not limited to the work of neophytes. One evening when I relaxed with a highly acclaimed medical thriller, I came across a description of an autopsy room as a beehive of activity and the new widow as wearing a ton of makeup. The investigating officer managed to fan his partner's anxiety to a fevered pitch, and another character felt that her fears had come to pass.

The clichés continued, each drawing part of my attention away from the story. Determined to discover why this clumsy, verbose author was so popular, I forced myself to spend two hours slogging through his best-seller before giving up. Each hour seemed like an eternity.

The popularity of this author and others like him should not make you complacent about your own forms of expression. It takes only a cliché or two on the opening pages of your submission to cause a frown to crease the brow of a busy screener.

INTENTIONAL TRITENESS

When you self-edit your manuscript, make an extra pass to catch all of its outworn, overworked expressions. Change them or get rid of them—with one exception: where you use them deliberately, as with characterization or parody.

For example, in Babs Lakey's first mystery thriller, *Spirit of the Straightedge,* the killer says:

> I felt proud of my self-control. *If it's worth doing, it's worth doing it right,* squawked a parrot-like cliché.   [p. 16]

Lakey acknowledges the saying as a cliché and makes fun of it, leaving no doubt that its inclusion is not an oversight. It's parody.

At times, an overused expression captures the perfect metaphor to sum up a novel's theme. Lisa Polisar makes use of that metaphor when introducing the killer in her first psychological thriller, *Black Water Tango.*

> Some men are capable of just one crime. One crime that evolves out of a crack in the glue of sanity and righteousness that binds together the healthy balance between the human heart and mind. And this crack happens as the result of one incident, one betrayal, a proverbial straw on the camel's back.
>
>   [p. 1]

In addition to calling attention to this overworked metaphor, Polisar demonstrates its usefulness to her novel's theme and gives it a fresh twist.

Similarly, Anne Rivers Siddons acknowledges the triteness of her method of describing a neighbor in *The House Next Door.*

> The man's voice was distinctly southern New Jersey, but his face, as the cliché goes, was the very map of Ireland.   [p. 84]

CLICHÉ AS CHARACTERIZATION

When clichés are confined to dialogue, their occurrence is interpreted as the writer's way of revealing something about the character who utters them. Like any idiosyncrasy, an impoverished vocabulary is representative of its speaker. To maximize the effectiveness of this speech habit, limit it to one role.

The next example departs from that recommendation by showing two rival law enforcement officers intentionally throwing a succession of trite sayings at each other. These duets are brief, however, and occur in only two scenes out of the many in which the two men interact. The following passages are taken from *Framework for Death,* the second Tory Travers/David Alvarez mystery by Aileen Schumacher. One speaker is the series character, Detective Alvarez, a Texan. The interloper is a federal drug enforcement agent from the Midwest. The bilingual Alvarez speaks first.

"I hate to rain on your New Year's parade, but I think you're
barking up the wrong tree. There's more weird shit to this case
than a three-dollar bill, but I don't think your guy did his wife."
    There was a pause. "Do you always talk like that?"
    "Only when I speak English. My partner taught me all the
clichés I know."   [p. 149]

Five chapters later the federal agent returns to the verbal contest.

"But there's no point sitting here crying over spilt milk,
while Boyce is out there making hay. See, I've been working
on some midwestern clichés for you."
    "Before we move on to greener pastures, so to speak, one last
thing. . . ."   [p. 217]

Alvarez again gets the last word.

Schumacher's technique functions on multiple levels. First, on the literal level the dialogue continues the men's discussion of the case. Second,
their verbal banter expands their rivalry into the arena of repartee. Third, as
characterization, that repartee shows the pair of crime-fighters equally
matched in quick-wittedness. Fourth, as entertainment, Schumacher's
parody is a tour de force proving the richness of her writing style.

CLICHÉ AS PLOT

A clichéd plot won't cause the immediate death of your submission,
because plot defects don't show up right away. Still, to round out our discussion of triteness, we ought to take a look at some clichéd situations.
"The butler did it" may not apply to your novel, either because it includes
no butler or you're aware of the jokes about this much-maligned domestic
servant. But many writers are basing their plots on scenarios such as these:

- the wrongly accused who is saved by the arrival of a long-lost
  twin;
- the sole witness for the prosecution who decides to walk her dog
  the night before she testifies and is not seen again (though Buster
  is found in a dumpster);
- the prostitute who will quit the profession as soon as she saves
  enough to become a real mom to the baby she gave up years ago;

●❖ the phone caller who has urgent information for the sleuth, but for some never-explained reason can't talk about it on the phone, and whose corpse the sleuth stumbles over, in great surprise, when he arrives for their clandestine meeting only an hour later;

●❖ the sleuth who is tied up and about to be killed when she cajoles her captor into bragging about the details of his crimes (which no one would otherwise know), and who is rescued at the very moment the killer conveniently supplies the final clue to his guilt;

●❖ the gorgeous blonde who slithers her way into the run-down office of a deep-in-debt, wisecracking private investigator, and in a husky voice tells him. . . .

You've been there before, often, so I'm sure you can think of many more examples. The clichéd situation, like the clichéd expression, is good for one thing—parody.

J. L. Abramo spoofs a medley of classic P. I. stereotypes in his Jake Diamond series, achieving both humor and intrigue. Here is the opening to Abramo's *Catching Water in a Net,* a Shamus award-winner for best first private eye novel.

The phone on my desk rang so unexpectedly that I nearly spilled the Mylanta onto my only unstained necktie.

It was my trusty assistant calling from her sentry post out front.

. . . .

"There's a woman here to see you."

I'd figured we had a guest. The place was small. Usually when Darlene wanted me she just hollered.

"Count to twenty, Darlene, and send her in," I said, determining that we were on a secure line.

"Is that one, two or one Mississippi, two Mississippi?"

I quickly assessed the condition of the desk.

"Make it one Montgomery, Alabama, two Montgomery, Alabama."

I tossed the bottle of Mylanta into the top drawer along with the plastic ashtray, remembering for a change to extinguish the burning cigarette. I opened a few dummy file folders and spread them across the desktop. No reason everyone had to know how slow business had been lately. I buried my face in the top folder, which incidentally held an unfriendly reminder from my ex-wife's attorney regarding past due alimony payments.

You've been here before, too, but never so imaginatively as listening to the dialogue taking place in the two-room office of Diamond Investigation. Jake asks his new client how he can help.

> "It's my husband."
> If I had ten cents for every time I've heard that phrase I could have all three ties dry-cleaned.
> "I can't find him," she added.
> "I assure you, Mrs. Harding, he's not here."
> "What?"
> "It's a joke I use to relax new clients."
> "It doesn't work."
> "I can see that. How long has your husband been missing, Evelyn?"
> "Since Saturday evening."
> "That would be four days."
> "I can see now why you came so highly recommended."
> Evelyn Harding was as personable as an Office Depot catalog.   [pp. 3–5]

APPRAISING PHRASING

The time to root out the wretched expressions from your writing is not when they fly from your fingertips as you romance the keyboard. Any words that come readily to mind serve as handy surrogates for thoughts that might vanish if you stop to self-edit. Clichés are shorthand that can help you get your first draft committed to paper or pixels. So keep writing; revising comes later. That's when you dump the dull-as-dishwater expressions and replace them with fresh.

Writers unable to distinguish the worn-out from the fresh might also be oblivious to what editors call a *howler:* the comical result of using an expression with a figurative meaning in a context that unexpectedly brings out its literal meaning.

> Whenever the boss's son walked in, Waldo was deep in thought, eyes closed. The young man would always say, "Stop daydreaming and get to work, Pops. You act like you got Alzheimer's."
> Waldo had half a mind to prove the kid wrong.

Detecting your own howlers and killer clichés is not easy. The computer program has yet to be designed that can redline outdated, gray-haired expressions. Without graydar, the next best way to detect overused expressions is with a thorough line edit of your manuscript.

One writer, whose book-length manuscript showed great storytelling skill, said he learned a great deal from his first editing experience about techniques he'd never been aware of. He wrote: "An avid reader does not necessarily make for a knowledgeable writer."

To get the most value from a professional edit, use it as a learning tool. Make a list of all the comments, recommendations, and kinds of weaknesses that editing points out to you. Add to it the specific expressions you use that others identify as clichés. Refer to the list when you self-edit your next manuscript.

DEADER THAN A DOORNAIL

Mark my words: expressions as old as the hills are the kiss of death. First and foremost, they cast a pall over your writing and yank the rug out from under your labor of love in the blink of an eye. They offer proof positive that the writer is wet behind the ears. If you've heard it once you've heard it a million times: one rotten apple can spoil the barrel.

Unless you are bending over backwards to tickle your reader's fancy, don't shoot yourself in the foot with those tried and true expressions. Needless to say, forewarned is forearmed. Last but not least is this hard and fast rule of thumb: avoid clichés like the plague.

FIND & FIX CLUE #20: KILLED BY CLICHÉ

- Eliminate as many trite expressions in your writing as you can find and get help in finding the rest of them.
- If a cliché benefits your story in some way, acknowledge its use so it doesn't seem like an oversight.
- Verify that any clichés used in dialogue are consistent with that character's speech pattern and the personality you want to project.
- Treat clichés in dialogue as you would any distinctive speech habit: sparingly—which requires being aware during self-editing of every word you've written.

"Only a few writers take the time to learn about style, and usually they learn it after studying everything else about writing. Smart writers, though, create a crisp style and produce tight, polished manuscripts that pull ahead of the pack. . . . If style makes the difference, why don't all writers improve their style and succeed in any way they define success? Simple. Few people have the capacity to evaluate their own writing."

Bobbie Christmas, *Write In Style* [56]

CLUE #21: GESTURED TO DEATH

Gestures are handy little devices that anchor characters in their settings and furnish quickie images for readers to visualize. Because everything in a mystery exists for a reason, the well-crafted gesture, mannerism, or display of body language is purposeful.

That purpose is to enhance meaning by suggesting what a character may be doing or feeling at the moment.

Regrettably, most submissions suffer from what I call *gesturitis,* a glut of pointless, stereotyped movements. One character paused and took a deep breath, another wiped away a tear. He ran a hand through his hair. A frown creased her brow. He nodded and smiled. She shrugged and shook her head. They sighed and sat down. She laughed and stood up. He smiled and looked around. She looked at him. He looked out the window. I yawned.

The same predictable busyness fills manuscript after manuscript, none of it adding insight or characterization. On the contrary, under such a burden of meaningless perpetual motion, plot and character differences fade.

Identical images and phrasing make the majority of submissions seem written by the same person. Busy screeners get a sense of *déjà view*—the feeling that they are viewing the work of the same writer day after day.

VALUE ADDED

When revising your manuscript, take a good look at the gestures and mannerisms you assign.

- Do they add value to the story by deepening your characterization?
- Or do they merely add an assortment of tics and fidgets?

Know why you select one gesture over another. Analyze the function you want each to serve. Characterize the whole person.

231

. . . Like many a cop, he could say all this through his teeth, barely parting his lips. It's an art.

Max Allan Collins, *Blood and Thunder*   [pp. 26-27]

Kate said, "You probably know the ins and outs of all the careers."

Kate could measure the flattery when he hooked both thumbs in his jeans pockets and rolled forward from the hips.

Cecelia Tishy, *Jealous Heart,* first mystery novel   [p. 45]

Make each observation fresh and original, like these from *Monkeewrench,* the first mystery from P. J. Tracy.

Bonar sucked at the inside of his cheek for a minute, thick eyebrows working like a pair of caterpillars.   [p. 6]

The priest looked up, found his memory on the ceiling.

[p. 9]

Gestures often take the form of beats or tags to accompany dialogue. But they are not mere substitutes for *he said/she said.* An effective mannerism or glimpse of body language can build tension and reveal feelings or attitudes that a character keeps hidden or is unaware of.

. . . He carried a cap in his hands that looked several sizes too big for him, which he kept mashing together and pulling apart as if it were an accordion.

Martha Grimes, *I Am the Only Running Footman* [p. 213]

Little behaviors not only add meaning to what is said; they also imply what isn't.

"You know what gets me?" Kate said. The coffee Owen had poured for her was getting cold.

Deborah Adams, *All the Great Pretenders*   [p. 213]

. . . He smiled a rueful Baptist minister smile.

Walter Sorrells, *Will to Murder*   [p. 20]

Body language can show contradictions between spoken words and unspoken feelings.

> "Sure, I'd be happy to do that." She bit her lip.

Avoid mannerisms that can be interchanged with any of a dozen others without affecting the story. If a gesture does no more than mirror the words it accompanies it is redundant.

> "That's very puzzling." He frowned and scratched his head.
> "It sure is," she said, nodding in agreement.

Almost every manuscript submitted by a first-time writer contains more than one "nodding in agreement," further reinforcing the "yes" effect of nonconfrontational, symmetrical dialogue (CLUE #16). Repetitive, meaningless, empty gestures weaken a manuscript. Weak writing quickly becomes uninteresting, and uninteresting writing remains unpublished.

SHOWING NOT TELLING

Meaningful body language allows readers to draw their own conclusions about a character's feelings instead of your interpreting those feelings for them.

> The detective looked like he didn't believe me.

This is the narrator telling us that the detective was doubtful. Maybe the writer doesn't know what not believing looks like and hasn't given it much thought. *Telling* is easy; *showing* takes imagination.

Catherine Coulter uses both showing and telling in the following example from *The Edge,* fourth in her FBI series featuring Ford MacDougal.

> Detective Castanga didn't believe me. He turned to Laura, a
> dark eyebrow cocked up a good inch.   [p. 148]

If for whatever reason you cannot show the appropriate body language, at least try to come up with a creative representation of it—which is how Coulter handles another of Mac's observations.

> Detective Castanga slowly straightened. He was surprised, I
> could see it in the sudden twitch in his cheek, the slight hitch in
> his breathing.   [p. 147]

There's more than one way to present a "look" even if you can't quite
describe it. Here's one from Denise Swanson's *Murder of a Small-Town
Honey,* nominee for an Agatha award for best first mystery novel.

> . . . Glancing at her as if she were something he'd scraped off
> the bottom of his shoe, the boy selected the biggest stone from
> his pile and threw it as hard as he could.   [p. 51]

Originality counts. Here's a look Chassie West offers in *Sunrise:*

> . . . Mr. Sheriff gazed at me as if my pilot light had gone out.
>   [p. 61]

Metaphors and similes offer unlimited opportunities for bringing creativity to your gestures. Walter Sorrells offers this comparison in *Will to
Murder:*

> . . . He looked blanched and worn for a minute, like laundry
> that had been out on the line too long.   [p. 31]

In *Prime Witness,* Steve Martini shows this response by a D. A. to a
defense attorney's probing:

> . . . He stops in mid sentence, calms down and looks at me. "I
> am assuming," he says, "that the witness is a male?" He stands
> there, a big-eyed question mark.
>   I offer him the social intercourse of a chimney brick.
>   [pp. 277–78]

SUBTLETY OF GESTURE

The next series of excerpts comes from Elizabeth George's fifth novel
in the Thomas Lynley and Barbara Havers series, *For the Sake of Elena.*
Unobtrusive gestures show how the author's two New Scotland Yard de-
tectives feel about an elusive suspect.

Inspector Lynley says to Havers:

"... So if he did kill her, I imagine he'd have set himself up with an iron-clad alibi, don't you?"

"No, I don't." She waved her teacake at him. One of its raisins dropped with a plop into her coffee. She ignored it and continued. "I think he's clever enough to know we'd be having a conversation just like this." [p. 124]

Havers' ability to ignore a consequence of her hand gesture shows how focused she becomes about a case. Moments later the Inspector's body language and a gesture underscore his feelings about the murderer.

... He shoved his coffee cup to one side. "What we need is a witness, Havers."

"To the killing?"

"To something. To anything." He stood. "Let's look up this woman who found the body." [pp. 124–25]

Consider for a moment the words *he shoved* in comparison with these alternatives: *he moved* his coffee cup; *he placed* his coffee cup; *he shifted* his coffee cup.

Elizabeth George captures Lynley's determination in his shove—no adverbs, other verbs, or further description needed.

His next action, *he stood,* suggests his resolve to get on with the investigation. By itself, getting up might mean little; most submissions overflow with standing up and sitting down. Here, Lynley's standing follows a forceful *shove* and the clipped reply, "To something. To anything."

Taken together, these small movements work in concert to strengthen our insight into the inspector's feelings. At the same time, these gestures are subtle enough to support his dialogue without overpowering it.

MOTION OR MEANING?

Not every movement must be pregnant with meaning. But a glut of position-shifting that serves primarily to stave off rigor mortis is not action. It's not even activity. It's fidgeting. It's author fatigue.

To see how often you repeat meaningless mannerisms, use your word processor's counting feature to search for the words *sat* and *stood,* as well as their assorted forms, *sit, stand,* and *took a seat.* Also search for "window," as in *walked to* and *looked out of.* Consider how well all that moving about contributes to either character portrayal or tension.

If you have difficulty self-editing for just the right gesture, examine each character's script and the agenda behind it. Consider exposing more of each hidden agenda through dialogue or body language. Reduce or eliminate empty gestures and the emptier chitchat they attempt to animate. Replace with gestures and dialogue that carry their own meaning. (Take another look at CLUES #15 and #16.) And come up with original observations, as these authors have:

> "You Casey?" she asked, snapping her gum as if the pop
> were a question mark at the end of her sentence.
>> Katy Munger, *Legwork,* first Casey Jones mystery
>>> [p. 78]

> Fallon stuck a finger in his ear, ran it around, examined it.
>> Nancy Means Wright, *Mad Season,* first Ruth Willmarth
>> mystery   [p. 90]

SUGGEST EMOTION

Favor gestures that reveal feelings. Here's an example from *Easy,* the first title in Phillip DePoy's mystery series featuring Flap Tucker, a private eye with a special gift for finding lost things. In the following extract, Flap is being let into the apartment of two murdered strippers by the building manager, who tells him:

> "You're damn right. But these places like the Tip Top"—she
> shoved the key into the lock like she was mad at it—"they got
> no sense of purpose." She threw open the door with the same
> disdain. "And these poor little girls, they got no purpose
> either."   [p. 91]

DePoy reveals the manager's feelings through dialogue and action, and he expands upon the verbs "shoved" and "threw open" by using a brief comparison.

Analyze how the authors of the next examples show feelings.

"All right, all right. . . . I'll concede that she probably would not have taken ecstasy or a look-alike. At least not knowingly."

As that one sank in, I dug the toe of my shoe into the sand, found a pebble, and kicked it with all my strength. When I spoke, my voice was shaking.

Jeanne Dams, *To Perish in Penzance* [p. 111]

"She was so full of life," responded the mother, her chin trembling and face beginning to crumple like a used paper bag.

G. Miki Hayden, *By Reason of Insanity* [p. 28]

". . . You're a lawyer, for God's sake."

"Was." He was shredding the bar napkin under his drink, rolling the damp paper into little bullets, lining them up side by side on the tabletop.

Kathy Hogan Trocheck, *Heart Trouble* [p. 141]

Examine the small behaviors in your own manuscript and the dialogue they accompany to see how you convey emotional meaning.

"So I'm guessing Winston Percival has talked to you already?" I said.

She laughed without moving her mouth.

Ruth Birmingham, *Atlanta Graves* [p. 196]

In a scene from Kathryn R. Wall's first mystery novel, *In for a Penny,* a mother is shown reacting to questions about her son's possible steroid use. What thoughts and feelings do you think her body language is communicating?

Bitsy picked a fallen twig up off the deck and began to strip the bark from it. "I think he's graduated up to some of those other things. . . ." [p. 136]

Is the mother worried, distracted, wrapped in thought? Is she trying to dissociate from painful reality, or working hard to control her emotions? All of the above?

The value of showing a behavior instead of telling about it is that no interpretation is necessary. Wall captures a mannerism so familiar that we recognize having stripped a few twigs ourselves. Certain experiences are universal, their associated feelings buried in our memories.

Famed mystery editor Ruth Cavin writes, "Borrow mannerisms from real life—*but only those that tell us something about the character you have created.*"[57]

The unskilled writer who attempts to dramatize a similar situation either tells us what the emotion is or inserts a vague, ubiquitous *pause,* which could mean anything or nothing.

Conventional wisdom says that readers enjoy crime novels because they like picking up the clues that let them try their hand at solving the mystery. Readers of fiction in all its forms also like picking up the clues to the emotional implications of a character's actions, body language, and dialogue. When you revise your manuscript, look for the specific ways you offer those deeper dimensions.

THE PAUSE THAT REGRESSES

Take the pause. Take it out in the alley and shoot it, I beg you. As a dialogue breaker-upper it can make a character seem hesitant when you want her to come across as pensive. An excess of pausing—including its first cousins "stopped to think for a moment" and "became silent for a bit"—creates a drag on the scene and makes the writing sound immature. Whenever I cross out pauses in a manuscript, the writing becomes stronger and the pace stops dragging, without feeling rushed.

One useful function for a pause (there aren't many) is to signal that a character is reversing himself or changing the subject.

> "I didn't go to her house that night." He paused. "Well, I sort of did. I drove by, but I didn't go inside."

A pause is not the only way to indicate a change or correction. Here's a slightly more imaginative alternative.

> "I didn't go to her house that night." He studied a hangnail. "Well, I sort of did. I drove by, but I didn't go inside."

If your scene is already busy with many little mannerisms like the above, a single pause in the right place might be a relief. A series of unrelated mannerisms could produce a choppy effect. But see what happens when you develop a theme that multiplies and unifies their effect.

> He studied a hangnail.
> "Well, I sort of did. I drove by, but I didn't go inside." His studies advanced to using one fingernail to clean under the nails of his other hand. "I saw the Honda parked in the driveway again. I wanted to, uh, you know, see what they were, ah, doing, but. . . . "
> With all ten digits accounted for, he graduated to picking at a scab on his wrist.

Watch how Elizabeth George shows reluctance and evasiveness in *For the Sake of Elena*. Inspector Lynley is interviewing Terence Cuff, the head of Elena's college, about the dead girl.

> "There were troubles?"
> Cuff took a moment to tap the ash from his cigarette into a porcelain ashtray. . . .   [p. 58]

When the inspector challenges one of Cuff's responses, it sets off a series of evasive actions.

> Cuff got up from his chair and went to the fireplace, where he lit the coals that formed a small mound in a metal basket. The room was growing cold, and while the action was reasonable, it also bore the appearance of temporizing. Once the fire was lit, Cuff remained standing near it. He sank his hands into his trouser pockets and studied the tops of his shoes.   [p. 60]

Twice more the head of the college is shown rearranging the coals before answering a question. One time he is said to shrug. This is not an indiscriminate physical gesture, nor the redundant "he shrugged his shoulders." George uses the verb in its figurative sense to clarify that:

> Cuff shrugged off both question and implication.   [p. 61]

In eight pages of stalling behaviors by the reticent Mr. Cuff, not one of them is a pause.

FREQUENCY DISTRACTS

Some gestures are so common they've become clichés. Many are also redundant, as in "he nodded in agreement" and "she breathed a sigh of relief." Vying for the redundancy award are "thought to himself"; "shrugged her shoulders"; "nodded her head"; and "hesitated a moment."

Watch those eyes. "Winked an eye" and "blinked his eyes" are redundant. Don't send anyone's eyes to unlikely places in improbable ways, such as "she threw a glance out the window"; "he cut his eyes to the knife on the counter"; "he cast his eyes ashore."

Congratulate yourself if you recognize that the last three examples are also *howlers.*

One editor grew so fed up with the expression "she tossed her head" that she took to writing "to whom?" in the margin of manuscripts.[58] My own method of raising awareness is not as amusing, but you can easily apply it to your own manuscript by running a computer search for certain overused gestures.

The list that follows is the product of a word search I performed on a single fiction manuscript of 83,000 words. Each numeral represents all forms of a word—that is, *sitting* includes *sat, sit, seated,* and *took a seat.*

This list totals 1,392 separate gestures, and I've probably missed a few.

5	guffawing	38	shrugging
5	gawking	43	breathing (as in took a deep
9	pausing		breath, *not* under his breath)
9	moaning	52	staring
14	gasping	63	standing
22	grimacing	80	nodding
22	shaking head	81	grinning
23	showing nervous-ness	83	turning (to, toward, away, around)
25	snickering	88	glaring
25	chuckling	94	sighing
27	bolting (from seat, bed)	98	sitting
		105	smiling
33	smirking	144	laughing
37	frowning	215	looking

Given that each verb requires at minimum one pronoun or other helper word, I can conservatively double this figure and say that 2,784 words out of a total word count of 83,000 refer to repetitive movements, fidgets, and twitches.

My electronic search of the same manuscript also turned up fifty-one mentions of the word "cigarette." I made no attempt to computer-count the many related actions, such as "struck a match," "lit," "took a drag," "smoked," and "tapped the ash." Of an estimated 300 words that went up in smoke, only one reference was plot-related.

Aside from weakening the writer's style, all this tobacco use seems to have caused no other harm: my computer counted only four coughs.

Computer-search your own draft using the above list. Your totals might indicate more repetition of insipid gesturing than you realize. Remedies:

- Sharpen your people-watching skills.
- Create more compelling action.
- Craft more purposeful dialogue.

BE OBSERVANT

A yawn, blink, scowl, or shrug is occasionally effective in the right situation, but original phrasing and fresh observations are preferred. Avoid sprinkling mannerisms like salt on popcorn. Instead, treat each one as you would herb seasoning to bring out the flavor of the main dish.

> "That's great," Waters said, leaping to his feet and pumping my arm like he was trying to bring up water.
> Katy Munger, *Legwork*   [p. 123]

> Mrs. Bradford was beating muffin batter, her arm slapping against the side of her chest.
> Deborah Adams, *All the Great Pretenders*   [p. 186]

When you're ready to revise your writing for its gestures, first assemble all your characters in a big circle. Ask them to do nothing for one full minute but nod, sigh, blink, yawn, scowl, grimace, and shrug. Visualizing this epidemic of tics and fidgets might lead you to select body language that speaks with greater literacy.

TIP: REVIEW YOUR GESTURES

Here's how to computer-count the most common gestures that you write. Start with the list of verbs on page 240.

1. Copy all your chapters into one backup file to facilitate a global search.
2. Instead of searching for whole words, determine the root letters common to all forms of a verb. For instance, the letters *paus* are common to *paused, pauses,* and *pausing.*
3. In your search-and-replace feature, type the same letters in both fields. If you search for *paus,* replace it with *paus.* This ensures that when you click "replace all," you replace every occurrence with itself. Your manuscript is unchanged, but your word processor shows the total number of occurrences.
4. Diagnose the way you present your characters' body language and correct as needed. Add other verbs that you often use.

FIND & FIX CLUE #21: GESTURED TO DEATH

- Make every gesture serve a purpose, just as you do with all the other details you select.
- Revise body language so it expands characterization, communicates attitude, or contributes a fresh observation, thereby adding value.
- Look for the specific ways you have your characters' body language offer clues to their emotions.
- Use your computer's search feature to see how often you repeat certain gestures, especially those used most often by most unpublished writers.

PART IX: LOOSE ENDS

"One of my mantras when I was in the submission phase was, 'If you're not getting a rejection a day, you're not submitting enough.' I don't know where I read that. But it helped me a lot. Each rejection proved I was one step closer to my goal."

Cindy Daniel, author of *Death Warmed Over*

CLUE #22: SNITCH VERSUS SPY

Old-time gangster films offer a useful contrast between two techniques that I think of as the Snitch and the Spy. One is a stool pigeon, a sniveling tattletale who explains e-v-e-r-y-t-h-i-n-g, as if readers couldn't size up your characters themselves by watching their behavior.

The other is a professional spy, a trained observer who lets audiences draw their own conclusions by watching your characters in action. The Spy's success comes from capturing this action with a tiny camera and a state-of-the-art sound system hidden in his pinky ring.

Which caricature does the audience cheer?

Review your manuscript to see that you take advantage of the Spy's talent for observing behavior and playing it back. (You still have to edit it, of course.) The triumph of Spy over Snitch demonstrates a basic principle in fiction: *show, don't tell.*

243

Writers find those three little words scrawled across returned manuscripts more often than any other editorial comment. That's because *showing* is the most misunderstood writing principle. New writers often let the Snitch take charge, and snitches love story*telling*. Where's the story*showing?*

Long time, no see.

SHOWING VS. TELLING

One reason for the misunderstanding is that novels contain a substantial amount of exposition, and exposition is the same as telling . . . or is it? No, not in the sense of "show, don't tell." See for yourself in the following passage of exposition. It comes from *Mama Rocks the Empty Cradle,* the sixth of seven novels in the Mama mystery series by Nora DeLoach.

> The fresh pork was seasoned with onion, garlic, and green pepper. . . . I knew, because its smell reminded me of how Mama cooked fresh neck bones for an hour before she added cleaned, cut collard greens.
>
> The aroma of what Rose was cooking sashayed through the door of her little kitchen, meandered to the front of the mobile home, and drifted on the wind until it passed the huge oak tree, the rosebush with red blossoms that had been planted in the middle of the swept yard, and the hedge of wildflowers that stood between the trailers. The scent of the pork landed at my Honda's window.   [p. 87]

Without a doubt, this is exposition, yet it *shows,* and most effectively. The passage is loaded with sensory details that evoke vivid smells, tastes, and images. And those details create considerable movement on their own.

So it isn't exposition *per se* to be wary of, it's the type of exposition—the kind that forms conclusions and makes judgments based on no evidence that would convince a jury. Instead of telling us that a billing clerk is a kind and generous person, show her volunteering at the rescue mission on her day off. Instead of telling us that a retired judge is a cantankerous old man, show us his interactions with others.

Patricia Sprinkle brings this judge to life in the second of her Sheila Travis series, *Murder in the Charleston Manner.* In the following excerpt, Judge Black and his wife, Annie, have just been offered a drink.

"Pour it quick, before my old woman objects. She's always going on and on about saving my heart. At eighty-nine, who the hell does she think I'm saving it for?" He cackled at his own wit.   [pp. 10–11]

The conversation soon turns to the host's resident nurse.

"She ain't full-time nursing." Judge Black chuckled. "Meeting Heyward under the magnolias in the dark. Probably takes him in the house, too, when you ain't looking."
"There's no such word as 'ain't,'" Annie burst out. "And why a man with your education and experience—"
"Woman, when a man has my education and experience, he can say any damn word he pleases. And what's got you so riled up ain't my language. It's the thought of what them young 'uns might be up to. . . ."
"I could kill him," Annie muttered. "Sometimes I could just kill him."   [pp. 11–12]

The judge's own words substantiate his temperament and let us experience his nature up close and personal. If this scene were told to us instead of shown, the richness of the judge's persona would be filtered through the narrator. Any intermediary puts distance between readers and characters.

SHOWING EMOTION

Showing enables readers to experience emotions for themselves.

Analyze the techniques Denise Tiller uses to show her protagonist's emotional reactions in this scene from her first mystery novel, *Calculated Risk*. The phone rings as the series protagonist, California actuary Liz Matthews, is making a salad for dinner with her boyfriend.

. . . "Elizabeth, this is your mother."
My cheeks burned as if she'd slapped my face. "I don't have a mother!"
I slammed the receiver down and pressed my hands against my ears to block the echoes of playground taunts. "We know what happened. . . . Your mother left because she didn't love you."

I squeezed harder. "It's not true. She's not my mother."

"Lizzie! Who was that?"

I jumped and dropped my hands when I saw Jack peering into my face. "Wrong number. I didn't hear you come back." I pulled a long knife from the block and dismembered a weak cucumber with savage chops.

Jack sucked in air. "Who's not whose mother?" He leaned against the refrigerator with his arms folded, waiting for an answer. Meanwhile I attacked a ripe tomato. Red juice and seeds sprayed across the counter.

"Thought you said your mother was dead."

"She is as far as I'm concerned," I muttered as I hacked. "She abandoned Dad and me when I was a baby. I haven't heard from her in almost thirty years." I waved the knife, dripping with juice, in his face. "And if that woman thinks. . . .

The phone rang and I slammed the blade into the cutting board. It stuck straight upright. . . .   [pp. 26–27]

We experience Liz's emotions through her senses (feeling her cheeks burn, hearing the taunts of her childhood) and through her actions (slamming the receiver down, attacking defenseless veggies). Reinforcing Liz's murderous impulses are Tiller's vibrant details: the juice of a ripe tomato spraying across the counter . . . a long knife dripping red waving in Jack's face . . . the blade slammed into the cutting board.

Notice that the backstory is brief and presented through dialogue, where it neither weakens the scene nor slows its pace.

THE UNSHOWABLE

Now that the Spy shows what can be achieved through exposition and dramatization, let's further expose the nefarious work of the Snitch.

He seemed a little uncomfortable.

In isolation, this statement tells of discomfort we cannot observe and interprets a supposition we cannot support from the evidence. To make a characterization convincing, show what "a little uncomfortable" looks like. Perhaps this fellow squirms in his seat, runs a finger around the inside of his collar, or dabs at his forehead with a grimy handkerchief.

Emotions that are *not* easily shown are more challenging. Here's another Snitch kind of statement:

> Naomi sat there with a vindictive expression on her face. "I guess so," she said.

What does vindictive look like? I can't picture Naomi's expression, can you? And the dialogue is of no help.

Not every emotion can be rendered through body language alone. Many need the context of the character's words or thoughts. Some need a little telling, too, with the telling and the showing complementing—not contradicting—each other.

For expressing complex meanings, a combined show-and-tell is often necessary. The following dialogue is from *Them Bones,* the first Mississippi Delta mystery by Carolyn Haines. Here, the series character, Sarah Booth, is being confronted by a man she is attracted to, though she suspects him of murder. The underlining is mine.

> "I heard you visited my sister." <u>There was both question and demand in his statement,</u> the stern master grilling his staff for an infraction of his rules.
>
> "What if I did?" I threw the challenge back. The delicate glass bottle Sylvia had given me for him was down in the parlor, safely tucked on the sideboard.
>
> <u>Though he appeared relaxed, I saw the turmoil in his eyes.</u> "My sister isn't well. You can't rely on anything she said. You certainly shouldn't trust her. She could get you in trouble."
>
> . . . .
>
> <u>Hamilton gave me a speculative look.</u> "Did she say anything about Mother?"   [pp. 219–20]

The exposition I underlined summarizes and interprets feelings, but it doesn't do so alone. Dialogue and action provide corroboration. Show and tell support each other. Symbiosis.

Another example of the unshowable and how it's shown can be found in Kris Neri's first mystery novel, *Revenge of the Gypsy Queen.* Tracy Eaton, the series character, has her accomplice, an Iraqi emigré, try on her husband's suit.

"Your husband's taste in clothes is. . ." It wasn't clear whether Nuri's inadequacy in English produced that struggle to find the right word—or tact.

"Dull," I offered. . . .

When Tracy thinks about Nuri's gesture she offers a substitute for its meaning's complexity.

"No, Tracy." Nuri tossed his hand in a throwaway gesture, which struck me as very Old World in nature, though I'd never seen its like from Tony. It was a gesture that conveyed the complex thought: We will never speak of this, though we both know it's true.   [p. 124]

As this scene confirms, *showing* loses none of its value even when some telling is needed to supplement the meaning. Just beware of over-telling: saying essentially the same thing in many different ways.

Jed felt relieved. "I'm glad you're not pressing charges," he said, smiling and leaning back in his chair. Joan saw his shoulders relax and the creases in his forehead fade.

Do you recognize that *Jed felt relieved* is a conclusion? It's also redundant, along with any three of the four images that supplement the dialogue and make the identical point.

OVERSHOWING

Because I point to instances of telling versus showing throughout the book, this CLUE is brief. The only passage I want to revisit appears way back in CLUE #1, where I turn a compact, effective hook into this deliberately amateurish example of excess.

I was lazily watching my tall, well-built bodyguard mowing the lush green lawn in her bright pink bikini when I heard a loudly buzzing small, private airplane flying overhead. When I looked up I saw the scary sight of a man's body falling from the cloudless sky.

Here's the hook to *Dead Over Heels* as Charlaine Harris wrote it:

> My bodyguard was mowing the yard wearing her pink bikini
> when the man fell from the sky.

Harris's brief original shows action, whereas my parody smothers the action and bludgeons readers with an epidemic of adverbosity and adjectivitis. Watch for signs of these disorders when you revise your own writing. For each modifier you find, question your reason for using it.

Typically, modifiers tell us how we should be viewing what the writer might be able to show more effectively. I've seen writers tell their readers that a poorly lit street is also very dark, deeply shadowed, inky, and dim—all on the same page. Footsteps don't merely echo, they echo loudly, repeatedly, and ominously.

Modifier overkill suggests performance anxiety in writers who don't trust their words to evoke the desired reader response, and who don't trust the readers to interpret behavior when it's dramatized.

> "Dramatize the story in scenes and dialogue, don't narrate it, which is a better version of the old 'show, don't tell.'"
>
> Win Blevins, author of *Stone Song* and *Heaven Is a Long Way Off*

If you write *what a frightening moment Harvey faced,* that's telling. It's also known as author intrusion, because it's your emotional interpretation of the scene, not Harvey's. The Snitch that lurks within you feels pretty smug about putting something over on you.

Instead of telling about a scene, show how your viewpoint character experiences it: the smell of uncollected garbage, the sound of a baby crying, the chill of the wind. Use sensory impressions to simulate the character's emotional responses, and present the dialogue and action that lets us see what provokes his or her reactions.

Keep your own emotions off the page. Show what your characters feel. Ideally, a subtle portrayal will evoke the desired feelings in your audience— as with this opening line from *Shards,* by Tom Piccirilli.

> *"I would never hurt you," he said, taking me in his hand, and hurting me.*

Would the same content have the same impact if Piccirilli chose to tell you about this situation instead of using dialogue and action to show you?

FIND & FIX CLUE #22: SNITCH VERSUS SPY

- ⬤◆ Look for examples in your manuscript of interpretations, conclusions, and summaries that tell readers what to think.
- ⬤◆ Avoid generalizing by showing behavior that readers can interpret for themselves.
- ⬤◆ Double-check that you portray your characters through their dialogue, actions, and thoughts.
- ⬤◆ See if your exposition includes sensory impressions that evoke vivid imagery.
- ⬤◆ Be aware of redundancy when you supplement what's shown with what's told.
- ⬤◆ Show your characters' feelings, not your own.

CLUE #23: MYSTERY DYSTROPHY

B y now, your self-editing is moving right along. Your hook is so well sustained that readers wouldn't think of getting away. There's no perilous prologue or toxic transcript to sidetrack your story's progression. Bloody backstory and fatal flashbacks are (ahem) things of the past.

You dumped those dastardly descriptions, jettisoned the juvenile gestures, and ousted every ounce of overwriting. All accidental alliteration has been axed, and all clichés clobbered—though the effort of doing so caused many a frown to crease your brow.

Actions and emotions are shown, not told, and conflicting agendas keep tension idling on every page. Your settings demonstrate a keen sense of place, and your point of view shifts only when you want it to.

Self-editing has greatly improved your manuscript. Still, you wonder what other weaknesses you might have overlooked. So you devour three books on characterization and three more on plot, conflict, and suspense. You know your manuscript is good, but is it good enough? Does it show enough *density?* What about *voice*—too thin? Too weak? Does your style show enough *style?* Does it have muscle? Maybe it lacks pizzazz. What *is* pizzazz, anyway?

Editors used to talk about talent, a quality inherent in the writer, not the manuscript. These days, it's risky to use the word *talent;* writers might interpret a rejection as suggesting they haven't any.

Pizzazz, on the other hand, is mysterious and indefinable, therefore safer. Moreover, the word seems to apply to the submission, not to some deficiency in the writer. One dictionary defines *pizzazz* as "glamour, vitality," but most resources, including a popular online dictionary, don't even list the word. It's indefinable, all right.

STYLE

How does a writer acquire indefinable qualities of voice, style, pizzazz? Accept the reality that most submissions seem written by the same person. Despite differences in character and plot, the writing style is nearly identical. That style produces a voice—even if you think you don't have one. To an editor, the sound of the typical fiction manuscript shouts *amateur.*

A key step in voice rehabilitation is to eliminate the evidence. That's why I want you to self-edit for the two dozen deadly techniques you are discovering. That alone will differentiate the sound of your writing from other submissions. Your voice may still be weak, but it's yours, and you can learn to strengthen it. Most writers need time and practice before their unique voice develops. Keep writing and self-editing; it's good exercise for developing weak muscles.

> "Editors can spot a good voice in a few paragraphs. . . .
> How? They read first for *mistakes!*
> They spot lack of craft in the first few paragraphs. . . . Unique voice sells the story. Lack of one begets rejection. Voice has substance. It is something you, the writer, can shape."
>
> Doris Booth, founder of Authorlink.com[60]

A basic step, following the advice of experienced authors, editors, and writing coaches, is to *read widely.* Pay special attention to the authors who stir excitement in your heart, who make your fingers itch to grab a pencil and get back to your own writing. They have style; perchance *pizzazz.*

I'm not convinced that voice is something to work at; the outcome could sound pretentious and overly literary, which some call "writerly." So I'm passing along the next idea in the event you want to use it.

A few writing coaches advocate the conscious parroting of the style of authors you admire. Not their content; write your own story, but do so in the manner *they* would write your story. The idea is to simulate the voice of one author at a time until you feel comfortable with his or her style. Then combine the best of your efforts. Through exercise and practice, you will eventually develop a voice you can call your own.

Skeptical? Prefer that I talk about talent? Would you believe me if I told you that while it is impossible to make a competent writer out of a bad writer, and equally impossible to make a great writer out of a good one, it is possible, with lots of hard work, dedication, and timely help, to make a good writer out of a merely competent one.

You might not believe *my* telling you this, but I think you'd believe Stephen King if you knew those insightful words were his. They are.[61]

I never met Stephen King; we attended the University of Maine at the same time and we both taught writing there, but on different campuses. I read the above words for the first time in King's autobiographical *On Writing,* published in 2000. Yet thirty years before that I had based my life's work as a teacher and editor on the very same belief that King articulates. I remain convinced of its truth because I keep seeing the results.

FIGURATIVE LANGUAGE

The rest of this CLUE reviews techniques such as figurative language, parallel structure, and symbolism—techniques that enrich your writing by taking it beyond a single layer of meaning. I'm not suggesting that depth and richness are a matter of technique alone. Style cannot be stuck onto a story like bows on a gift box. Still, effective writing can be cultivated.

You are already familiar with many types of figurative language. Its forms were introduced in junior high. Try the following in your writing, in moderation, and see how fresh and original you can be. Each construction should come naturally, or appear to, because struggling to devise a clever remark can make the words seem forced, or clumsy and foolish.

FAMILIAR FIGURATIVE LANGUAGE

- ●◆ A *simile* uses "like" or "as" to compare unlike things (Anne Grant's "looked like both sides of a bipolar personality"; Denise Swanson's "quivered like the curb feelers on a car").

- ●◆ A *metaphor* implies a comparison without stating it (Carolyn Wheat's "a cloud of expensive perfume"; George Orwell's "the insect voice of the clock").

- ●◆ An *extended metaphor* takes the original figure of speech (Nancy Bartholomew's "smelled worse than a rotten egg") and continues it by adding one or more related metaphors ("having my picture taken by a smelly egg").   *more...*

MORE FIGURATIVE LANGUAGE

- ☙ An *epithet* is a nickname that substitutes for another name or phrase (Margaret Maron's "Miss Big Ears"; Evelyn Coleman's "Tattoo Man and Biting Nails").

- ☙ A *symbol* is a word, concept, object, or theme with a number of associated meanings. These add to and deepen its figurative meanings while retaining its literal meaning (Vicki Hinze's "eagle paperweight [with its] dark shadows between the glints of light"; Jeffery Deaver's "tight, stubborn curls").

Over time, a variety of linguistic and structural techniques may become a natural part of your style. Their absence from your writing indicates no error on your part. Neither does their inclusion ensure success. But they *can* make your writing more exact, more interesting, more vibrant.

If nothing else, these techniques are fun to play with—a process that often reveals new ways to multiply the levels of meaning in a novel.

SECOND REFERENCES

Fundamental to both the art and the craft of writing is the ability to find relationships between unrelated ideas and create new meaning from them. A relationship can be as simple as a second reference to something mentioned earlier in a different context. This difference in context alters the meaning of the second reference and distinguishes it from mere repetition.

One thing that a second reference needs is a first one. To demonstrate, here's a scene from the first book in the Carlotta Carlyle series by Linda Barnes, *A Trouble of Fools*, nominee for the Anthony, Edgar, and Shamus awards. Carlotta is searching for money that her elderly client hid in a trunk in her attic.

> The door opened into shadow, not darkness, therefore the attic had a light source somewhere, one sadly insufficient for a search. I dipped into my shoulder bag—which weighs about a ton because I keep it crammed with picklocks, my trusty Swiss army knife, MBTA tokens, and stray lipsticks—in hopes of locating a flashlight. My first find [of] the right shape turned out to be a can of that old-style lacquery hairspray, which,

believe me, is just as off-putting to muggers as a can of Mace, much cheaper, and you don't need a license for it. I never use hairspray for anything else.   [p. 80]

If nothing from this paragraph were mentioned again, the stuff Carlotta carries in her shoulder bag would serve the purpose of adding humor and expanding characterization. Yet one item among all these other objects *is* mentioned again, in a different, unexpected context in Barnes's next chapter. It opens with Carlotta feeling nervous about carrying the money her client asked her to move from the trunk to a safer hiding place.

My favorite part of those Gothic suspense novels, aside from the climactic moment when our heroine gets a message from our hero and waltzes off to meet him at midnight in the old abandoned warehouse, is where the heroine goes outside carrying thousands of bucks belonging to some secret organization, armed only with a can of hairspray.   [p. 85]

The less remarkable an object's first mention, the more heightened its effect when the reader comes upon it in another context. The greater the difference in context, the more unexpected and enjoyable the encounter. The hairspray itself is of no importance; Carlotta doesn't use it for defense. Its value is as a rhetorical device, a second reference that sneaks up on readers and makes us appreciate the author's rich writing style.

PARALLEL ACTION

A more complex technique is parallel action, in which separate, often unrelated events are interwoven in the same scene. Each event multiplies the effect of the other. Let's say you are writing a scenario in which your crime-fighter summarizes what is known about the investigation so far. He is shown analyzing facts, weighing alternative theories, and contemplating new directions for the investigation. While all this introspective theorizing is taking place, what do you give your readers to visualize?

Give them a parallel action. Put it in the form of some tangible activity that needs no explanation, such as fixing a bike, shopping for groceries, wrapping presents, or leaving the office and heading for a parking garage. You want a simple, familiar activity that makes no demands on your readers and lets them stay focused on the workings of your sleuth's keen mind.

Pairing a cerebral process with an unrelated, parallel action establishes a symbiotic relationship between them: neither is compelling enough to support a scene on its own, yet each brings to the other greater interest, depth, and opportunity for increasing tension.

An effective use of this type of parallelism can be seen in Lisa Scottoline's second mystery novel, *Final Appeal,* which won an Edgar for best paperback original. Here, the protagonist, attorney Grace Rossi, is thinking through the puzzling death of her lover, Judge Armen Gregorian.

> I read the papers on the way to the Xerox machine. It's a complete sitting schedule, with Armen's initials crossed out next to his cases and a new judge's written in. All of Armen's cases, reassigned so fast it'd make your head spin.
>
> READY TO COPY, the photocopier says. I open the heavy lid, slap the paper onto the glass, and hit the button. The light from the machine rolls calcium white across my face.
>
> Suicide? I don't understand. They were going to file for divorce, if what Armen said was true. I feel a pang of doubt; would Armen lie? Of course not. Afterward we talked for a long time, holding each other on the couch. He was an honest man, a wonderful man.
>
> READY TO COPY. I hit the button. You don't kill yourself just because you're Armenian. Armen was a survivor. And he hated guns, was against keeping them in the house. Where did he get the gun?
>
> READY TO COPY, says the machine again, but I'm not ready to copy. So much has happened. We found and lost each other in one night. I stare at the glass over the shadowy innards of the machine; all I see is my own confused reflection.
>
> [pp. 51–52]

Scottoline's final paragraph continues the parallel threads of action and thought *and* goes further. It intertwines them. The "ready to copy" light, the reflective glass, and the "shadowy innards" take on symbolic qualities that suggest the depth of Grace's state of mind. Tension grows, and multiple meanings build density. *That's style.*

COUNTERPOINT

Actions that converge and inform each other with added layers of meaning approach a higher calling: counterpoint. Whereas parallel actions maintain their identities as separate, unrelated themes, counterpoint does that and more by creating a relationship between unrelated themes. The new relationship has no existence of its own until the writer creates it and gives it expression.

Analyze the counterpoint Michael Allen Dymmoch develops in the following scene from *The Man Who Understood Cats,* winner of the St. Martin's Press/Malice Domestic award for best first mystery novel. Dymmoch's series features two professionals, John Thinnes, an overstressed Chicago detective, and Jack Caleb, a gay psychiatrist.

Caleb wants to learn who murdered one of his patients, and Thinnes wants to learn if Caleb is the murderer. These personal agendas make it logical for the detective to offer—and the psychiatrist to accept—an invitation to ride along one evening as the police investigate an unrelated case. (The lone mention of Karsch, below, refers to a psychologist and police consultant.)

> They flagged an old Buick down on Division Street and followed it into an alley, letting it pull several car-lengths ahead. Thinnes and Caleb stayed in the car. Thinnes filled Caleb in on the case, while Crowne got out and walked up to lean against the Buick and talk to the driver, a former gang member in his twenties, who sometimes gave them useful information. As they watched, Thinnes asked Caleb, "What does a psychiatrist actually do?"
>
> "If he's successful," Caleb said, "he helps people solve their personal problems."
>
> A Karsch kind of answer, if ever there was one, Thinnes thought. "Yeah, but how? What exactly do you do?"
>
> "There's nothing exact about it. When a client asks me to help, I have him describe the problem. I listen to what he says. I study his body language for discrepancies. I try to notice what he doesn't say."
>
> He paused as they watched Crowne take out a cigarette and

then hand the pack to his informant. Crowne lit up with a green plastic lighter, which he also handed over. The informant took a cigarette, lit it, and put both pack and lighter in his pocket.

Thinnes could read neither approval nor disapproval on Caleb's face as he continued. "If there's any suggestion of organic impairment, I send him to his physician for a thorough physical, and I test him myself for drugs and anything I think his doctor may have missed."

Down the alley, Crowne walked around the informant's car and got in the front seat. His gestures became mildly threatening, and he leaned toward the informant as the man spoke.

Caleb waited, perhaps for Thinnes to comment, then went on. "If I don't find drugs or any physical cause for the problem, I dig into his family history and try to determine what purpose the problem serves, either for the client or for significant others in his life."

In the informant's car, Crowne shook his head vigorously, almost as if disagreeing with Caleb. He listened to the informant for a moment, then shrugged.

"Motive, opportunity, and method," Thinnes said. "Basic detective work, huh?"

"That, and a bit more. A detective's finished when he's discovered who did it and presented his evidence. At that point in the investigation, a therapist still has to determine if his subject really wants to change, and if he's serious, how to help him do it."

"Sort of a one-man criminal justice system."

"That's one way to put it, although it's more frequently described by critics as playing God."

Crowne got out of the Buick and started back toward them, poker-faced, but Thinnes could tell he'd struck out. Thinnes kept his eyes on Caleb and said, "What do you think, Doctor. Did he score?"

"I doubt it."

Then Crowne opened the door and threw himself into the passenger seat with a resounding "Damn!"   [pp. 84–85]

A great deal is going on in this well-crafted scene. For parallel action, two unrelated events are unfolding side by side. The dominant event is a technical explanation of the process of psychiatric observation—an abstraction. The subordinate event, starring a minor character, Crowne, provides the necessary action to sustain visual interest and support the abstraction.

Dramatic irony grows as Thinnes watches Caleb in an attempt to read the psychiatrist's body language, while the psychiatrist explains the psychoanalytical method of trying to read the body language of a client.

Each man, it soon becomes clear, is engaged in a form of detective work. The similarity between the men's professions develops, and we realize that Dymmoch is presenting parallel *themes* in addition to parallel actions.

The irony deepens when the themes cross over.

> In the informant's car, Crowne shook his head vigorously, almost as if disagreeing with Caleb.

In less skillful hands than Dymmoch's, a technical presentation of the psychoanalytic process might come off as a lecture. However, what Dymmoch does so effectively is to introduce parallel themes, carry them out through parallel actions, interweave them, add strains of dramatic irony, and produce a well-orchestrated whole greater than the sum of its already substantial parts. What style!

As in music, counterpoint entwines two separate themes that enrich each other and create a third entity that multiplies the effect of the whole.

SYMBOLISM

My final example of a rich rhetorical device has much in common with parallel themes and counterpoint, but it adds more layers of meaning through the power of symbols. The following scene comes from *Sad Water,* the third novel in the Gale Grayson series by Teri Holbrook, winner of numerous awards. One of the story's main characters is Chalice, a sculptor, who is unable to speak because of an injury to her tongue.

> . . . she sat in the workroom of Markham Studio and examined the clay mask she was fashioning. Kitschy, and not at all her style, but the masks kept her employed. This one's working title was "The Yeller," because of the taut gape of the mouth.
>
> [p. 40]

The symbolism of the gaping mouth seems to suggest the feelings of the mute sculptor. Chalice's hands continue to reshape the mouth as she listens to the conversation between her sister, Totty, and her employer, Olivia. They are talking about the search for a body.

> Olivia laughed. "That's generally how I feel about the police. They certainly can't come in here without leaving their slobber about."
> Chalice placed her fingers inside the mask's mouth and gently pulled. The clay gave and the lower jaw extended a fraction of an inch.   [p. 41]

Because Totty appreciates Olivia's having employed her mute sister, she often avoids telling the owner of the studio what she thinks.

> Chalice knew what her sister was thinking: *Not bloody likely.* But Totty would never say that to Olivia. Totty was too grateful. Beneath Chalice's fingers the lips on the mask cracked. She quickly dipped her fingers in water and ran them over the clay.
>   [p. 43]

The symbolism intensifies as complex meanings continue to develop. Not the least of these is the irony of Totty's ability to speak but choosing not to, compounded by Chalice's knowing what her sister is thinking and why she chooses to figuratively hold her tongue. Additional meanings become apparent as we probe the question of whose lips are cracking, those of Totty? Chalice? Or Olivia—an opportunist who uses the power of speech to hurt others? Perhaps all three of the above, each in her own limited way.

The power of a symbol is that the more one contemplates its possible interpretations, the more meanings swirl and ripple from it, without explaining it. An effective symbol is so rich that mere words are too restrictive to represent its scope and depth.

DENSITY

When you self-edit, try different techniques. Experiment. You'll discover relationships among ideas that you hadn't realized were there. Truthfully, they *aren't* there. You bring them into existence through your vision as a writer. Your unique vision discerns potential connections between dissimilar concepts. That insight won't let you rest until you find a way to explore the possibilities.

Don't be in a hurry to get the process of self-editing over with. Your heightened awareness of the variety of techniques within your grasp will help you approach your manuscript from a fresh perspective.

Metaphors be with you.

FIND & FIX CLUE #23: MYSTROPHY DYSTROPHY

- ●◆ Experiment to see how you might enrich your writing with the judicious use of similes, metaphors, extended metaphors, second references, and epithets—in moderation.
- ●◆ Look for potential parallels that create visual interest for cerebral content lacking its own imagery.
- ●◆ Continue working with parallel actions to see what multi-layered relationships you can develop among different themes.
- ●◆ Explore the possibilities offered by counterpoint and symbolism to deepen your meaning.
- ●◆ Read many authors in different genres and study the techniques, style, and voice of each writer you admire—and a little of those you dislike.
- ●◆ Write, rewrite, and rewrite again.

"In the late 1990s after completing the last novel
in my first mystery series—Patricia Delaney, Computer
Gumshoe—I wrote two stand-alone suspense novels.
Neither was published, although one came close.
At the time I was devastated, partly because I
couldn't figure out what I was doing wrong.

What I'm writing now helped me realize the fatal
flaw of those two stand-alones. I wrote them to be scary,
for scary's sake, because I thought "scary" would sell.
After, just for fun, I wrote about a quirky character,
and in doing so I hit upon voice. Or at least the start of
finding voice in my writing. That novel,
Death of a Domestic Diva, was the first in
my current Stain-Busting mystery series.
If I ever write another stand-alone, it would
have to be a novel of the heart, and I think the
only way for me to do that would be to find,
again, voice in my characters.

The bottom-line, simple-sounding yet difficult
in reality, is: follow your heart, find your voice,
and write whatever story that leads you to."

Sharon Short, Stain-Busting Mystery Series,
including *Hung Out to Die*

D.O.A.

CLUE #24: WORDS & MISDEMEANORS

For big-time help with small-time search and destroy missions, there's nothing like a word processor's search feature. It lets you quickly find and fix the culprits that lurk in your expressions.

"Words are the clothes that thoughts wear," wrote Samuel Butler. If so, the thoughts of some writers are disheveled and threadbare. Or—to stretch the metaphor—the reader's perceptions and the writer's intentions match as well as a plaid shirt and striped slacks.

If you fail to arrest the clashes that follow, your submission is not doomed; plenty of untidy writing gets published, as we know. And some readers who sense the disconnects and ambiguities in a story sometimes think it's *them*. Alert screeners, however, recognize the clues to sloppy writing and are grateful to have any reason to lower the piles of never-ending submissions.

"SUDDENLY"

One "suddenly" per book, please. More frequent use reduces its effect the one time it might be justified. The word also suggests the kind of writer who probably uses other "ly" adverbs to bolster action that is too feeble to provide its own effect.

The good news is that an effective scene written to surprise readers and catch them off guard doesn't need the word.

A technique recommended by senior editor Michael Seidman is to set up the paragraph *before* the surprise to make readers leap to a conclusion that's different from the one you intend.[62]

What conclusions do you leap to as you read the following extract from *Authorized Personnel Only,* by Barbara D'Amato? It's late afternoon in Chicago, and police officer Suze Figueroa and her partner are taking a break at a neighborhood bar.

263

"Be right back," Figueroa said. She went to the women's rest
room, way down the hall from the men's. It was less convenient, and although she had never been in the men's room, she
heard their room was bigger.

She figured a bathroom break right now would be a good
idea because she and Norm were going to go back out and
spend several hours hiding in the alley. It would also be a good
idea to call home. She had told them she'd be back by midnight, which was stupid of her. She should have realized it
could take longer.

Yeah, take longer and maybe achieve nothing, she thought.

Still, with Maria in charge and Kath as backup, and Robert
getting home by twelve, there shouldn't be a problem.

She'd call anyhow.

She washed her hands, dried them on one of the brown paper
towels from the dispenser, and grabbed one of the prepackaged
towelettes that had appeared in a dispenser in the washroom a
year or so ago.

She gave her face a good, brisk wiping off. Nice lemon
fragrance.

Lemon fragrance? Oh, my god!   [pp. 299–300]

I won't comment on the last line, which, you can tell, makes an impact.
Instead, let's analyze D'Amato's techniques for building up to that impact.

Every detail in this scene works as a diversion to set us up for the surprise in the last line. Beginning with the image of "way down the hall," our
expectations are misdirected. What mystery reader would not become alert
to a possible attack on a woman as she enters a long, deserted corridor?

With Suze's mind wandering to the disparity between the men's and the
women's facilities, then to the long night's stakeout ahead, the pace slows
and our apprehension grows. Suze, pay attention here!

When her walk down the hall proves uneventful, our expectations turn
to what might happen when Suze opens the door to the women's room.
Will a dead body fall from a stall? A live one leap from behind the door?
Pay attention, puh-leeze. But again our fears are unfounded.

With Suze thinking of home and family, D'Amato continues to slow the
pace, and our tightly coiled springs begin to loosen. Five sentences of

whether or not she should phone home force us to concentrate on her decision-making. Add to that the minutiae of hand washing and drying, and our anticipatory antennae relax even more. We are lulled into accepting the scene as an ordinary visit to a restroom.

Wham! Wrong again. There *is* a surprise, and it's not at all what D'Amato's techniques led our imaginations to expect. The suddenness of this development gains power from the author's having set us up for it.

And she does so with nary a "suddenly."

Search your own manuscript for the "s" word and see what happens when you delete it. If you find that its absence reduces your scene's impact, you will have learned an important lesson: it's the *scene* that needs work.

DIES LAUGHING

Showing characters joking with each other is one way to portray personalities and relationships. Clowning around also lightens a scene's gloom and doom—if that's what it needs. Some writers, perhaps thinking to increase the comedic effect of a scene, go beyond showing these actions to telling us that a line of dialogue was *laughed.*

Words can be said with a laugh or while laughing, but words cannot *be* laughed. Neither can they be smiled, chuckled, snorted, grinned, grimaced, or guffawed. If you use one of these verbs, write it into a beat, not a tag. Beats help us see the speaker; tags help us hear how the speaker sounds. Whenever I read the tag "he laughed" I imagine the character's words sounding like a horse's whinny. As for "snorted," I won't even go there.

When your intention is to have your audience share in the merriment, don't show the characters cracking up; show only what is causing them to do so. In this way you let your readers react to whatever strikes *them* as funny.

If you want to show characters laughing at their own jokes, underplay your protagonist's reaction—as in the next extract. It's from Sandra Balzo's *Uncommon Grounds,* which received an Anthony nomination for best first mystery. The protagonist, Maggie Thorsen, is talking with her tax preparer.

> ". . . I suppose I'm going to get killed on taxes," I ventured.
> "Well, we'll see. You know what they say, Uncle Sam wants you—and everything you've got." She was still laughing, freshly buoyed by accountant humor, as I left. [p. 43]

This passage's humor owes much to Maggie's leaving without laughing. Underplaying—or in this case ignoring—is a cool, above-it-all response.

When you do portray laughter, make it give value, as Katy Munger does in this clever line from *Legwork,* her first Casey Jones mystery.

> Slim Jim began to laugh and I listened as his merriment gave
> way to the sound of his truck motor fading down the lane.
>
> [p. 219]

Laughter's value in the next scene lies in what it adds to a professor's characterization. In the first title of the Ben Candidi mysteries by Dirk Wyle, *Pharmacology is Murder,* Ben is a Ph.D. candidate being interviewed by the head of the pharmacology graduate program. Each man tries to outdo the other with his erudition and wit.

> "Yes, I see," he said flipping back to my transcript. "You also
> received an 'A' in philosophy. Say, tell me, Mr. *Candidi,* what
> philosophy did they teach you in that course? That it is the Best
> of All Possible Worlds!" His laugh rattled the file cabinets.
>
> A flash of inspiration furnished a reply. "Yes, that's exactly
> what they did teach. The prof's name was *Dr. Pangloss."* Dr.
> Taylor smiled at my snide answer, so I upped the ante. "At this
> point could I ask *you* how well am I standing up to the *Grand
> Inquisitor of Lisbon?"*
>
> This brought out another booming laugh. His chest heaved,
> and he literally bounced in his chair.   [pp. 47–48]

Readers unfamiliar with Voltaire's *Candide* who miss the allusions central to the characters' repartee are nonetheless entertained by Wyle's imagery. The passage is able to appeal to readers on several levels.

I can't tell you how to write humor. I wish I could. What I *can* share with you are two general principles for effectively conveying emotion.

- Underplay the emotional reaction of others.
- Select details that evoke the emotion in your readers.

Observe what you find humorous when you read. Analyze the techniques of the authors who make you laugh. If you want your readers to laugh out loud, write scenes that are inherently funny.

Comedian Bob Newhart says that with TV's canned laughter, "The writers don't write as well because they have that crutch." [63]

I suspect that writers who prop up their dialogue with *he laughed* use the tag as their crutch, similar to propping up weak action with adverbs, adjectives, and gestures. After all, if writers *tell* what others are feeling, they don't have to create dialogue and action to *show* those feelings.

The same applies to *he smiled*, except that frequent, habitual smiling has the added disadvantage of causing characters to look like silly fools and making the writing seem adolescent. Avoid this construction: *"That's a lively dog," Pam smiled.* Alternatives include *she said with a smile* and *he said, smiling.* Or convert the tag into a separate sentence—a beat.

> "That's a lively dog." Pam smiled.
> Angie returned her sister's smile. "I agree."

Sappy writing, but you get the idea. Better still, select verbs that expand the action and characterization instead of echoing the dialogue.

> "That's, uh, one cute little dog you've got there." Pam smiled
> and quickly sidestepped the leash about to encircle her ankles.

Look to your purpose. If the reason for showing a smile or a laugh is to keep readers from misinterpreting the attitude with which a character delivers a line of dialogue, something is lacking in the dialogue and the characterization. Work on those issues first.

THE POINT IS?

Like the word *suddenly*, the exclamation point can be overdone. Here's advice from the respected *Chicago Manual of Style:*

> An exclamation point is used to mark an outcry or an emphatic
> or ironic comment. To avoid detracting from its effectiveness,
> however, the author should use this punctuation sparingly. [64]

This mark of punctuation is appropriate for true exclamations, such as "Oh!" "Gosh!" "Help!" and "Watch out!" If a computer search of your manuscript shows a frequent or indiscriminate use of the exclamation point, experiment with different words and word arrangements until the emphasis you want doesn't come from punctuation but from placement.

That is, place the key words or phrases you want to emphasize at the ends of sentences. Endings vibrate power. Where possible, place key sentences at the ends of paragraphs. Gary Provost's advice to writers is to arrange sentences with tension in mind.[65]

For an example of a power arrangement, consider this ending to Chapter 22 from *The Heat of the Moon,* the first novel by Sandra Parshall.

> In the closed alcohol-reeking ambulance, with the keening siren deafening me to all other sound, I forced myself to turn my head and look at the stretcher next to mine.
> The medic bent over her, blocking her upper body from my sight. As I watched, he sat back, shoulders slumping. He remained that way for a moment with his head bowed. Then he shifted and I caught a glimpse of her pale cheek before he drew the blood-soaked sheet over her face.

Compare Parshall's phrasing with this much weaker rewrite of mine, in which I change only the word order within each sentence:

> I forced myself to turn my head and look at the stretcher next to mine in the closed alcohol-reeking ambulance, with the keening siren deafening me to all other sound.
> The medic blocked her upper body from my sight by bending over her. He sat back, shoulders slumping, as I watched. He remained with his head bowed that way for a moment. Before he drew the blood-soaked sheet up over her face, I caught a glimpse of her pale cheek when he shifted.

See how my word order ends each sentence on a weak note? My version would be even weaker if the blood-soaked sheet were drawn over the woman's face at the beginning of the sequence.

And think how infantile my version would become if I ended it with an exclamation point! Exclamation points in *abundance* produce the *same effect* as *too* much *italicizing:* after a while, readers *wonder* if the writer *thinks* we are *deaf or dense.* Literary critic B. R. Myers says that unnecessary emphasis is the classic sign of a writer who lacks confidence.[66]

Evidently, many writers lack confidence in their ability to get their point across! Maybe they doubt their audience's ability to read! A few seem to turn almost every line into an exclamation! That produces a most unusual effect!! *Stop it!!!*

RANGES

For superlatives—the biggest, the smallest, the most, the least, and so on—there is only one of its kind. That *one* cannot also exist as a range of possibilities. Do not write:

"This may seem like a fine point, but fine points can draw blood."
Theodore M. Bernstein

- ❧ The victim was at least seventy-five or eighty years old.
- ❧ When he reached the scene, as many as twenty or thirty bystanders had gathered.
- ❧ The child holding the gun couldn't have been more than ten or twelve.

Pick one. Say: the victim was seventy-five years old, there were as many as thirty bystanders, and the child couldn't have been more than twelve.

Or drop the "most-least" definers and keep the range:

- ❧ He guessed that the victim was seventy-five or eighty years old.
- ❧ When he got to the scene, twenty to thirty bystanders had gathered.
- ❧ The child holding the gun was ten or twelve.

When using a range, additional hedging words such as "about," "around," or "approximately" are redundant.

DOUBLED PREPOSITIONS

Another insidious form of redundancy is the doubled preposition. The protagonist sits *down on* the couch, reaches *up over* his head, stands *out in* the driveway, and climbs *up onto* the roof. He is constantly going *over to,* walking *over toward,* looking *over at,* and driving *over across.* Sometimes the habit manifests in triplets, as in looking *down below at* the street and coming *on over to* the house.

If this is your usual manner of speech, no problem. It won't affect your literary career, as long as you vigorously self-edit your writing. But if your multiple-prepositioned manuscript lands in front of someone whose job requires lowering a towering pile of submissions, any wordy habit adds to the perception that the writer's style is, at best, average.

Average writing is amateur writing. One of its obvious characteristics is imprecision in the choice of words. Because words are a writer's tools, evidence of tool mismanagement furnishes the quickest route to rejection.

Most instances of doubling can be cut in half. An occasional pair of twins may be allowed to take up residence in your manuscript if doing so improves the effect of certain passages, such as dialogue. Their presence must be intentional, however, not accidental.

Learn to recognize these uninvited guests. You are their host, so keep them from spreading their stuff out over and around about on everything.

FINALLY

This final tip may seem more nitpicky than my other observations, but picking nit is part of what editors do.

> "Nit: the egg of a parasitic insect, esp. of a louse."
> Webster's Encyclopedic Unabridged Dictionary

Take the word "finally"—one of the nits that can louse up any action. It belongs at the end of a series of challenges, not in the middle. Yet the word keeps popping up whenever a character overcomes any intermediate hurdle in a chain of events. Two manuscripts I edited used "finally" on page 1. Here's a condensed version of the typical mis-usage.

> Yvonne struggled to undo the rusty lock on the outside cellar doors. Finally she got it open. Slowly, cautiously, she made her way down the rickety ladder to the basement, listening for any sound. When she finally felt the dirt floor beneath her feet, she stumbled around until her foot hit wood and her groping confirmed a handrail.
>
> Yvonne climbed the stairs leading to the first floor. After quietly checking out each room and finding them unoccupied, she finally came across the doctor's home office. In the light from a streetlamp on the corner, she saw that all three filing cabinets held four drawers each. Just as she thought. Her search was first beginning.

For something first beginning, each *finally* sends a contradictory message. By now, readers have as much faith in the writer's accuracy as in a storefront banner proclaiming "Final Clearance."

"Finally" implies a hurdle overcome, a challenge met, anticipation satisfied. The implication triggers a temporary release of tension. You want to build tension, not alleviate it.

Consider the use of the more accurate "eventually" or "gradually." Better still, cut out the adverbs and show the character's feelings. Make readers experience the same emotion the character does at each step in the sequence—frustration, anger, a momentary sense of relief for contrast, then growing anxiety and fear. Note that I said to *show* these feelings. Not tell.

When should "finally" (or "ultimately") be used? Save it for the end of a series of challenges when you want tension to drop. Its overuse echoes the voice of an amateur.

As a TV host and his contestants were known to say with numbing regularity, this is my final answer.

FIND & FIX CLUE #24: WORDS & MISDEMEANORS

- Use your computer's search feature to see how often "suddenly" pops up in your own writing, and rewrite the action to surprise readers by making them anticipate a different outcome.
- Type the letters *laugh* into your search feature and analyze each occurrence, asking yourself why you are depending on some form of the word to tell an emotion that the dialogue could be doing a better job of revealing. (For a simple search method, see the TIP on page 242.)
- Repeat the above search using the letters *smil.*
- To intensify emotion in the reader, underplay it in the character.
- Search and destroy exclamation points and rearrange a sentence's word order until you produce the desired emphasis.
- To cure an excess of exclamation points, look on your keyboard for the period. Use it.
- Finally, search for the word "finally" and make sure it isn't overused, misused, or mindlessly reused. Reserve it for when you want readers to feel a true sense of finality.

"Creativity is the best revenge.
Let's finish our books."

Stone Altman, writer

PART X: POST-MORTEM

SUPPORTING TESTIMONY: ENDNOTES

PART I: DEAD ON ARRIVAL

1. Leonard Pitts, "First thanks go to my first reader," in *Greensboro News & Record,* April 10, 2004, p. A9.
2. "Slush," a 1982 essay in *Editors on Editing,* Gerald Gross, ed., Harper & Row, New York, 1985, p. 120.
3. For an explanation of genres, see the books by Carolyn Wheat and G. Miki Hayden listed in *Recommended Nonfiction,* Exhibit B.
4. I presented the original "shopping for a good fit" parable July 15, 2000, as part of the "Crisis!" panel at the Southern Mystery Gathering/Harriette Austin Writers Conference, University of Georgia. Since then variations of it have been quoted by others, some of whom credit the source.
5. "Talking with Justin Kaplan," by Lisa Burrell, in *Copy Editor,* 14:6 (Feb-Mar 2003), p. 3.
6. One exception is the belief that once an author's sales get into the millions, writing well is no longer a prerequisite for publication.
7. Based on letters from agents that writers have graciously shared with me.
8. *The First Five Pages,* Fireside, 2000, p. 13.
9. Kathie Fong Yoneda, *The Script-Selling Game,* Studio City, CA: Michael Wiese Productions, 2002, p. 2.
10. Jason Epstein, *Book Business,* New York: W.W. Norton, 2002, p. 43.
11. Barbara Gislayson, agent, at MWA's "Of Dark and Stormy Nights."
12. Quoted by Jennifer King, F&W Publications, in the newsletter of Mid-America Publishers Association, July 1996, p. 1.

PART II: EVIDENCE COLLECTION

13. "The Plot Quickens," by Sandra Wales, in *SPAN Connection,* VII:11, Nov 2002, p. 5. (Wales writes fiction under the name Haley Elizabeth Garwood.)
14. Interview in *Publishers Weekly,* Feb 14, 1999.
15. From a presentation by Elizabeth Daniels Squire at the North Carolina Writer's Network Conference, Asheville, Fall 1999.

PART III: FIRST OFFENDERS

16. John B. McHugh, "Self-Publishing for Individuals: How to Evaluate the Economic Realities and Ten Things to Do," 1999, BookZone.com.
17. Foster-Harris, University of Oklahoma Press, 1960, p. 80.
18. Foreword to *The American Claimant,* Charles L. Webster & Co., 1892.
19. Since 1982 the English Dept. at San Jose State University has sponsored the Bulwer-Lytton Fiction Contest to write the worst opening sentence to a novel. The contest was begun by Prof. Scott Rice, who unearthed the source of the line "It was a dark and stormy night." www.bulwer-lytton.com.
20. Research conducted on the DorothyL listserv.
21. Interview with Jessica Faust, Bookends, May 17, 2002, via e-mail.
22. E-mail from Jim Huang dated Jan 22, 2004.
23. Carolyn Wheat, *How to Write Killer Fiction,* compares mystery and thriller.
24. *How to Grow a Novel,* p. 229.
25. *The 38 Most Common Fiction Writing Mistakes,* pp. 11–12.
26. New York: Harper & Row, 1955, p. 21.
27. "Good Writing is Good Editing," in *AMWA Journal,* 17:1, p. 28.

PART IV: KILLING TIME

28. Sol Stein, *Stein on Writing,* New York: St. Martin's Griffin, 2000, p. 144.
29. *Technique in Fiction,* Harper & Row, 1955, p. 155.

PART V: THE LINEUP

30. Remarks by Lawrence Block at MWA 2003 Mid-Atlantic Region Conference, as reported by Peter Abresch.
31. Speaking at the MWA Skill-Build, Aug 16, 2003, Columbia, SC.
32. "Bruce Holland Rogers," a review in *Wisconsin Regional Writer,* 52:4, Winter 2004, p. 2.
33. *The 38 Most Common Fiction Writing Mistakes,* p. 11.
34. "Newsmakers," interview in *Newsweek,* Dec 23, 2002, p. 75.
35. "Standing in the Line of Fire," interview in *Newsweek,* July 5, 2004, p. 56.

PART VI: CHANGE OF VENUE

36. Posted on "10 Mistakes List," www.holtuncensored.com.
37. *Writing Crime Fiction,* London: Teach Yourself, 2003, p. 10.
38. "Fred Chappell," by Maria C. Johnson, in *Greensboro News & Record,* Sunday, Jan 19, 2003, p. D2.

PART VII: THE USUAL SUSPECTS

39. Quoted in "The Spooky Art," *Newsweek,* Jan 27, 2003, p. 64.
40. *The 38 Most Common Fiction Writing Mistakes,* p. 31.
41. Patricia Highsmith, *Plotting and Writing Suspense Thrillers,* p. 65.
42. Isabel Zuber, "Mining the Memory," in *North Carolina Writers' Network News,* Nov/Dec 2002, p. 20.

43. *From Pen to Print: The Secrets of Getting Published Successfully.* New York: Henry Holt, 1990, p. 32.
44. For readers who might not recognize this reference, it's to "The Pit and the Pendulum" by Edgar Allen Poe.
45. No need to write to tell me that pornography and erotica are not the same. I took some license here for the sake of a little humor. Very little, I agree.
46. "The Sport of Fiction" in *Writer's Digest,* Oct 1992, p. 32. Provost authored thousands of articles and dozens of books covering almost every genre.
47. In mythology, Hero was a woman. Her courage was so outstanding that her name was also applied to men who exhibited extreme bravery. Today the word is understood to apply equally to men and women.
48. "Suspense," unidentified contributor, in *The Mystery Writer's Handbook,* Mystery Writers of America, Harper, 1956, p. 105.
49. "Fiction," in *Mensa Bulletin* #461, Jan 2003, p. 14.
50. In Chapter 18; p. 186 of the Pocket Books edition, 1939.

PART VIII: ROGUES GALLERY

51. Carl T. Bogus, "Guns in the Courtroom," in *The Nation,* Mar 31, 2003, p. 40.
52. Erica Jong, "The Artist as Housewife," in *Ms. Magazine,* I:6 (Dec 1972), p. 66.
53. Interview of S. J. Rozan by Qui Xiaolong on www.mysteryreaders.org/athome.html, *Mystery Readers International.*
54. Original publisher, University of Louisiana Press. Reprinted 1987 by Grove Weidenfeld.
55. "Fallacies of Anti-Reformers," by Sydney Smith, 1771-1845, who proposed the idea of *The Edinburgh Review* in 1798 and wrote for it for 25 years.
56. *Write in Style,* Union Square Publishing, 2004, p. 7.

PART IX: LOOSE ENDS

57. *Writing Mysteries,* ed. Sue Grafton, p. 210. Emphasis is Cavin's.
58. Renni Browne & Dave King, *Self-Editing for Fiction Writers,* New York: Harper Perennial, 1994; revised 2005.
59. Source unknown.
60. Presentation at Harriette Austin Writers Conference, Athens, GA, July 2002.
61. Stephen King, *On Writing,* p. 136.
62. *Editing Your Fiction,* Cincinnati: Writer's Digest Books, 2001, p. 128.
63. "Bob Newhart," by Tim Williams in *TV Guide,* July 17, 2005, p. 15.
64. 14th ed., University of Chicago Press, p. 162, §5.17. The 15th ed., p. 260, §6.76, adds: "should be used sparingly to be effective."
65. *Make Your Words Work,* p. 245.
66. B. R. Myers, "A Reader's Manifesto," in *Atlantic Monthly,* 288:1 (Jul-Aug 2001), 104.

EXHIBIT A: STANDARD MANUSCRIPT FORMAT

Always follow the preferences stated by your submission's recipient. If none are stated, use these industry standards.

Double-spaced typed text: This does NOT mean one-and-a-half lines of space. It means that for 12 point type, spacing or leading should be 24 points. The same for quotations and footnotes.

Margins: Minimum 1" top and bottom, 1.25" sides. Large margins make it easier for an editor to write notes and for the author to read them.

Alignment: Flush left, also known as ragged right. Never justify.

Paragraphs: Don't skip lines between. To separate scenes within a chapter, hit "return" once and type # (or * * *) in the center of the line.

Paragraph indents: One tab or 5 spaces.

Tabs: Use for paragraph indents, not for columns, tables, or centering titles. Instead, use the word processor's features meant for these functions.

Font: `Monospaced, as a typewriter,` not proportional, as in typesetting. This is 12 pt Times New Roman; it's proportional. `This is 12 pt Courier (not Courier New); it's monospaced.` Times is for a quick read; Courier, for a quality manuscript edit. Use Courier unless you are instructed otherwise. To mimic typesetting is to look like an amateur. On a typewriter, "pitch" refers to characters per inch [`pica = 10 pitch or 12 points; elite = 12 pitch or 10 points`].

Serif font: Courier and Times have little "feet" that make them easier to read, so never use a sans serif font (like this one) for manuscripts. Go easy on the *italics;* avoid ALL CAPS and *decorative or display type.*

<u>Underscore:</u> This tells copyeditors and traditional typesetters to set words in italics (a separate font that might not be the same as your keyboard shortcut). Use for most foreign words and for the names of books, plays, movies, and TV series. (Use quotation marks for articles, chapters, acts and scenes, short stories, and TV episodes in a series.) To de-italicize set type, underscore and write <u>rom</u> (for roman) in margin.

Bold face: May be used for headings and subheadings, never in text. If emphasis is required, <u>underscore</u> to represent italics.

Dash: Show as a double hyphen--without spaces.

Ellipsis: Show with 3 periods, with or without spaces; 4 periods when quoted material falls at the end of a sentence. Turn off the keystroke feature that creates 3 condensed dots. (For using dots vs. dashes, please see the TIP on page 177.)

Hyphenation: Off.

Page numbers: Must be in sequence throughout, including front matter. No pages missing, repeated, or out of order. (Use the auto-numbering feature that's part of your word processor's header and footer options). If necessary, hand write page numbers on the printout; never type them on individual pages in a word processing program—they become scrambled within the text when text changes are made.

Footnotes (for nonfiction): If the work is being submitted for editing, use your word processor's footnote or endnote feature and set all notes and bibliographic material to print the same as other text: 12 pt Courier double-spaced. Or type the actual note directly into the text where you want it referenced, and enclose it in parentheses, without numbering.

Graphics: Avoid embedding charts, tables, figures, etc., in the main text. Number each graphic, and show where it belongs by typing a corresponding number in the text and the line: "Insert figure x here."

Paper: Standard white 8-1/2" by 11"; no pin-feed tear-offs or hole punching. Avoid erasable bond, which smudges. Avoid heavy bond; the added weight increases shipping costs and suggests to editors that the length is excessive).

Printing: One side of the paper only; one column of text.

Black ink: Use a laser or ink cartridge that produces clear, sharp text. If submitting a photocopy, it should be a first generation copy. Handwritten text must be typed; if accepted for publication, it must be available electronically, so use a computer. Scanning is not recommended.

Binding: None. Loose pages only, not stapled, not clipped, not bound in a looseleaf or any kind of binder. Punched holes get in the way of an editor's marginal notations. Use a big rubber band.

END: Type this word at the end of your manuscript. This, together with consecutive page numbering, lets the editor and typesetter know they have the entire manuscript.

Never send photos without permission, or your only copy of anything.

EXHIBIT B: RECOMMENDED NONFICTION

EDITING FICTION

Bickham, Jack M. *The 38 Most Common Fiction Writing Mistakes (And How To Avoid Them).* Cincinnati: Writer's Digest Books, 1992.

Browne, Renni, & Dave King. *Self-Editing for Fiction Writers.* New York: Harper Perennial, 1994; revised 2005.

Christmas, Bobbie. *Write in Style: Using Your Word Processor and Other Techniques to Improve Your Writing.* New York: Union Square Pub., 2004.

Gross, Gerald. *Editors on Editing, 3rd ed.* New York: Harper & Row, 1985.

Lukeman, Noah. *The First Five Pages: A Writer's Guide to Staying Out of the Rejection Pile.* New York: Simon & Schuster, 2000.

Obstfeld, Raymond. *Fiction First Aid,* Cincinnati: Writer's Digest Books, 2001.

WRITING FICTION

Bickham, Jack M. *Setting: How To Create and Sustain a Sharp Sense of Time and Place in Your Fiction.* Cincinnati: Writer's Digest Books, 1994.

Block, Lawrence. *Telling Lies for Fun and Profit: A Manual for Fiction Writers.* New York: William Morrow & Co., 1981.

Lukeman, Noah. *The Plot Thickens.* New York: St. Martin's Press, 2002.

Orr, Alice. *No More Rejections: 50 Secrets to Writing a Manuscript that Sells.* Cincinnati: Writer's Digest Books, 2004.

Provost, Gary. *Make Your Words Work.* Cincinnati: Writer's Digest Books, 1990; Author's Guild Backinprint.com edition, 2001.

Stein, Sol. *How to Grow a Novel.* New York: St. Martin's Press, 1999.

WRITING MYSTERY

Ephron, Hallie. *Writing and Selling Your Mystery Novel: How to Knock 'Em Dead with Style.* Cincinnati: Writer's Digest Books, 2005.

Grafton, Sue, ed. *Writing Mysteries: A Handbook by the Mystery Writers of America.* Cincinnati: Writer's Digest Books, 2001.

Hayden, G. Miki. *Writing the Mystery.* Philadelphia: Intrigue Press, 2001.

Highsmith, Patricia. *Plotting and Writing Suspense Fiction.* Boston: The Writer, 1966; New York: Writer's Library, 1990.

King, Stephen. *On Writing: A Memoir of the Craft.* New York: Scribner, 2000; Pocket Books edition, 2002.

Neri, Kris. *Writing Killer Mysteries: 8 Lessons to Get You Into Print.* Valencia CA: T2G Productions, 2006. (Format: DVD)

Tapply, William G. *The Elements of Mystery Fiction: Writing the Modern Whodunit.* Boston: The Writer, Inc., 1995; Poisoned Pen Press, 2005.

Wheat, Carolyn. *How to Write Killer Fiction.* Santa Barbara: Perseverance Press, 2003. Outstanding comparison of mystery and thriller, plus a useful guide to genres and subgenres.

CHARACTER BUILDING & BEHAVIOR

Ballon, Rachel. *Breathing Life into Your Characters: How to Give Your Characters Emotional and Psychological Depth.* Cincinnati: Writer's Digest Books, 2003.

Douglas, John E., and Mark Olshaker. *Anatomy of Motive: The FBI's Legendary Mindhunter Explores the Key to Understanding & Catching Violent Criminals.* New York: Scribner, 1999.

Groetsch, Michael; ed. Chris Roerden. *He Promised He'd Stop.* Brookfield WI: CPI Publishing, 1997. Profiles the types of men who abuse women.

Kress, Nancy. *Dynamic Characters.* Cincinnati: Writer's Digest Books, 1998.

Samenow, Stanton E. *Inside the Criminal Mind.* New York: Crown Publishing, 2004.

Tannen, Deborah. *You Just Don't Understand: Women and Men in Conversation.* New York: Ballantine Books, 1991.

CRIMINAL INVESTIGATION

Brown, Steven Kerry. *The Complete Idiot's Guide to Private Investigating.* New York: Penguin Group, 2003.

Campbell, Andrea. *Making Crime Pay: The Writer's Guide to Criminal Law, Evidence, and Procedure.* New York: Allworth Press, 2002.

COPYRIGHT

Kozak, Ellen. *Every Writer's Guide to Copyright and Publishing Law,* 3rd ed. New York: Henry Holt, 2004.

MARKETING THE MANUSCRIPT

Brogan, Kathryn S. *Guide to Literary Agents.* Cincinnati: Writers Digest Books, 2005.

Herman, Jeff. *Guide to Book Publishers, Editors, and Literary Agents.* Waukesha WI: The Writer Books, 2005.

Maass, Donald. *The Career Novelist: A Literary Agent Offers Strategies for Success.* Portsmouth, NH: Heinemann, 1996.

Page, Susan. *The Shortest Distance Between You and a Published Book.* Broadway Books, New York. 1997.

Sands, Katharine. *Making the Perfect Pitch: How to Catch a Literary Agent's Eye.* Waukesha, WI: The Writer Books, 2004.

WRITER'S LIFE

Kelner, Steve. *Motivate Your Writing!* Lebanon, NH: University Press of New England, 2005.

EXHIBIT C: POPULAR INTERNET SITES

Mystery Writers of America, *www.mysterywriters.org,* is the oldest organization of crime writers in the world. Membership is open to professionally published as well as unpublished writers and others in the book industry. Online discussion groups. Links to regional chapters, many with their own annual conferences and workshops for writers. Annual Edgar® Awards. List of approved publishers that qualify members as professionally published.

Sisters in Crime, *www.sistersincrime.org/index.htm,* is a membership organization for women and men offering networking and advice to mystery writers, published and not-yet-published. Mission is to combat discrimination against women in the mystery field. Local chapters, online discussion group, beginners group.

The Private Eye Writers of America, *www.thrillingdetective.com,* is an organization of fans, writers, and publishing professionals devoted to private-eye detective fiction. Annual Shamus awards.

American Crime Writers League, *www.acwl.org/index.html,* provides member-recommended links.

Crime Writers of Canada, *www.crimewriterscanada.com/index.htm*

International Association of Crime Writers, *www.crimewritersna.org*

International Thriller Writers, *www.thrillerwriters.org,* is the first organization for professional writers of thrillers. Sponsors Thrillerfest.

Science Fiction and Fantasy Writers of America, Inc., *http://sfwa.org*

Horror Writers Association, *www.horror.org,* is a worldwide organization of over 1,000 writers and publishing professionals. Free online articles on writing plus links.

Romance Writers of America Kiss of Death Chapter, *www.rwamysterysuspense.org,* is for murderously inclined romantics.

ClueLass, *www.ClueLass.com,* provides details on hundreds of mystery bookstores, organizations, events, authors, and more. Lists new and recent mystery fiction releases. Listings are interlinked so author pages list their books, and book pages include links to mystery booksellers.

Writer's Medical and Forensics Lab, *www.dplylemd.com,* lists specialized medical and forensic knowledge.

Dorothy L, *www.dorothyl.com,* is a discussion and idea listserve for lovers of the mystery, created by women librarians in honor of Dorothy L. Sayers. Over 3,000 members worldwide. Free.

Femmes Fatales, *http://femmesfatalesauthors.com,* is a fun, free, online mystery newsletter run by female mystery authors about the trials, tribulations, and the finer points of writing mysteries.

FictionAddiction, *http://fictionaddiction.net,* offers networking among writers, publishing news, finding a literary agent, Ask the Expert section, free articles, and links to author-related sites and resources.

Malice Domestic, *www.malicedomestic.org,* is held annually in Washington, DC, saluting traditional mysteries typified by Agatha Christie.

Bouchercon World Mystery Convention, *http://bouchercon.net,* is run annually by fans for fans.

Predators & Editors, *www.anotherealm.com/predators,* provides information and contacts for writers seeking publication, any genre; lists good and bad agents, some editing services. Links to writers' forums and discussion lists, contests, conventions, resources, workshops, and more.

Agent Query, *www.agentquery.com,* is a database of literary agents actively seeking clients, searchable by genre, plus sample query letters.

Literary Agents, *www.literaryagents.org,* is a part of Fiction Writers Resource Web. Includes pages of Agents Actively Looking, Top Agents, addresses, and free articles on finding an agent and cover letters.

Corrections and additions to this resource list are welcomed for future editions of this book. See the contact information at
www.MarketSavvyBookEditing.com/contact.html

EXHIBIT D: BIBLIOGRAPHY OF FICTION CITED

Abramo, J. L. *Catching Water in a Net.* New York: St. Martin's, 2002.

Abresch, Peter. *Bloody Bonsai.* Aurora, CO: Write Way Publishing, 1999.

Adams, Deborah. *All the Great Pretenders.* New York: Ballantine, 1992.

Albert, Susan Wittig. *Lavender Lies.* New York: Berkley Prime Crime, 1999.

Anderson, Beth. *Murder Online.* Denver: Amber Quill Press, 2003.

Andrews, Donna. *Murder with Peacocks.* New York: St. Martin's, 1999.

Avery, Morgan. *Act of Betrayal.* New York: Pinnacle Books, 2000.

Baker, Deb. *Murder Passes the Buck.* St. Paul, MN: Midnight Ink, 2006.

Ballard, Mignon F. *Shadow of an Angel.* New York: Minotaur, 2002.

Balzo, Sandra. *Uncommon Grounds.* Waterville, ME: Five Star, 2004.

Barnes, Linda. *A Trouble of Fools.* New York: Hyperion, 1987.

Barr, Nevada. *Liberty Falling.* New York: Putnam, 2001; Berkley Books, 2002.

Barrett, Kathleen Anne. *Milwaukee Winters Can Be Murder.* (New York: Thomas Bouregy, 1996); in *Homicide for the Holidays.* Aurora, CO: Write Way Publishing, 2000.

Bartholomew, Nancy. *Drag Strip.* New York: St. Martin's Minotaur, 1999.

Bickham, Jack M. *Dropshot.* New York: Tom Doherty Associates, 1990.

Biehl, Michael. *Doctored Evidence.* Bridgehampton, NY: Bridge Works, 2002; Berkley mass market ed, 2003.

Birmingham, Ruth. *Atlanta Graves.* New York: Berkley Prime Crime, 1998.

Bland, Eleanor Taylor. *Done Wrong.* New York: St. Martin's Press, 1995.

Bone, Patrick. *A Melungeon Winter.* Johnson City, TN: Silver Dagger, 2001.

Brod, D. C. *Error in Judgment.* New York: Walker Publishing, 1990; Diamond ed, 1991.

Brown, Dan. *The DaVinci Code.* New York: Doubleday, 2003.

Brown, Sandra. *The Alibi.* New York: Warner Books, 1999.

Brown, Steve. *Hurricane Party.* Taylors, SC: Chick Springs Publishing, 2002.

Browning, Pat. *Full Circle.* iUniverse, 2001.

Buchanan, Edna. *Miami, It's Murder.* New York: HarperCollins, 1994.

Buffa, D. W. *The Prosecution.* New York: Henry Holt, 1999.

Burke, James Lee. *A Morning for Flamingos.* Boston: Little, Brown & Co., 1990; Avon Books, 1991.

Burke, Jan. *Flight.* New York: Simon & Schuster, 2001; Pocket Books, 2002.

_____. *Goodnight, Irene.* New York: Simon & Schuster, 1993; Pocket Books, 2002.

Carson, Leah. *Sons of Lazarus.* Dousman, WI: Excellent Words, 1997.

Child, Lee. *Die Trying.* New York: Putnam, 1998; Jove ed, 1999.

Chittenden, Meg. *More Than You Know.* New York: Berkley Sensation, 2003.

Churchill, Jill. *The Merchant of Menace.* New York: Avon Books, 1999.

Coben, Harlan. *Tell No One.* New York: Dell, 2001; Delacorte Press ed, 2002.

Coleman, Evelyn. *What a Woman's Gotta Do.* New York: Simon & Schuster, 1998.

Collins, Max Allan. *Blood and Thunder.* New York: Signet, 1996.

Connelly, Michael. *The Black Echo.* New York: St. Martin's Press, 1992; Warner Books ed, 2002.

Connor, Beverly. *A Rumor of Bones.* New York: Cumberland House, Nashville, TN, 1996.

Cook, Dawn. *First Truth.* New York: Berkley, 2002.

Cornwell, Patricia. *Black Notice.* New York: Putnam, 1999.

Coulter, Catherine. *The Edge.* New York: Putnam, 1999; Jove ed, 2000.

Cruse, Lonnie. *Murder in Metropolis.* Martinsburg, WV: Quiet Storm, 2003.

D'Amato, Barbara. *Authorized Personnel Only.* New York: Tom Doherty, 2000.

_____. *Killer.app.* New York: Tom Doherty Associates, 1996.

Damron, Carla. *Keeping Silent.* Aurora, CO: Write Way Publishing, 2001.

Dams, Jeanne. *Body in the Transept.* New York: Walker, 1995.

_____. *To Perish in Penzance.* New York: Walker, 2001; Worldwide, 2002.

Daniel, Cindy. *Death Warmed Over.* Martinsburg, WV: Quiet Storm, 2003.

Deaver, Jeffery. *The Coffin Dancer.* New York: Simon & Schuster, 1998.

DeLoach, Nora. *Mama Rocks the Empty Cradle.* New York: Bantam, 1998; Bantam mass market ed, 1999.

DePoy, Phillip. *Easy.* New York: Dell Publishing, 1997.

_____. *The Devil's Hearth.* New York: St. Martin's, 2003; Worldwide, 2004.

Dietz, Denise. *Footprints in the Butter: An Ingrid Beaumont Mystery Co-starring Hitchcock the Dog.* Lee's Summit, MO: Delphi Books, 1999; Worldwide, 2003.

du Maurier, Daphne. *Rebecca.* New York: Doubleday, 1938; Avon Books ed, 1971.

Dymmoch, Michael Allen. New York: *The Man Who Understood Cats.* New York: Avon Books, 1993.

Estleman, Loren D. *Sinister Heights.* New York: Mysterious Press, 2002.

Evanovich, Janet. *One for the Money.* New York: Scribner, 1994; HarperPaperbacks ed, 1995.

Fairstein, Linda. *Final Jeopardy.* New York: Scribner, 1996; Pocket Books, 1997.

Frommer, Sara Hoskinson. *The Vanishing Violinist.* New York: St. Martin's, 1999; Worldwide, 2000.

George, Elizabeth. *For the Sake of Elena.* New York: Bantam, 1992.

Glatzer, Hal. *A Fugue in Hell's Kitchen.* McKinleyville, CA: Perseverance Press, 2004.

Grafton, Sue. *"P" is for Peril.* New York: Ballantine Books, 2002.

Grant, Anne Underwood. *Multiple Listing.* New York: Dell Publishing, 1998.

Grant, Linda. *A Woman's Place.* New York: Ivy Books, 1994.

_____. *Lethal Genes.* New York: Ivy Books, 1996.

Grimes, Martha. *I Am the Only Running Footman.* New York: Dell, 1986.

Haines, Carolyn. *Them Bones.* New York: Bantam Books, 1999.

Hall, Parnell. *Murder.* Canada: General Publishing, 1987; New American Library/Onyx ed, 1989.

Hampton, Lynette Hall. *Jilted by Death.* Johnson City, TN: Silver Dagger, 2004.

Harris, Charlaine. *Dead Over Heels.* New York: Worldwide/Scribner, 1998.

Hayden, G. Miki. *By Reason of Insanity.* New York: Free Range Press, 1998.

Hellmann, Libby Fischer. *An Eye for Murder.* New York: Berkley Prime Crime, 2002.

Helms, Rick. *Voodoo That You Do.* Weddington, NC: Back Alley Books, 2001.

Highsmith, Patricia. *The Blunderer.* London: William Heinemann Ltd., 1956; Penguin Books, 1988.

Hinze, Vicki. *Duplicity.* New York: St. Martin's, 1999.

Hoffman, Jilliane. *Retribution.* New York: Putnam, 2004.

Holbrook, Teri. *Sad Water.* New York: Bantam Books, 1999.

Hunter, Ellen Elizabeth. *Murder on the Candlelight Tour.* Greensboro, NC: Writers' Group of the Triad, 2003.

Hunter, Gwen. *Delayed Diagnosis.* Ontario: Mira Books, 2001.

Jance, J. A. *Desert Heat.* New York: Avon Books, 1993.

Johansen, Iris. *Long After Midnight.* New York: Bantam Books, 1997.

Kellerman, Faye. *Moon Music.* New York: William Morrow, 1998; Avon, 1999.

Kellerman, Jonathan. *The Clinic.* New York: Bantam Books, 1997.

Kelner, Toni L. P. *Down Home Murder.* New York: Kensington Publishing, 1993; Kensington Paperback ed, 1999.

Kennett, Shirley. *See* Morgan Avery.

Konrath, J. A. *Whiskey Sour.* New York: Hyperion, 2004.

Krich, Rochelle. *Blues in the Night.* New York: Fawcett, 2002; Ballantine, 2003.

Kronenwetter, Michael. *First Kill.* New York: St. Martin's Minotaur, 2005.

Lakey, Barbara. *Spirit of the Straightedge.* Minneapolis: A.M.F. Publishers, 2002.

Lane, Vicki. *Signs in the Blood.* New York: Bantam Dell, 2005.

Lehane, Dennis. *Gone, Baby, Gone.* New York: Avon Books, 1998.

Leonard, Elmore. *Glitz.* New York: Mysterious Press, 1985; Warner Books, 1986.

MacDonald, John D. *The Deep Blue Good-by.* Greenwich, CT: Fawcett, 1964.

Maron, Margaret. *Bootlegger's Daughter.* New York: Mysterious Press, 1992.

_____. *Southern Discomfort.* New York: Mysterious Press, 1993.

Martini, Steve. *Prime Witness.* New York: Putnam, 1993; Jove ed, 1994.

Matthews, Alex. *Death's Domain.* Philadelphia: Intrigue Press, 2001.

McBain, Ed. *There Was a Little Girl.* New York: Warner Books, 1994.

McCullough, Karen. *A Question of Fire.* Ontario, Canada: LTDBooks, 2000.

McDermid, Val. *A Place of Execution.* Great Britain: HarperCollins, 1999; New York: St. Martin's Paperbacks, 2001.

Mosley, Walter. *Bad Boy Brawly Brown.* Boston: Little, Brown, 2002; New York: Warner Books, 2003.

Mucha, Susan P. *Deadly Deception.* Augusta, GA: Harbor House, 2005.

Muller, Marcia. *The Cheshire Cat's Eye.* 1983; New York: Mysterious Press ed, 1990.

Munger, Katy. *Legwork.* New York: Avon Books, 1997.

Myers, Tamar. *The Ming and I.* New York: Avon Books, 1991.

_____. *Too Many Crooks Spoil the Broth.* New York: Doubleday, 1994; Signet ed, 1995.

Neri, Kris. *Revenge of the Gypsy Queen.* Highland City, FL: Rainbow Books, 1999; Worldwide, 2003.

Nicholson, Scott. *The Red Church.* New York: Pinnacle Books, 2002.

Orwell, George. *Nineteen Eighty-four.* New York: Harcourt, Brace, 1949; Signet Classic, 41st printing.

Paretsky, Sara. *Bitter Medicine.* New York: William Morrow, 1987; Ballantine Books, 9th printing 1990.

_____. *Blood Shot.* New York: Delacorte Press, 1988; Dell, 1989.

Parshall, Sandra. *The Heat of the Moon.* Scottsdale: Poisoned Pen, 2006.

Patterson, James. *Cat & Mouse.* Boston: Little, Brown, 1997.

Peters, Elizabeth. *Naked Once More.* New York: Warner Books, 1989.

Piccirilli, Tom. *Shards.* Aurora, CO: Write Way Publishing, 1996; first paperback ed, 1997.

Pickard, Nancy. *No Body.* New York: Pocket Books, 1986.

Pickens, Cathy. *Southern Fried.* New York: Thomas Dunne, 2004.

Picoult, Jodi. *Plain Truth.* New York: Pocket Books, 2000.

Polisar, Lisa. *Blackwater Tango.* Boonsboro, MD: Hilliard & Harris, 2002.

Prospero, Ann. *Almost Night.* New York: New American Library, 2000; Onyx ed, 2001.

Proulx, Suzanne. *Bad Luck.* New York: Ballantine, 2000.

Reichs, Kathy. *Death du Jour.* New York: Scribner, 1999; Pocket Books ed, 2000.

Reuben, Shelly. *Weeping.* Cambridge, MA: Kate's Mystery Books, 2004.

Riggs, Cynthia. *Deadly Nightshade.* New York: St. Martin's, 2001; Signet ed, 2003.

Rozan, S. J. *A Bitter Feast.* New York: St. Martin's, 1998.

_____. *Winter and Night.* New York: St. Martin's, 2002.

Sandford, John. *Rules of Prey.* New York, Putnam, 1989; Berkley ed, 1990.

Saums, Mary. *Midnight Hour.* Johnson City, TN: Silver Dagger, 2000.

Schumacher, Aileen. *Framework for Death.* Aurora, CO: Write Way Publishing, 1998; Worldwide, 2000.

Scoppettone, Sandra. *My Sweet Untraceable You.* New York: Little, Brown, 1994; Ballantine Books edition, 1995.

Scottoline, Lisa. *Final Appeal.* New York: HarperCollins, 1994.

Sebold, Alice. *The Lovely Bones.* Boston: Little, Brown, 2002.

Shaber, Sarah R. *Snipe Hunt.* New York: St. Martin's Press, 2000; paperback edition, 2001.

Siddons, Anne Rivers. *The House Next Door.* New York: Random House, 1978.

Singer, Gammy L. *A Landlord's Tale.* New York: Kensington Publishers, 2005.

Sorrells, Walter. *Will to Murder.* New York: Avon Books, 1996.

Spencer-Fleming, Julia. *To Darkness and to Death.* New York: Thomas Dunne Books, 2005.

Sprinkle, Patricia Houck. *Murder in the Charleston Manner.* New York: St. Martin's Press, 1990; Worldwide Mystery edition, 1993.

Squire, Elizabeth Daniels. *Memory Can Be Murder.* New York: Berkley Prime Crime, 1995.

_____. *Who Killed What's-Her-Name?* New York: Berkley Prime Crime, 1994.

Swanson, Denise. *Murder of a Small-Town Honey.* New York: Signet, 2000.

_____. *Murder of a Sweet Old Lady.* New York: Signet, 2001.

Sweeney, Leann. *Pick Your Poison.* New York: NAL/Signet, 2004.

Tiller, Denise. *Calculated Risk.* Allen, TX: Timberwolf Press, 2000.

Tishy, Cecelia. *Jealous Heart.* Nashville, TN: Dowling Press, 1997; Signet, 1999.

Todd, Charles. *A Test of Wills.* New York: St. Martin's, 1996; Bantam ed, 1998.

Toole, John Kennedy. *A Confederacy of Dunces.* Louisiana State University Press, 1980; New York: Grove Weidenfeld, Evergreen ed, 1987.

Tooley, S. D. *When the Dead Speak.* Schererville, IN: Full Moon Publishing, 1999.

Tracy, P. J. *Monkeewrench.* New York: Putnam, 2003; Signet, 2004.

Trocheck, Kathy Hogan. *Heart Trouble.* New York: HarperCollins, 1996; HarperPaperbacks, 1996.

Vidler, Ellis. *Haunting Refrain.* Johnson City, TN: Silver Dagger, 2004.

Viets, Elaine. *The Pink Flamingo Murders.* New York: Dell, 1999.

Vogt, M. Diane. *Six Bills.* Beverly Hills: New Millennium Press, 2003.

Wall, Kathryn R. *In for a Penny.* Beaufort, SC: Coastal Villages Press, 2001.

West, Chassie. *Sunrise.* New York: HarperPaperbacks, 1994.

Wheat, Carolyn. *Fresh Kills.* New York: Berkley Prime Crime, 1995; paperback ed, 1996.

Woods, Stuart. *Blood Orchid.* New York: Putnam, 2002.

Wright, Nancy Means. *Mad Season.* New York: St. Martin's, 1996.

Wyle, Dirk. *Pharmacology Is Murder.* Highland City, FL: Rainbow Books, 1998.

CROSS-EXAMINATION: INDEX

A

Abramo, J. L. 226
Abresch, Peter 40, 126
accidental crime fighter 47, 167
Adams, Deborah 232, 241
adjectives, adverbs 187, 248
Aehl, Roxanne 101
Albert, Susan Wittig 215
allusion 136
Altman, Stone 272
anchoring 143–49
Anderson, Beth 30, 32
Andrews, Donna 37
anticipation 163, 165
Arnston, Harry 40
attribution 187–98
author intrusion 249
Avery, Morgan 36

B

background 55
Baker, Deb 207
Ballard, Mignon F. 32
Balzo, Sandra 265
Barnes, Linda 254
Barr, Nevada 31, 125
Barrett, Kathleen Anne 123
Bartholomew, Nancy 97, 140, 205, 253
beat 188
Bernstein, Theodore M. 269
Bickham, Jack M. 54, 104, 151, 206
Biehl, Michael 213
Birmingham, Ruth 146, 237
Bland, Eleanor Taylor 86
Blevins, Win 249
bloat 154
Block, Lawrence 93
body language 187–89, 231
body on page one 46
Bone, Patrick 217

Booth, Doris 252
braiding 125
Brod, D. C. 115
Brohaugh, Bill 20
Brown, Dan 43
Brown, Sandra 67, 195
Brown, Steve 202
Browning, Pat 46, 97
Buchanan, Edna 31
Buffa, D. W. 32
Burke, James Lee 97
Burke, Jan 16, 47, 80

C

calendar of events 91
Carson, Leah 31
Cavin , Ruth 238
Chappell, Fred 150
character development 169
Child, Lee 35
Chittenden, Meg 43, 125
Christie, Agatha 188
Christmas, Bobbie 230
Churchill, Jill 176
clichés 37, 223–29
cliffhanger 49
Coben, Harlan 48
Coleman, Evelyn 206, 254
Collins, Max Allan 232
computer tips, see TIPS
conflict 163–82
   internal 169–72
Connelly, Michael 134
Connor, Beverly 99
contradiction 106
Cook, Dawn 131
Cornwell, Patricia 36
Coulter, Catherine 233
counterpoint 257
crowd scenes 195
Cruse, Lonnie 164

D

D'Amato, Barbara 157, 263
Damron, Carla 94
Dams, Jeanne 101, 237
Daniel, Cindy 215, 243
Deaver, Jeffery 96, 100, 254
DeLoach, Nora 244
density 23, 25, 56, 59, 65, 100, 260
DePoy, Phillip 31, 236
description 93–119, 121–24, 134–38
dialect 215
dialogue 21, 175–86
    shortcuts 161
    tags 187–98
Dietz, Denise 35, 42, 122
digression 160
dilemma 169
direct address 192
diversity 207–209
dramatic irony 181, 259
du Maurier, Daphne 83
Dymmoch, Michael Allen 257

E

editing, types of 18
Edson, Margaret 219
elements of the novel 25
Ellison, J. T. 52
Ephron, Hallie 142
epithet 98, 205
Epstein, Brett Jocelyn 183
Epstein, Jason 13
Estleman, Loren 138
Evanovich, Janet 120, 161
exclamation point 267

F

Fairstein, Linda 37, 218
Faust, Jessica 42
figurative language 253
filter through narrator 127, 245

"finally" 270
Fitting Room, The 6
flashback 63–70
Fleisher, Leon 211
follow-through 115
foreboding 36, 49
foreshadowing 49, 82
foretelling 49
formatting 18
Foster-Harris 29
Frommer, Sara Hoskinson 55

G

genre 4–5
George, Elizabeth 234, 239
gesturing 231–42
Gislason, Barbara 17
Glatzer, Hal 179
Goodman, Ellen 199
Grafton, Sue 16, 90
Grant, Anne Underwood 108, 121,
    253
Grant, Linda 50, 143, 152
Grant-Adamson, Lesley 128
Grimes, Martha 232
grounding 143–49

H

had-I-but-known 49
Haines, Carolyn 247
Hall, Parnell 169
Hampton, Lynette Hall 136
Harris, Charlaine 29, 248
Harte, Bret 215
Hayden, G. Miki 237
head-hopping 128
Hellmann, Libby Fischer 107, 158
Helms, Richard 109
Highsmith, Patricia 11, 152, 159
Hinze, Vicki 170, 254
Hoffman, Jilliane 206
Holbrook, Teri 259

Holt, Patricia 121
hook 27–39
howler 227, 240
Huang, Jim 44
Hunter, Ellen Elizabeth 28
Hunter, Gwen 64

I

impression 95–97, 108
information exchange 138, 179
internal conflict 169–72

J

Jance, J. A. 130
Johansen, Iris 29
Jong, Erica 208

K

Kaplan, Justin 9
Kellerman, Faye 36
Kellerman, Jonathan 31
Kelner, Toni L. P. 95
Kennett, Shirley 36
King, Stephen 253
Konrath, J. A. 38, 123, 132
Kozak, Ellen M. 160
Krich, Rochelle 180
Kronenwetter, Michael 32

L

Lakey, Babs 223
Lane, Vicki 215
Lanning, George 54, 72
laughter 265
leapfrogging 125
lecturing 160
Lehane, Dennis 177
Leonard, Elmore 29, 104
light, changes in 87
lost opportunity cost 10
Lukeman, Noah 12

M

Maass, Donald 196
Macaulay, Robie 54, 72
MacDonald, John D. 123, 212
Mailer, Norman 151
Maine, University of 253
Maron, Margaret 110, 217, 254
Martini, Steve 234
Matthews, Alex 140, 183
McBain, Ed 191
McCullough, Karen 105
McDermid, Val 135
McHugh, John B. 27
mechanics 4, 18, 197, 276
Melnick, Arnold 62
metaphor 98, 234, 253
mirror device 121–22
misconception 106–107
modifiers 187, 248
mood 33
Mosley, Walter 37
motivation 163–74
Mucha, Susan P. 31
muddle maneuver 201
Muller, Marcia 28
Munger, Katy 236, 241, 266
Myers, B. R. 268
Myers, Tamar 140, 218

N

naming characters 199–210
Neri, Kris 247
Newhart, Bob 267
Nichols, John 24
Nicholson, Scott 29

O

Orr, Alice 84
Orwell, George 73, 148, 253
overwriting 151–62

P

pace 146, 153–55, 185, 238
parallel actions, themes 180, 255–59
paraphrase 157–59
Paretsky, Sara 36, 59
Parker, Robert B. 200
Parshall, Sandra 268
Patterson, James 32
pausing 238–40
Peters, Elizabeth 88
phony dialogue 56
Piccirilli, Tom 249
Pickard, Nancy 37, 76
Pickens, Cathy 123
Picoult, Jodi 32
Pitts Jr., Leonard 3
pizzazz 11, 251
planting 155
point of view 44, 121–32
Polisar, Lisa 224
Potter, Clarkson viii
POV, *see* point of view
preposition doubling 269
professional crime-fighter 46, 167
progression 54
prologue 41
Prospero, Ann Reaben 135
Proulx, Suzanne 213
Provost, Gary 167, 268
publishing 3–13
PUGS 18
punctuation 196, 267
purpose
    of story elements 25
    of each character 166
Puzo, Mario 131

Q

question-and-answer 177, 196
quotation marks 197

R

raising stakes 167
range, with superlatives 269
realism 155
red herring 155
Redbird Studios 14
redundancy 188, 233
Reichs, Kathy 200
rejection 6
resources 14, 278–86
restaurant settings 138
Reuben, Shelly 207
revision methods 15
Riggs, Cynthia 181
Rogers, Bruce Holland 101
Rozan, S. J. 87, 137, 208
rules
    for submitting 12
    for writing 3, 20

S

Sandford, John 69
Saums, Mary 33
Schumacher, Aileen 224
Scoppettone, Sandra 219
Scottoline, Lisa 256
screening process 3–10
Sebold, Alice 35
second reference 254
Seidman, Michael 263
self-description 121–24
sense data 145, 244, 249
sequencing 90
setback 166
setting 133–42
    interior 136–38
    regrounding 143–49
Shaber, Sarah 58, 176
Short, Sharon 262
shortcuts in dialogue 161

show v. tell 99, 187, 233, 243–50
Siddons, Anne Rivers 224
Simons, Rayanna 4
Singer, Gammy L. 29
Smith, Sydney 222
Sorrells, Walter 232, 234
speaker identity 191–96
Spencer-Fleming, Julia 99
Sprinkle, Patricia Houck 244
Squire, Elizabeth Daniels 26, 54, 87
stakes 165–68
Stein, Sol 48, 64
stories-within-a-story 72
style 230, 252
submission guidelines 5, 12–14, 18
"suddenly" 263
summaries 50
suspense 163, 165
Swanson, Denise 98, 234, 253
Sweeney, Leann 35
symbiotic relationship 247, 256
symbolism 254, 259–60

T

telephone conversation 128, 182
telling, *see* show v. tell
tense: past perfect 68–69
tensile strength 33
tension
    borrowed 181
    on every page 163–74
Tiller, Denise 245
TIPS
    reviewing gestures 242
    swapping names 205
    tagging habits 191
    using dots and dashes 177
tipsheets, *see* submission guidelines

Tishy, Cecelia 232
Todd, Charles 217
tone 32
Toole, John Kennedy 216
Tooley, S. D. 36
Tracy, P. J. 232
transitions 152
Trocheck, Kathy Hogan 237
Twain, Mark 37, 215

U

unity 45, 148

V

verbatim transcripts 71–78
verbs, active 98–100, 187, 190
Vidler, Ellis 129
Viets, Elaine 31
villain 47, 167
Vogt, M. Diane 80
voice 252, 262

W

Wales, Sandra T. 22
Wall, Kathryn 237
weather 35
Weinberg, Barry 211
West, Chassie 189, 234
Wheat, Carolyn 116, 253
Wilson, Kim 91
Woods, Stuart 129
wordiness 30, 151–62
Wright, Nancy Means 127, 236
Wyle, Dirk 266

Z

Zuber, Isabel 159

THE WITNESS BOX

I solemny swear that hundreds of readers and writers helped this book materialize by providing encouragement and giving me practical feedback, even when it meant their slogging through early, unedited, work in progress.

I'm grateful to the very talented mystery writers Alex Matthews, Anne Underwood Grant, Jeanne Dams, and Steve Brown, who took time from their own writing to offer gentle criticism and generous advice. Your experience and insight have been invaluable to me.

Enormous appreciation goes to Linda Lemery, Terri Scalf, Chris Antenen, Lonnie Cruse, and Rebecca Evans for patiently reviewing my manuscript at different stages of its development. Your excellent suggestions helped keep me on track.

Special gratitude to Rod Hunter for your expertise and good-natured support.

How fortunate I am to know Bill Kozlowski, Carrie Whitehead, and Joe Terrell—you have reminded me of important information to include.

Thank you to my good friend, Kim Wilson, a talented author in her own right. Your keen observations and questions always challenge my thinking.

Above all, my deepest gratitude to my dearest friend, Pat Meller, my most tolerant first reader, astute business partner, and tireless supporter. Your role in helping me produce this book has been above and beyond expectations.

Chris

THE PERPETRATOR

An accomplished editor, writer, and teacher, Chris Roerden shares knowledge gleaned from more than 40 years in niche publishing—a career that began at age 16 upon her graduation from New York City's H. S. of Music & Art. It took publication of her first book some years later for Chris to act on the urge to go to college— which produced a BA in English *summa cum laude* and an MA. All her honors work and her Master's thesis focused on technique in fiction. She remained at the University of Maine–Portland as an instructor of writing, and later supervised the writing of independent study students for Empire State College of SUNY.

Eventually returning to publishing, Chris left a busy managing editor's position in 1983 to become a busy independent book editor. Yet she made time every year for community service, including a summer of teaching communication skills in South Korea and eight years of teaching night classes in writing and publishing at the University of Wisconsin-Milwaukee. She was president of a trade association of 250 Midwest publishers and served nearly six years on the southeast regional board of Mystery Writers of America.

Chris is a long-time member of Sisters in Crime, Publishers Marketing Association, and Mensa, and a proud grandparent of three little boys who live in Boston with her son Doug and daughter-in-law, Laura, also an editor. Chris has three granddogs who live with her son Ken in Los Angeles.

Now settled in Greensboro, NC, Chris enjoys seeing pansies bloom in February and not having worn snow boots since the 20th century.

P. M.

Also available from Bella Rosa Books

The Dark Side Of Heaven, by Tamar Myers
ISBN 1-933523-01-8; Hard cover
The poignant, yet uplifting tale of a naïve Amish woman's banishment from her community and her passage into the *real* world. It is the story of her struggle to come to terms with life-altering decisions. It is a novel about religious conflict and hard choices.

Blackwater Secrets, by Gwen Hunter
ISBN 1-933523-02-6; Hard cover
Geneva swore she would never return to Louisiana, but her failed marriage leads her back—to a teenage romance re-explored and an investigation into secrets of the past, secrets that are broken open and brought to light by a child's love for her tortured mother. This midlife coming-of-age story of a love that was never fulfilled, never forgotten, is a story of hope that will leave you crying and cheering for joy. For it is never too late to chase your dreams—or to fall in love.

Death Of A Dunwoody Matron, by Patricia Sprinkle
A Southern Mystery, Fifth in the Sheila Travis series
ISBN 1-933523-06-9
What does a Dunwoody matron wear to a funeral? Her black tennis dress. Sheila finds her emotions stirred by an undeniably appealing man with a disturbing connection to the crime. Her maverick investigation startlingly reveals the biggest secret of all.

The Fugitive King, by Sarah R. Shaber
ISBN: 978-1-933523-21-7
Deep in the North Carolina woods beneath the Blue Ridge Parkway, a forest ranger finds the remains of a young woman who disappeared forty years earlier, entombed in an old pickup truck. The confessed killer, serving a life sentence in Raleigh for her murder, now asks Professor Simon Shaw to help prove his innocence.

By Blood Possessed, by Elena Santangelo, Agatha Award Finalist
ISBN 1-933523-04-2
Pat Montella, sick of her office job and looking for any shortcut to early retirement, receives a mysterious summons from a lawyer. A stranger intends to bequeath a 200-acre estate to Pat. The catch is, she must first spend a week there with Miss Maggie, a retired history teacher. The past comes alive for Pat, but in ways neither she nor Miss Maggie expect: phantom aromas of Union army chow, sounds of soldiers felling trees . . . and nightmarish visions of horrific battles. But while Pat delves into the saga of Bell Run and the family who gave their lives to protect it, she finds, stalking her through the bewitching Virginia woodlands, a much more terrifying present-day murderer.

Spider Blue, by Carla Damron
ISBN 0-9747685-6-1; Hard cover
Social worker Caleb Knowles grapples with two horrendous crimes: a nurse found stabbed to death in the yard of her suburban home and a mill worker who inexplicably opens fire on his fellow employees. Caleb's ties to these murders are both personal and professional, and he soon finds himself a reluctant witness and victim to dark events in the underbelly of his hometown.

Secrets & Ghost Horses, by Holly McClure, a Low Country Mystery
ISBN 0-9747685-7-X
When twin sisters Hannah and Aislinn learn they have to spend the summer in a dilapidated house in the mysterious Low Country of South Carolina, they could not be more miserable. Then they meet Donovan, the most gorgeous boy they have ever seen—although the fact that he is a ghost takes some getting used to. When he asks them to help bring his murderer to justice, how can the girls refuse?

BellaRosaBooks
www.bellarosabooks.com

Printed in the United States
135846LV00004B/111/A